YOU WILL WEAR A WHITE SHIRT

YOU WILL WEAR A WHITE SHIRT

From the Northern Bush *to the* Halls of Power

SENATOR NICK SIBBESTON

Douglas *&* McIntyre

Douglas and McIntyre (2013) Ltd.
P.O. Box 219, Madeira Park, BC, VON 2H0
www.douglas-mcintyre.com

Edited by Silas White and Lacey Decker Hawthorne
Indexed by Stephen Ullstrom
Text design by Carleton Wilson
Dust jacket design by Anna Comfort O'Keeffe
Printed and bound in Canada

BRITISH COLUMBIA
ARTS COUNCIL
An agency of the Province of British Columbia

Canada Council   Conseil des Arts
for the Arts   du Canada

Canada

Douglas and McIntyre (2013) Ltd. acknowledges the support of the
Canada Council for the Arts, which last year invested $157 million to
bring the arts to Canadians throughout the country. We also gratefully
acknowledge financial support from the Government of Canada through
the Canada Book Fund and from the Province of British Columbia
through the BC Arts Council and the Book Publishing Tax Credit.

Cataloguing data available from Library and Archives Canada
ISBN 978-1-77162-055-0 (cloth)
ISBN 978-1-77162-056-7 (ebook)

To Karen and my children,
Glen, Randy, Murray, Janice,
Jerald, Laurie and Shane

And to George Braden (1950–2015),
the first modern-day premier
of the Northwest Territories

Contents

Prologue

MORE THAN TEN years ago, I was escorted into the senate chamber for the first time by my old friend Senator Willie Adams, from Nunavut, and by Senator Bill Rompkey of Newfoundland. Both have since retired, but I'm still here going to work every day, attending to the business of government.

I sit in my comfortable office in the east block on Parliament Hill and wonder, amazed at how I came here from such humble beginnings. Earlier today I was questioning the government on changes to the Fisheries Act. Later this week I'll speak to the third reading of the Northwest Territories Devolution Act. The draft speech, prepared by my policy advisor Hayden Trenholm in his office down the hall, is sitting on my desk, awaiting my review and amendment. I can hear Renee Allen, my executive assistant, on the phone in the adjoining room making arrangements for visiting northerners to have lunch with me in the parliamentary restaurant.

There's always something to do here on the Hill: speeches to make in the chamber, questions to ask of witnesses at committee meetings, or meetings with colleagues or constituents on a wide range of issues affecting the Northwest Territories. Today, however, I'm content to gaze out my window and ponder the long winding course of my life.

A dozen years ago my wife, Karen, and I were happily running Bannockland, our bed and breakfast on the banks of the Liard River. We were working hard but we were our own bosses, answerable to no one.

Twenty-five years ago I was completing my term as premier of the Northwest Territories and was preparing for the fall election—my last, as it turned out.

Thirty-five years ago I set up my practice as the first northern-born Aboriginal lawyer in Canada.

Fifty years ago, I became the first Native kid from Fort Simpson to ever graduate from high school.

Sixty years ago I was torn from the arms of my family and taken away to residential schools where I suffered loneliness and abuse—and survived, though at a terrible cost.

And sixty-five years ago I was a young boy living with my mother and grandmother in Fort Simpson. I was three years old but I can distinctly remember my mother telling me, "Someday you're going to wear a white shirt." As a child those words did not mean anything, but as they were repeated year by year, I came to realize that I would be *somebody*, different from my relatives, someone like the teacher, the storekeeper or perhaps the occasional government person who visited the community.

It was remarkable that my mother, who was raised in a traditional Dene home with only a grade two education and who could barely read and write, had this "white shirt" dream for me. It is almost beyond imagining. There was no man in our house. My grandfather and uncles were trappers, hunters who spent their winter months in the bush working for a living. In the summer they and other Native people would come to town looking for outdoor labour jobs, often living in tents. White people had the inside jobs. The best a Native person could aspire to was to be an interpreter, a store clerk, a riverboat pilot or perhaps a school janitor.

While the bush life in its entirety was exuberant and fulfilling and provided a good living for those who hustled, I never had a chance to experience it. People came out from the bush healthy, with dogsleds full of furs. They were eager to get out of town again once they had bought their supplies, having socialized and attended church services. I never aspired to that way of life. Instead, from an early age, I had this idea that I would go right from the bush to a warm inside job. I was not to be like the trappers struggling for a living. I was to be more educated and have a different lifestyle.

And here I am. Every morning, I walk over the Alexandra Bridge from my small condo in Gatineau to my office on Parliament Hill.

The eternal flame flickers in front of the Peace Tower and people mill around on the front lawn: visitors, protestors or merely students playing a game of Frisbee. The clock in the Peace Tower strikes an hour, the chimes ringing and echoing across the city. From my second-floor office window, I can see the Château Laurier and a bit of the Rideau Canal. In the distance the wide expanse of the Ottawa River flows, the water dark and flecked with foam. This is the only feature that resembles my home in the North, where I live along the banks of the Liard River and see in the distance the high riverbanks and the Mackenzie flowing northwards. Every day I wear a dress shirt—though often not white—and often a suit as well, though some days I prefer my beaded caribou-hide vest. When I walk past the security staff they salute me. Everyone calls me "Honourable."

And I smile and think, "Man, this is a long way from Fort Simpson."

And I remember how it all began.

Part One:

CHILDHOOD

Chapter 1: Origins

I GREW UP in Fort Simpson, a village at the junction of the Mackenzie and Liard Rivers in the Northwest Territories. It sits on an island; a small stream (a snye) separates it from the mainland, though now it is joined by a permanent causeway. These days it is primarily a government town and most people, Aboriginal and non-Aboriginal, work for the federal, territorial, municipal or First Nation governments. Lots of tourists come through on their way to Nahanni National Park during the summer. A mine to the west of the community holds out some hope for a more diverse economy. There is an airport with regularly scheduled flights to Yellowknife and a highway south (though we still rely on a ferry in summer and an ice road in winter to make the connection). Television arrived in the mid-seventies and we have internet and cellphone service, though these appeared only in the last few years.

This is not the Fort Simpson of my childhood. In those days, the Roman Catholic church was the dominant institution, much like government today. The village had a hospital, a school, a church, mission buildings, warehouses, barns, cattle, horses, chickens and large gardens to support the hospital and all of its personnel. Government was in its infancy and consisted of the Indian agent, a federal experimental farm, an army signals facility, a few teachers and two RCMP officers. The church and government were the domain of white people, as were the other major institutions in the community—the Hudson's Bay Company (HBC) and independent traders like Jimmy Cree and Harry Brown. Andy Whittington, a white trapper with a flair for business, cut logs up the river and whipsawed boards to build a hotel and dance hall. My uncle Charlie Hansen, a Dane who married my aunt, arrived by walking along the shore into town one fall after his boat got iced in as he was making his way up the river. He became the only contractor in town, cutting and hauling wood and doing anything else required of him. When he decided to settle in the community, he drove a small Caterpillar tractor all the way from Waterways, Alberta, and started a sawmill.

The community swelled with people in the summer as hunters and their families set up their tents on either ends of the island. The Mackenzie and Liard Rivers came to life with boats after the spring break-up. In spring, the boats brought fresh fruit and other food; later in the summer they brought merchandise and dry goods to the stores in town. The summer months were a hive of activity as barges passed down the river carrying cargo as far as the Arctic coast.

Throughout the summer, square dances in Andy's hall competed with tea dances and hand games on the flats. The first signs of fall, usually a frost or ducks flying south in late August, saw Native people starting their "kickers" and moving their families in loaded scows and canoes out to their camps to resume hunting and trapping. As winter took hold, the rivers froze and the village settled into hibernation with only a few Métis and Dene families and the white population occupying the island.

Because of its location at the junction of two great rivers, Fort Simpson was always a good camping location for the Dene who travelled the rivers. The HBC was the first to make it into a trading post, followed by other traders. The community slowly developed into a trading centre, where the Dene people exchanged furs for supplies. The missionaries, both Catholic and Protestant, arrived in the mid-1850s. Schools were built by both denominations, and the Catholic Church built a hospital in 1916 and gradually all the infrastructure to support their work.

Over time the Indian agent and the RCMP arrived on the scene, as well as the army signals and experimental farm personnel. Métis and white trappers and other people from the south swelled the village's population. In the early 1940s, the US Army came to build the airport; my grandfather George Sibbeston trudged through the bush to help locate a suitable site. For the most part, Dene people lived along the rivers and lakes and didn't move into town until the 1950s. What brought them out of the bush into the communities was the school for their children and opportunities for employment.

By 1943, when I was born, the community was well-established. A dirt road along the river served the few vehicles in town and was the main route for walking the length of the island. Houses were situated along the river and, in some areas, further inland. The mission gradually cleared the thick bush on the back side of the island to create an extensive farm operation.

The island was prone to flooding. My mother often tells a story she heard from elders of a flood that occurred when there was only the HBC post and a few Dene people camped on the island. Ice and water had covered virtually all the island, with only the southern tip left dry. The traders were desperate as the water rose around their post and they finally gave an old man who was reputed to have "medicine" some tobacco to put a stop to the flooding. The old man chanted and stuck a stick at the edge of the water; the water receded. My mother laughed about how even the white people reverted to Indian medicine to save themselves. There have been a few floods since this one, but not as high as the one the old man stopped.

The Catholic mission had a large hospital, a nurse's residence, a church, a school, a power plant, warehouses, garages, barns and a chicken coop. To feed everyone in the mission and hospital, they kept cows, a bull, horses, chickens and large cultivated fields and gardens. Before my time they even had pigs. One of my early memories is seeing cattle far away in the fields and once seeing a cow close up in the early morning grazing next to our house. The cows wandered in the bush towards the snye, and my grandmother would sometimes run across them when getting wood or visiting her snares.

My mother, Laura Sibbeston, had me out of wedlock so I didn't have a father, but the home where I grew up was loving and comfortable. My mother and I lived with the woman I knew as my grandmother Ehmbee. I was a teenager before Ehmbee told me how she became my "grandmother." Ehmbee had lived with my real grandparents, Ama and Papa (Harriet and George Sibbeston), when she was a widow mourning the death of her husband, Betsedia, and their baby girl. From the time my mother was born and brought home, Ehmbee looked after my mother like her own child. One fall when Ehmbee moved down the river to live with another family, my mother cried and was inconsolable. Papa had to go down the river amongst the ice flows to get her to Ehmbee. From that time on they were inseparable and Ehmbee raised my mother as her own daughter.

Eventually Ehmbee moved back to Fort Simpson and married Joe Hope, an Ojibwa man from Manitoba. He was the chief in Fort Simpson in the 1930s until he died in the flu epidemic of 1937. Their house, built by Joe, was a well-crafted, square-logged structure, half-way down the island from the flats and some distance behind Ama and Papa's house. Except for some of the Métis homes, Ehmbee's was one of the better houses built and owned by Native people in our community.

Life with Ehmbee and my mother was idyllic. A young boy could not have had a better upbringing. The house was warm and we always had food. I was pampered with nice warm clothes, moosehide mitts and moccasins. Meat—moose or caribou—was given to us by relatives and friends, and Ehmbee caught rabbits in her snare line, which started at the back of her house, ran south along the back road, then cut into the bush by Cli's house, past 'Mena iih's house into thick bush. The trail passed through a stand of birch and poplar and down a hill into dense spruce before ending in the willows by the snye.

I loved going with Ehmbee on the snare line. Rabbit trails ran all along Ehmbee's path in the bush. In winter, it was easy for me to see the trails where the rabbits ran back and forth, but in summer, only Ehmbee could spot them. We would be walking along and she would suddenly stop and say, "See this trail?" I could see nothing until I got down on my knees and saw jellybean-sized droppings and an indentation amongst the leaves and twigs.

Having found the trail, Ehmbee would leave the path and use her axe to clear an area of small trees and willows. She would strip a nearby small tree of its branches and bend it into the clearing. Then she would attach one end of a string snare to the top of the tree and twist a small stick halfway along the snare around a nearby willow to keep the tree from springing up. It looked like a bow. She would then place twigs on each side of the rabbit trail and attach the string, making a round loop the size of the rabbit's head. The string had been rubbed with moss to take away the human scent. When a rabbit ran along the trail its head slipped into the loop and tugged the line. The stick on the willow would let go, the tree would spring upright, and the rabbit was flung into the air hanging by its neck.

I often ran ahead of Ehmbee to see if there was a rabbit hanging from a tree, occasionally surprised to find a spruce grouse instead. When a rabbit was caught I would wait for Ehmbee and she would reach up and bend the tree to take it down. I carried a pack sack, and the rabbit would be put in it. It always felt good, especially if the rabbit was still warm, to know that we would be eating the rabbit as soon as we got home.

We would eat our lunch in the open by the snye, where there was just sand and water. Big logs served as chairs while we ate our bannock and tinned meat. We drank cold water that I fetched from the river in a lard pail. Once, while we sat, a whisky jack came and landed right by us. Its head bobbed from side to side as if it was telling us that it was hungry. Ehmbee said that whisky jacks were greedy and they ate the eyes and sometimes other parts of the rabbit if it was on the ground. If I had had any bannock left, I would have given it a piece.

Heading home, Ehmbee chopped dry willow trees to put in the sack on her back. A pond lay to the left at the bottom of a small hill. I followed Ehmbee, moving carefully and quietly through the moss. We could hear the splash of water and quacking of ducks. Ehmbee's back was bent close to the ground as we snuck to the edge of the pond. At the far end two ducks chased each other. Closer by, a muskrat left a trail in the water as it swam from its mud-pile house. "Next spring," Ehmbee said, "I'll set some traps for the muskrats for when the little ones become big. Muskrats taste good."

In the spring, Ehmbee would carry lard pails to gather sap from the birch trees and boil it into syrup. Sometimes we could hear drumming away in the bush, and we might come across a chicken (grouse), which she called a *talleh*, beating its wings on its breast. Ehmbee said it was a boy chicken and that if we waited long enough, a girl chicken would come and they would make eggs. I wanted to wait, but Ehmbee never let me stay.

Also in the spring, Ehmbee worked on a moosehide at the back of our house. The hide was stretched on a large frame and she scraped it, taking all the hair off until it became nice and white. Then she and I would go into the bush and get bags of old rotten wood, which she burned to tan the hide with smoke. When she was finished she had a nice brown hide which she used to make moccasins, mitts and other things. My mother made me a dogwhip from a piece of hide, which I used to swing and make a cracking noise. My mother also sewed nice uppers for moccasins using coloured beads or threads. Sometimes when my grandmother was sewing, she would help me to sew and to make small cloth bags.

Our summer garden provided potatoes, carrots, turnips and other vegetables that Ehmbee and my mother put up for use year-round. We caught fish with nets down the bank, and in the fall, before the ice was too thick, loche lines were set through holes. Berries, eaten fresh or stored for winter, included summer strawberries in the nearby fields, late summer raspberries along the back road, and rosehips and cranberries throughout the bush in the fall. Bee stings were often a risk, and Ehmbee always warned me to be careful in a berry patch. One kind of berries, which Ehmbee called *eh theen lu*, were red and filled with sour juice. She said they liked people, as they always grew on the edge of bushes where people lived.

Ehmbee got tea, rice, a bit of baking powder and flour from the Indian agent. Later, she took her old-age pension cheque to Jimmy Cree's store to buy powdered milk, butter, lard and cans of meat and fruit. Even though we were poor, we lacked for nothing and had a happy life.

On the days when Ehmbee wasn't visiting snares, gardening or doing other work, she sat outside looking at catalogues or one of the *Life* magazines she got from Papa. She couldn't read but she liked looking at pictures. Sometimes I watched her examining boxes, bottles or cans she got from the store, turning them over and over and marvelling at them.

My mother spent her days caring for me. She cooked porridge in the morning and meat soup or rabbit for dinner. She baked tasty bread and buns which were quickly eaten. Hot tea brewed on the stove constantly, and bannock was available all day. I don't ever remember not drinking tea.

I was an only child and my mother was protective. Sometimes she tied me like a puppy in a harness, afraid I might otherwise wander down the bank and drown. The *nah gah*, the bogeyman, was lurking in the nearby bushes, she said, waiting to steal me away if I wandered too far from home. In winter she stuffed rabbit skins in my underwear to protect me from getting cold. If I felt any cold, I was to come in immediately, lest "they" freeze and drop off.

My grandmother Ehmbee was filled with love and affection. In the winter, she rose first to get the fire going. My mother and I would get up only after the house was warm. Ehmbee talked to me constantly to tell me I was a good boy or to show me things in the bush. Late at night she told stories about her early life or of our people. I liked to hear about *Eh son tsea*, a great Dene warrior, who led our people in fighting against neighbouring tribes, particularly the Cree. Arrows and bullets bounced off his chest. When the last arrow had fallen, he went amongst them and killed them all with a wooden club. It made me happy to know that the Dene had a great warrior. He was the reason why the Dene were a strong, proud people.

Ehmbee enjoyed taking me along when she visited her relatives and friends. We were always given tea and something to eat, and I played with whatever other children were there. I also went with Ehmbee to church, where we sat in the very back pew. She didn't understand Latin, French or English, but she watched the priest conduct mass at the altar as if she understood what was going on. Once in a while, a priest spoke Dene, and she would bend her head to one side to hear. She smiled when the father mispronounced Dene words, but most of the time she was serious. She didn't sing with the sisters in the loft, but she enjoyed the music. At communion, she went to the front to get what I thought was a white round candy. Once, when she returned, I reached into her mouth to get some of the candy and cried when I found out that there was nothing there. Ehmbee said that she used to go to the other church, the Protestant church along the river, but after it burned down she started going to this one.

Ehmbee's house was next to a trading post with a large warehouse and what they called an Indian house—a small house the trappers stayed in when they came to trade their furs. Traders often dropped by Ehmbee's house to visit us, as would patients or their visitors from the nearby hospital. As the widow of the former chief, Ehmbee was a generous hostess, giving people tea and bannock or anything she had cooking to eat.

The elder Emily George often stayed with us and, when we went to the snare line, enjoyed watching me run over the snow with my little snowshoes. I would duck under a spruce tree and shake all the snow off. Baptiste Betsedia from Willow River visited too. Once, we played a card game for matches. Baptiste won all of the matches, and I cried, "Oh, Ehmbee is going to be mad with me!" so he gave them back and I put them back into Ehmbee's matchbox. Joa Boots often came to stay with us from Willow River Lake. When Chief Joe Hope was alive, he would go with Joa to the trader to ensure that he got a fair deal for his furs. This was one of the roles of the chief in the old days, to make sure that the traders dealt fairly with everyone.

Not all our visitors were calm and quiet. One memorable old man called *Mah cellais* came in out of the cold one day and stayed upstairs in our house. Even though he was a trapper, he was always dressed in fancy dress pants and white shirt. *Mah cellais* was a bachelor and a "gentleman trapper," walking along the front road looking distinguished in his good clothes. As children we often asked him for *sahts tsogha*, some coins, and he was usually generous by giving us ten cents or sometimes a quarter. One evening while staying with us he started singing, quietly at first but before long he was creating a real racket. Ehmbee said he was making *ehn kho*, Indian medicine. I wanted to peek, but Ehmbee told me to sit still. Eventually, Ehmbee told him to be quiet as we were going to sleep. I always imagined him to be a strong medicine man. I admired him and wondered what medicine he had made upstairs in our house.

Sometimes people stayed with us and became part of our family. Jim, Shorty and Rita Wrigley moved in for a time after they returned from residential school. Their parents had both died while the three siblings were away at school. For me, it was like having big brothers and a big sister. In fact, Rita called me her little brother ever after. They helped with the household chores, getting wood from in the bush and water from down the bank.

My cousins Eddy and Thomas Hope stayed for a while after their father died and their mother left town. One night we were awoken by a loud popping sound coming from a small storage area at the bottom of the stairs. Ehmbee used a flashlight to open the door and discovered a bunch of bottles that had popped their corks and spilled with a fizzing sound onto the floor. It was homemade brew. Ehmbee was angry, as she didn't allow alcohol in her house, and Eddy, who made the brew, had to throw out all his bottles.

Unbeknownst to me at the time, I almost became a Tulita Mountain Dene. Paul Wright from Tulita was a tuberculosis patient at the hospital, and when he was cured and ready to go home, he asked my mother if he and his wife, Mary Rose, could adopt me. Thinking, I guess, that having a father in my life would be good for me, my mother agreed. But when Paul came to get me a few days later, Ehmbee would not let me go, saying, "I would be so sad and lonely if you took him from me." Paul didn't have the heart to take me away.

As I grew my horizons expanded. A narrow path led along a potato patch to Papa's house. The Goodalls, to our right, had a myriad of houses. The main one along the riverbank contained the post office and a small store. My uncle Philip Lafferty often claimed that the Goodalls' house was getting bigger every year. It looked funny with its many additions and the numerous stovepipes sticking out from its roof. Behind our house was an open field and then bush all the way to the snye. My mother ordered me a tricycle from the catalogue so I could ride and play in our yard and the adjacent fields.

Our dog Lily was tied at the edge of the bush. As I got bigger, I brought food to her every evening. Along the back road to the south was Jimmy Cree's store. North was the Roman Catholic mission and hospital. From our window I could see the brothers hoeing gardens and herding cows. At meal times, the priests and brothers in their long black cassocks walked in single file from their residence to the hospital. Closer to the river, patients at the hospital sat on a veranda sunning themselves while sisters in white nurse uniforms or grey and brown dresses went about their work, caring for the patients, hanging clothes or weeding the gardens.

My cousins lived in a house attached to ours. Kenneth and Bertha were my age and were my constant companions. We made nests for birds hoping that one morning eggs or baby birds might appear in them. In the spring we played along the edge of a flooded field with little sailboats and chased the sandpipers newly arrived from the south. We set traps for them, watching from inside our porch until we saw a flutter of feathers. We brought our prizes to Ehmbee, who would wring their necks, clean them and boil them into soup. Robins' nests, filled with blue eggs, were found at the edge of the bush. We would visit them every few days until little birds hatched. We gathered flies and bugs to feed the chicks.

In the fall, as the birds gathered into flocks to fly south, we tried to catch them to keep as pets. We set up a large tub with a stick holding one side up and a long string attached to it. We put rolled oats all around the box to attract the birds and we hid and waited patiently in the porch until they came. When they went under the tub, we pulled the string. Once I caught three of them and kept them through the winter, letting them loose in the spring.

My seemingly idyllic childhood had one ineradicable blemish, a sore that would one day infect me, too: alcohol. My mother often went out on weekends to drink, and sometimes she would not return for a few days. I often cried as she left with one of her friends. *Tso leh*, Jonas Lafferty's wife, was the one who came most often to get her. *Tso leh* always arrived in a happy mood, and she and my mother laughed and giggled as they left our house. Ehmbee consoled me on these occasions, telling me stories, pointing to the shadow shapes cast on the wall by the candle and helping me look for angels until I fell asleep.

One time when my mother came back after a few days, Ehmbee scolded her for drinking and told her she was going to tell the priest. Not wanting to listen, my mom took me by the hand and left our house, walking down the back road into the bush. When she found a clearing, she sat down with me and showed me a picture of a man in army clothing. Perhaps, I thought, it was a picture of my father. We didn't go home until it was dark.

Chapter 2: A Year in Providence

I REMEMBER THE day my idyllic life changed forever: one day in the early fall of 1949 my mother told me I would be going on a boat to Fort Providence to go to school. I had never heard of the Fort Providence school; I had always thought I would go to the school in town next to the hospital. But my mother explained to me that she was sick and would have to go far away to a hospital in the south, and that Ehmbee was too old to look after me. Ehmbee seemed perfectly well to me, walking daily to her snare line and coming home with big sacks of wood strapped to her back. And when there was a tea dance on the flats, she danced almost the whole night.

But I didn't think about it too much. After all, I was just five years old. All I could think was "I'm going on a boat!" I skipped along with my mother as we bought new clothes from the store. We filled a small cloth bag that I would take with me. Mitts, a parka and mukluks made by my mother for the cold winter were placed carefully at the bottom of the bag.

On the evening I left Fort Simpson, I walked with my mother and Ehmbee along the river road up to the landing where the mission boat was tied up. Ehmbee remained at the top of the hill overlooking the river while my mother walked with me down the bank to where the boat was tied by long ropes to the shore. People rushed about, untying the boat and putting other children aboard. Many of the children were crying as their mothers and fathers wailed and said goodbye, but I didn't cry or cling to my mother as the others did; I was too excited. My mother hugged me, told me to be a good boy and said she would see me when she returned from the hospital. A long plank led from the shore to the barge, and with a last glance at Ehmbee on the hill, I clambered down into the dark interior. I didn't know that I would not see my grandmother again for a whole year nor my mother for six years.

Down in the boat, two women in long dresses yelled at everyone to be quiet and motioned for us to lie on the mattresses scattered on the floor of the barge. Cold blankets covered us and I snuggled among the other boys. I woke in the morning surrounded by a crowd of other children, with the sisters yelling for everyone to wake up and kneel for prayers. It was then that I realized I was away from home, and I burst out crying. Everything seemed wrong. Where was my hot porridge dished up in comfort before a blazing hot wood stove? Where was my tea served in a glass tumbler? Strange boys pushed against me in a cold windy barge. I needed to go pee, to get warm, to sit by Ehmbee while she put on my moccasins. A bigger boy, Dolphus I learned, put his arms around my shoulders and told me to be quiet or the "sisters," as he called them, would spank me. I didn't know what spanking was—I had never been hit—so I kept crying. I was not the only one; others covered their faces to muffle their cries. One sister yelled and motioned we should kneel, make the sign of the cross and recite words of prayer. The boat rocked and the motors growled as water swished along the barge. The porridge they served was like nothing I had ever tasted before. I didn't like it, but I ate because I was hungry.

The morning wore on. From time to time, a sister opened the door of the barge and we could see the riverbanks go by slowly. Finally, we came to a bend in the river where tents and cabins lined the bank, smoke drifting from stovepipes. Dogs barked and people rushed about on shore. One of the bigger boys said that it was Jean Marie River. The boat inched towards the shore. Someone moved across the roof of the barge. At last he jumped ashore and tied the boat to some big rocks.

Soon people lined the bank, talking as their children cried. Mothers moved slowly down the hill, the children dragging their feet. As soon as the children were within reach, men grabbed them, carried them up the plank and handed them to the sisters. Before long, all of the children in the barge were crying. Up on the hill dogs barked, mothers wept, covering their faces with their handkerchiefs, and fathers stood silently next to them.

The door slammed shut, leaving us in the dark of the barge as the engines roared to life. We were on the river again. Some boys tried to open the door, and a nun pulled them away and yelled for quiet. Some little boys called for their mothers; others screamed for their sisters, corralled with the other girls at the far end of the barge. A nun clapped her hands over two boys' mouths, trying to make them stop screaming. Most of the children curled up on the mattresses; some fell asleep. I stayed by Dolphus and tried not to cry.

We were in the barge for days as the boat made its way up the river. We weren't allowed to move except to go to the "toilet"—a tub in one corner. Food was brought in large buckets and trays in the morning after we rose, at midday and at night before it became completely dark. When it wasn't raining or the wind blowing too hard, the door might open and we could see the trees in the distance. When night came, the boat stopped and tied up, starting again at first light. After a few long days, the bigger boys told us we were at Mills Lake, a large lake we had to cross to get to Fort Providence. The doors were slammed shut so we couldn't see outside. Water tossed the barge from side to side and up and down. Pots were passed around as many of us were sick. I was too sick to eat anything that day. As darkness fell again and we tied up for the night, the barge finally stopped swaying. Sister told us we would be in Providence the next day.

The jarring of the barge as it left the shore woke me. Soon the sisters yelled at us to get up. One motioned for us to get dressed, get our bags and sit still. No food was served that morning, even though we were terribly hungry, as many of us hadn't been able to keep anything down the previous day. At long last the barge stopped and the door was flung open. Houses dotted the shore and many priests, brothers and sisters hurried to meet us.

The girls walked off across the long plank first. I held tight to my small bag of clothes as I waited amongst the other children. Soon we boys began moving, and a woman wearing a long grey dress with a black top and a bonnet came and pushed me up the hill to join the other boys. I had never seen a nun so close, only from a distance in Fort Simpson. She scared me, and I wondered why she grabbed me so hard. I was never treated like this by Ehmbee or my mother.

As we came to the top of the hill, the sisters blew whistles and motioned for the boys and girls to line up and climb the hill toward some large houses. We wound our way up silently past two large buildings, which I learned later were a warehouse and the father's house. Finally we reached a multi-floored tin-covered house with many windows; it looked a bit like the hospital in Fort Simpson. Inside, we boys climbed the stairs to a big room with many beds in a row, a blanket and a pillow on each of them. I had never seen such a large room and so many beds. A row of sinks and toilets lined one wall. At home, we had only a small wash basin, which we filled with a dipper, and an outside toilet. I was curious to see how these indoor ones worked. I found out later they were only used when it was too dark or cold to go outside.

Sister said something I didn't understand, but I watched the other boys and did whatever they did. They took their clothes off and put them into one big pile, so I did the same, taking off my moccasins, jacket, new shirt and pants, and underwear and adding them to the pile. Then Sister lined us up with the smaller boys at the front. Each of us got a gob of smelly, greasy stuff from a can wiped into our hair. Then we were pushed toward a large washtub in the corner. I climbed in beside another boy who had water up to his neck. The water was cold and it looked as if there was lard at the edge of the tub. I shook from the unfamiliar cold. Another sister, kneeling beside the tub, rubbed my hair and pushed my head under the water to rinse it. I was nudged to climb out and then I stood to one side while I dried off. Once everyone was bathed, sisters herded us into the corner of the room.

Washtub sister pulled a hair clipper out of a cupboard. I knew what it was, as my mother also used one to cut my hair. My mother clipped carefully, using a comb as she worked to clip my hair neatly. Sister, on the other hand, worked rapidly, yelling at each boy to *"Vite! Vite!"* The clipper went *click, click* as my hair fell, making a pile on the floor. When Sister was finished my head felt light. All the other boys looked bald with little tufts of hair at the tops of their heads. I wondered if I looked the same. I found out when Sister told us to go to the sinks and wash our hair again. Mirrors hung on the wall above the sinks. I had never seen my reflection so clearly before. I was surprised at how different I looked from the other boys. They were brown and had black hair. I was white and had brown hair. I had always thought I looked like my mother and Ehmbee, who were also brown and had black hair.

Some bigger boys brought armloads of clothing and shoes and placed them beside our big pile of clothes. I wanted to get back into my own clothing but Sister handed me long underwear, dark coveralls with metal buttons all down the front and a pair of cowhide shoes that were too big. The coveralls felt stiff and rubbed uncomfortably on my belly.

Next we filed down the stairs to a large room, our playroom. Benches lined two walls; tables with drawers were along a third. The last wall, closest to the stairs, was lined with cupboards. Two boys carried our clothing from upstairs and placed it in a pile in the middle of the room. Sister motioned for us to get our own clothes and put them into our bags. I found the little bag my mother had so carefully packed with my mukluks, parka and underwear and added the clothes and moccasins I had taken off. The older boys put the bags in the highest of the cupboards and shut the doors. I thought I would be given my warm clothes back when it got cold. Little did I know this was the last I would see of them until the following summer, when we were put on the boat to go home.

A loud whistle blew from outside and a stream of boys rushed into the room. I've never seen so many boys, most bigger than me. They all had black hair; mine was the only brown. The sisters herded us downstairs into a large room with long tables and chairs. Some girls were eating at the far end of the room. When I last saw them marching up the hill, they were in dresses and kerchiefs of various colours and had long hair. Now they all looked like little nuns, only without bonnets. Their hair had been cut short and grey skirts hung almost to their feet.

The smell of cooked fish filled the room. I liked fish and my stomach growled at the aroma. We couldn't eat until we prayed. We filed past a table where a sister stood putting fish and potatoes on every plate. I got a fish head and I ate the eyes, the inside, the cheeks and all the parts I could just as Ehmbee had taught me. When we were done, we said another prayer and scraped all the bones and skin into a big pail before we were sent outside.

Some boys were at the far end of the field chasing birds, shooting their arrows into the flocks of snowbirds who took flight to escape them, just to land again a dozen feet away. I only knew Dolphus, but he was playing with boys his size. I stood by the entrance watching the boys on the swing or throwing a ball back and forth until a sister yelled at me to join them. Instead, I walked along the rows of stacked wood that stretched to the back of the yard, feeling sad, thinking of Ehmbee and my mother.

Another whistle blew and everyone started running to a sister standing by the convent waving everyone inside. Back in the play-room we gathered on the benches. Sister called out names from a paper. As each boy's name was called, he stepped forward. Many names were called: Dolphus, Daniel, Joseph, Albert, Jimmy, Charlie, Freddy. Towards the end, I heard "Nic-ko-law." The sister looked at all the boys before she pointed to me. "*Tu! Viens ici!*" she said, scowling and motioning for me to come over. "*Tu es Nic-ko-law.*" Some boys laughed. I wondered what I had done wrong, tears coming to my eyes. Then I realized that this was my name: Nicholas. My mother and grandmother called me Walkie, the only name I'd ever known. At that moment I wished that my mother had given me a name like the other boys.

Before we were allowed into our beds, Sister made each of us fold our arms and make the sign of the cross. I had seen my grandmother and the priests at church so I was able to do as Sister wanted. Some of the small boys didn't know how and started crying, and Sister took their hands and made them touch their forehead, heart, left shoulder and right shoulder. Then she took out her rosary. Again I knew what that was because my grandmother had one and she used it to pray when I went to church with her. She prayed in Dene and I always understood her. I liked the way Ehmbee prayed because it sounded like singing. Sister began praying but I couldn't understand her and it didn't sound like singing; it sounded more like she was angry, and she got louder and louder as she walked back and forth across the room. The bigger boys knew what responses to say during Sister's praying, which lasted a long time. Some of the boys fell asleep and the sister slapped them in the head to wake them up. I was tired but kept my eyes open from fear. Finally it was over. "Amen," Sister said, making the sign of the cross.

As soon as she finished she yelled, "Tow-let! Tow-let!" I followed the other boys' lead as we all rushed outside. It was cold and the sun was going down. We ran to a narrow building with many doors. It was dirty inside, not like our clean toilet at home. When I was done, I ran back to the convent just in time as the door slammed shut behind me.

A sister at the far end of the upper room was showing the boys which beds were theirs. I quickly did as the other boys did and took off my coveralls, shoes and socks and put them at the foot of my bed. Some boys were already in bed, but the sister waved her arms, yelling, "*Prier! Prier!*" making every one kneel beside their bed. I had never prayed kneeling down before, but I did as Sister said. A large cross hung on the wall, and the sister made the sign of the cross before it and began a prayer saying, "*Mon dieu, Jesu, Jesu.*"

As soon as we were done praying the light went out. I lay awake in the dark for a few moments thinking of my mother and grandmother, how they would talk with me and put my blankets over my head before going to sleep. They usually had a candle lit by their beds. Beside me a boy started crying. Before long others joined in. Sister yelled and when they didn't stop, began slapping the boys until they were silenced. I put my head under my blanket and covered my mouth to keep from whimpering until I fell asleep.

I woke up to Sister clapping her hands and yelling "*Réveiller! Réveiller!*" It was a harsh awakening from my dream of being at home playing with Lily. I jumped out of bed onto my knees like the other boys. Sister prayed, and then we made our beds, washed and dressed. Before letting us into the dining room, Sister made us go outside to the toilet. Back in the dining hall we prayed again and were given bowls of porridge. My mother had always made porridge for me in the morning, so I thought it tasted good, although I wished I had some sugar in it and bannock with jam.

Back we went to the playroom, where piles of clothes were heaped in the middle of the floor. Sister handed out pants and shirts, saying they were our going-to-mass and school clothes. She gave each boy a number and marked the number on the inside of the pants and shirt. I was one of the last and one of the smallest, so Sister couldn't find pants and a shirt that fit me. Finally, she took one of the pairs of pants and cut the legs shorter, marked "36" on them and threw them to me. I had a hard time keeping them up, so sister gave me a string as a belt. The shirt was also too big, but it was soft and I liked its red colour. I remembered the pants and shirt that my mother had bought for me. They fit me just right, and I wished that I could wear those. Sister told us to put our new clothes in our drawer, so I went around the room looking for "36" and put my clothes in it.

Outside again, I walked alone in the shade of the woodpile and watched the other boys. I missed my cousins Kenneth and Bertha; I didn't want to play with anyone else. I sat on the ground and built little houses out of sticks. After I was by myself for a long time, a boy named Georgie came to sit with me. He was small like me. We talked in Dene while we built more houses. He had a big brother named Archie and sisters named Celine and Marie Jane. He was lonely and wanted to see his sisters but wasn't allowed. We could hear the girls playing on the far side of the woodpile but we were forbidden to see them.

By the convent, a sister who had stood still as a statue watching us blew a whistle, calling us in for lunch, a watery soup with bits of cabbage in it. It tasted strange and unpleasant, so I set down my spoon and looked around at the other boys. Most were just staring at their soups and not eating. Sister became angry and yelled at us to eat, administering a few slaps until we all picked up our spoons and forced the stuff down. Back home, no one made me eat something I didn't like, but then again, I liked everything at home; the food there was always good.

Back in the playroom, Sister stood in the middle of the room and talked, pointing to each of the boys, then pointing up or down. Georgie told me that Sister was telling the boys which grades they were in and where their classes were. I didn't understand French but I heard her say *école* many times and the words *un, deux, trois*, which I learned were numbers. She pointed for me to go sit in the corner. Soon all the boys went to their drawers, put their school clothes on and left the room. I was alone; I would not be going to school. Sister held up her hand with her fingers spread out and said, "*Cinq.*" I was only five years old, too young to go to the classroom. I was sad because I wanted to go with my new friend Georgie and I was curious about what the boys did in school.

From that day, I spent my time with Sister Lapierre. She mended clothes at a sewing machine on a raised platform in the corner of the playroom. She was a skinny woman who never smiled and hardly ever spoke to me. She prayed a lot, her lips moving without words coming out, and I had a hard time getting her to look at me when I wanted to go to the toilet or get some water. I played with blocks with numbers and letters on them, and every afternoon a small mattress and a blanket appeared from one of her cupboards, and I lay down until the boys returned from class. It was a terribly lonely existence for a small boy.

One afternoon I woke up from my nap and Sister was gone. I looked in a boy's drawer next to mine and found a jar filled with something that looked just like lard though it had a sweet smell. I had seen a boy put it on his face, so I did the same. Then I put some in my hair hoping it would turn my hair black. When Sister Lapierre came back she laughed at me. It was the first time I had heard her laugh. But her face changed as she moved her head side to side and soon had an angry look on her face. She said I was a bad boy and told me that what I did was stealing. She slapped my hands, and when the other boys came back from school she stood me in front of everybody while they laughed at me, as she told me not to do that again. After that, Sister Lapierre spoke to me more often when we were alone and taught me numbers and letters of the alphabet. It didn't take long before I was able to understand what she was saying and could answer her when she spoke. I wondered what Ehmbee would say when I talked French to her.

A few days after we got to Providence we started going to mass in the mornings. Sister woke us early in the morning and we would get into our church clothes and walk quietly downstairs to the chapel.

The boys would go on the left side and the girls on the right. I sat at the very front. Father Denis or Father Posset said the mass. Sister made everybody sing. I didn't know the words or the songs but pretended to sing so Sister wouldn't get mad.

After mass came breakfast. Sometimes we had beans for our breakfast, which I liked. If I found a piece of bacon in the beans, I ate it fast so no one could take it from me. Next came chores. Some boys swept the floor, the stairs and the place where we slept and played; others straightened our beds, washed the sinks and cleaned the night toilets. My chore was to pick up anything on the floor in the playroom and to sweep by Sister's sewing machine. If our chores were done well, we were allowed to go outside for a while until school started. I had to stay behind with Sister, and I was sad I had no one to play with.

The schoolyard was big. The far end of the field, fenced by bush, was as far as we were allowed to go. To the left were big houses, beginning with the fathers' house, where all the fathers and brothers lived. Next were a warehouse and a shop where brothers kept their tools, and a small building where Brother Marcheseau worked with an engine that made electricity. Near the line of bush the brothers kept machines, horse sleds and wagons in a large shed. The horses and cows lived in a barn, which marked the other limit to our world. I watched a brother lead horses pulling wagons to the far fields, and I wondered what lay beyond the barn.

One day Sister told us that we were going to pick potatoes. She took us along the fence, past the barn and into some fields. A brother used a horse-drawn plow to lift all the potatoes to the top of the ground in long rows, stretching as far as I could see. The big boys were given pails or sacks while small boys stayed close to the sister putting little potatoes in a pile. Even the girls picked potatoes in a field past some bushes. We could see them with the sisters bending and picking potatoes with their dresses flying in the wind. When we finished after many days, the brother came with horses and a wagon to pick up the sacks. Sister said that we would have lots to eat in the wintertime.

It got colder each day. One day after school Sister went with us to the snye, which was covered with ice. We had to be careful as it was slippery. We could sometimes see a big fish swimming under the ice, and we would chase it until it went into the middle where the water was deep and we couldn't see it anymore. Sister stood on the shore and blew her whistle when we went too far from the edge. She tried to make me stay close to her but I drifted as far away as I could so I could play with the other boys.

When winter came, Brother Gosellin hauled big trees from the bush on a horse-drawn sled and piled them in our yard. I was fascinated by the streams of hot breath puffing from the nostrils of the strong horses as they dropped off the trees by the convent. When Brother finished hauling all the wood, men cut it using a tractor and a big round noisy saw. Every day after school the boys piled the wood or brought some to the big stoves that kept the convent warm. Even I helped, loading up my arms with small pieces of wood.

Now that there was snow, we went sliding every day after school in the yard or on the hill by the barn. On days there was no school we slid on the riverbank onto the ice. We used cardboard or made sleds or skis from wooden barrels. The boys tied skis to their feet and went fast down the hill. One time a big boy was sliding with his head facing the back on the sled and he hit a sister standing at the bottom of the hill. She looked funny on her back, not able to get up until some boys helped her. Albert, the boy who hit Sister, was not allowed to slide for a long time, and all the boys were told not to slide backwards.

When the snow was deep, the boys could go in the bush to set snares for rabbits or squirrels. Most of the boys went along the snye to the big island or to the mainland where the boys' shack was situated. Boys set their snares for rabbits amongst the willows and for squirrels amongst the big spruce trees. Georgie and I went together to set snares across from the boys' shack. We didn't set snares with string like Ehmbee did, but with wire that I bought from the HBC store with money my mother had sent me in a letter. Georgie and I were excited thinking about how many rabbits we would catch. I imagined that there would be a rabbit in every snare. But when we visited our snares after a few days, we hadn't caught any, as we had set the snares too high. We reset them closer to the ground, and the next time we checked we had caught one rabbit. Father Denis gave us five cents for the rabbit, and we bought candy with it. After that we didn't catch any more, and finally we gave up and just played in the bush.

If we stayed out too long in the bush, we could freeze our feet. When that happened, pus-filled blisters formed on the bottom of our feet. In a few days, the skin would tear off, making our feet sore and hard to walk on until new skin grew again.

One day, Sister woke me early in the morning and told me that it was my feast day, St. Nicholas Day (6 December), and to put on my good clothes. I hurried downstairs to the chapel where a few sisters and brothers were gathered for their early mass. I went up to the front where I usually sat with the boys, and Father Posset smiled at me. When mass was finished he told me I should be happy because I had a good patron saint. St. Nicholas was a jolly man who gave toys to children and was known as Santa Claus. Ehmbee and my mother had never told me I had a patron saint!

Finally it was almost Christmas. Everybody dressed in their school clothes and went to the refectory to watch the plays and hear the classes sing Christmas carols. All the fathers and brothers were sitting in the front rows; in the back were sisters and people from town. I sat on the floor at the front. A big curtain hung in front of the stage and I was eager to see what was behind it. All the lights went out except one at the front shining on the stage. Sisters said, "Shhhh," and put their fingers by their lips. The curtain opened. Georgie was standing in the front row of a bunch of young boys and girls, and I waved my hands at him and made him laugh. Sister told me to stop because he might make a mistake.

A big sister stood in front of the class and she waved her arms up and down and sideways as the children sang. When they were finished the curtain closed and everyone clapped their hands. When the curtain opened again, boys and girls were dressed up in costumes portraying the Nativity scene. They said their lines and sang more Christmas carols, ending with everyone on the stage singing "Silent Night, Holy Night."

A few days later Sister sent us to bed early. She woke us in the middle of the night so we could go to midnight mass at the church instead of the convent chapel. The church was almost full when we got there. We boys went to the front pews. We weren't supposed to look back, but I peeked and saw sisters and girls singing upstairs. In the front, spruce trees covered with ribbons and lights surrounded the crèche. It looked just like the church in Fort Simpson when I went to mass with Ehmbee at Christmas, making me feel a strange mix of happiness and sad longing for Ehmbee.

After, we had a hot chocolate and a piece of candy each. Sister told us that next day was Christmas and we would all get a present. I was excited, because back home I never got a present. My mother would make me a new pair of moccasins, but that was all. I never got a toy from the store. We didn't have a Christmas tree or lights. All we had was a coal oil lamp and candles.

In the morning, a big tree stood in the playroom with lots of presents around it. We had boiled eggs for Christmas breakfast. Sister called our names as she handed us each a small box wrapped in coloured paper. I got a small truck. It was red and could roll on the floor. Georgie's truck was blue. Many of the small boys had the same toy in different colours, though the bigger boys had different, bigger things.

Later that day, Georgie and I made little roads in the snow for our trucks. We tied strings to them and pulled them along the trails in the snow by the woodpile and along the fence to the barn.

When school started up again in January, I was able to go because I was now six years old. The class was held in the refectory by the girls' eating area. Pictures, numbers and letters covered the walls. I was surprised to find that boys and girls were in the class together. The teacher was tall, skinny Sister Gagnon.

Sister Gagnon spoke in English, of which I barely knew any words. Ehmbee spoke to me in Dene, and Sister Lapierre spoke to me in French. With Georgie and the other boys I spoke Dene. That first day, Sister brought me to the front to find out how much I already knew. I didn't understand her words, but I nodded as if I knew what she was saying. "Nicholas, do you know the numbers?" I nodded and started writing the letters "A, B, C, D …" on the board. Everybody laughed. "No. The numbers—one to ten." I wrote the numbers to ten. Again everyone laughed because "3" was backwards and I mixed up "6" and "9." Even Sister laughed. I put my head down, feeling embarrassed, but sister said I did fine—I just had to get all of the numbers the right way. I was astonished that she didn't get angry with me. She wasn't like Sister Lapierre, who never smiled or laughed. Sister Gagnon put me by Albert, a bigger boy, and told him to teach me the numbers and tell me what she was saying to the class. I learned fast, and it wasn't long before Sister moved me up to the front of the classroom. I liked school and tried to do everything that Sister asked me to do. By Easter, I could speak and understand English, and when Sister asked questions, I often raised my hand to answer.

Easter was a major holy week at the school. Sister Gagnon told us that a long time ago some bad people killed Jesus because he preached that he was the son of God. Sister pointed to a picture on the wall of an old man with a beard sitting in a big chair in the clouds. We drew pictures of Jesus and God with crayons, and Sister hung them on the walls in our class. I took some of my drawings to show Sister Lapierre, but she didn't say anything, and I put them in my drawer thinking that I would show them to Ehmbee when I went home in the summer. I wondered if she knew who God was.

We went to mass in the chapel every day during Easter. On Saturday night, we went to church at midnight just as we had at Christmas. Everything seemed sad, even the songs. There were no decorations, and all the statues and the cross were covered with purple cloth. Father Posset talked about how bad we all were and how Jesus was whipped and beaten, carried a cross and died for our sins. I wondered what sins were and why we were so bad. When Father finished, a brother took down the purple cloths off all the statues and cross. The songs grew more lively and louder. Father Denis, who was saying mass, kept saying "Alleluia! Alleluia!" and almost yelling *"Dominus vobiscum,"* telling us that Jesus had risen, making us all feel better. By the end, the girls and sisters up on the second floor were singing happy songs again and a sister standing in front of us waved her arm, urging us to sing louder. When mass was over, we all went outside and filed back to the convent. I was thinking that everything would be new and different and that we might even see Jesus. Instead we went straight to our beds. In the morning I woke up to Sister yelling at us to get up. Nothing had really changed. There were no gifts, but when we went down for breakfast, we were served boiled coloured eggs.

I could now speak English and do all the things that the other children did in class. I could read the books, could count up to a hundred and was learning to add and subtract numbers. I often got teased about being "white" and called names such as "Yellow Hair," but when I cried and told Sister, the bigger boys in my class would get angry and take it out on me in other ways. One boy, Freddy, teased me a lot; one day he took chalk from the classroom and put it in my soup at lunchtime. I knew that if I didn't eat it, he would hit me and make me cry, so I broke the chalk into pieces and swallowed it down with the soup without chewing it.

The days got longer and the snow started to melt. We had fun in the soft snow making snowballs and forts, waging war with one another. When all the snow melted, big ponds filled the field. The big boys carved boards into boats with their knives. A stick in the middle was hung with paper sails so the wind could push it across the pond. I was too small to have a pocket knife, but I asked a bigger boy to make one for me. We had races every day until the water dried up. Then we were set to work cleaning the yard. Starting near the bush we picked up all the sticks and rocks and put them in a pile. Bigger boys raked the dry grass into a different pile. When the yard was clean, the bigger boys had to scrub the row of toilets with pails of water and heavy brushes.

The seagulls, ducks and geese returned, landing in the snye. Robins, blackbirds and songbirds began making their nests. We found nests in the woodpile, out in the bush in small spruce trees or, for killdeers, on the ground.

Out on the river, the ice broke up. When the river was clear again, boys began running to the riverbank every day and looking upriver for the mission boat, which would be coming soon to take us home.

All the school books went into cupboards; we kept only our scribblers in which we wrote our letters and numbers. I was eager to go home and show Ehmbee how much I had learned. I could speak French and English, and I even knew a few Latin words that the priests said in mass, like *Dominus vobiscum*.

Finally one morning the *Santa Anna* arrived and we were told to get ready to go home. I was so happy. Our own clothes were brought down out of the cupboards, and there amongst the suitcases was my little bag, with "Walkie S" written on it. My pants, shirt and jacket still fit, though they were a little tight. I had to squeeze my feet into my moccasins. I wanted to run down to the boat right away, but Sister said we could go only after we'd eaten and put our coveralls and school clothes away.

After breakfast sister walked us to the boat, telling us to be good during the summer and to come back in the fall. She told us to make sure that we told our parents that we liked it here at school and that the sisters were nice to us. What she said didn't matter. I would tell Ehmbee the truth, that the sisters were mean and I hated eating fish all the time. The girls were already on the boat when we arrived. We walked up the boards onto the barge and up a ladder to the roof. A new sister made us all sit down while brothers loaded boxes on the front. Then the engines started and the barge powered away from the bank. Sisters on the shore and the children on the barge sang "Ave Maris Stella" ("Hail, Star of the Sea").

Soon the singing faded and now all we could hear were the engine and water swishing against the side of the barge. No one cried no matter how much the boat rocked. I doubt that any of us felt sad to leave the convent. It was a happy moment when we went around a point of land and could no longer see Fort Providence.

We stayed on the roof of the barge for three days, all the way to Fort Simpson. During the day the sun kept us warm, and at night, when it got cold, sister put a big canvas cover over us as we slept.

Sister on the boat was nice. She could not speak English well, only French. She came from Montreal but was heading north to teach at the convent away up in Aklavik. She was young and happy to be with us for the boat trip. She sang merry songs and was always smiling and laughing. The riverbank drifted by as we children talked about what we would do in the summer. A brother brought up big pots of porridge in the morning, soup and bread at noon and bread and meat before we went to sleep.

The morning we reached Fort Simpson was foggy, but slowly the houses emerged from the mist and grew bigger as we approached. Brother blew the horn, making sure that everyone knew we had arrived. We landed up by the HBC store, and I looked amongst the gathered people for Ehmbee, but I didn't see her.

A truck came from the mission, and Father told us to climb on. I scrambled off impatiently as soon as we got to Father's house and ran to Ehmbee's, which was not far across a field. I burst in and found Ehmbee on her knees washing the floor. A huge smile split her face when she saw me: *"Aeh, aeh, ce jaa!"* ("My boy!") She hadn't been expecting me until the afternoon. I ran into her arms. Ehmbee hugged me tight, kissing me all over my head and cheeks. I had not been hugged since I left home the previous year, and I felt as if I never wanted to leave Ehmbee's embrace. But I smelled a pot of rabbit soup simmering on the stove, and fresh bannock, and soon Ehmbee had me sitting with a big bowl of delicious soup. I ate all four legs and two bowls of soup.

After eating I was eager to go find my cousins Kenneth and Bertha, but first Ehmbee gave me a present, a small bag full of coins she had saved up for me all winter. All afternoon Kenneth and I played by the house, and we went out again after supper and played until bedtime. My own bed! I pulled it right up next to Ehmbee's bed, and she spoke quietly to me until I fell into a deep, warm, happy sleep.

It was such a joy to wake up at home. Sunshine filled the room, and there was an appetizing food smell. When Ehmbee saw me, she laughed. "You sure slept long!" and adding, "We will eat and then go visiting." I took my time enjoying my porridge, bannock and tea, and then we walked along a path on the riverbank to the road leading to the far end of the island. When we reached Jim Lafferty's house, rows of tents, one after the other, stretched as far as I could see. Dogs barked as we came to the entrance of the first tent. Outside, Deh'si was adding wood to a campfire, a pipe hanging from his mouth. Inside, Ka'hle rearranged their beds while two girls bigger than me washed dishes. They came out to shake Ehmbee's hand and mine, all saying how tall I had grown. Ehmbee looked proud and told them that I had just come back from school in Providence. I sat with Ehmbee on the spruce boughs inside the tent until the girls brought tea.

Soon, the girls could be heard laughing outside as they played, and when a rag ball landed by me I picked it up and chased after the girls as they ran screaming into the bush. We played until Ehmbee called me to go visit more friends. At an opening along the river a small tent stood. A dog tied in the bush barked. Gae'lih, a girl I had played with last summer, was playing in the entrance. A man and a woman came out of the tent and shook our hands. Ehmbee called the man Tan'che. The woman set out a cloth on the floor and brought a big plate of fish and put it in front of us. The fish smelled so good that I started eating fast with my fingers without saying anything. Tan'che laughed and said he could get more fish from his net down the bank. Gae'lih called then, so I went out with her to play tag.

We went further down the road until we reached the last tent along the river. It was the home of Baptiste Betsedia, who had played cards with me and won all the matches. While Ehmbee visited, I played kick-ball with all the other children. Every once in a while, I ran back to the tent to make sure Ehmbee was still there. Ehmbee finally called me to have meat and bannock and cold water. Then it was time to go home. The sun was going down and there was a cloud of dust along the road where the children were playing. I was tired, but blissfully happy after my first day back home.

For the rest of the summer I enjoyed my time with Ehmbee. Every few days we would check her snares for rabbits, leaving early in the morning and sometimes stopping to visit at 'Mena iih's house. A new trail led to a beaver pond, and Ehmbee showed me the big pile of mud and sticks that was their home. Sometimes we saw a beaver come up from the water and climb onto the house where it would clean itself with its little paws. Ehmbee told me that this was the father beaver; the mother was in the house with their babies. Some days Ehmbee caught no rabbits; other days there were two and she would give one to Papa. On the days we caught a rabbit, Ehmbee would make a big fire in the kitchen stove and cook the rabbit in a frying pan with bacon.

I also had fun with my cousins. We played hide-and-go-seek, made teepees amongst the willows or chased each other to a big warehouse or the ice house the teacher had in his yard. When there were enough children, we played anti-over, throwing a ball over a roof and trying to hit someone on the other side with the ball. Sometimes we picked raspberries with Ehmbee on the back road past Jimmy Cree's store. Once Ehmbee came running out of the bush and we thought bees were chasing her, but she had seen a bear eating berries in the bushes. From then on, we always watched for bees *and* bears. Ehmbee made jam with the berries that we ate with a spoon or put on our bannock.

I often went with Ehmbee to Jimmy Cree's store for canned food and flour or rice. She would tell me what she wanted in Dene and I would tell Mr. Cree in English. He would pile the items on the counter. Some cans and jars had pictures on them. Ehmbee knew that a cow on a can meant milk, a bee meant honey and a squirrel meant peanut butter. She could also guess by the colour of the tin cans or the size of the glass jars. The red milk cans had milk for my porridge; the white cans had thick sweet milk; the yellow cans, powdered milk. Ehmbee also knew which jar had sweet pickles, which she liked. When we were all done, Mr. Cree added up the price and I helped Ehmbee get out the right amount of money. I felt proud that I knew how to count so I could help her.

Too soon, Father Lesage came to tell Ehmbee that the mission boat would be in town in a few days to take all the children back to school. Father spoke a little bit of Dene, using the words *eh lah* and *jah te quon*, which meant "boat" and "Providence." Ehmbee asked if I could stay with her, explaining that she was getting old, and I felt a brief moment of hope. But Father said no, and as he walked back to his house across the field Ehmbee wiped her tears away with her handkerchief and didn't look at me. I sat by her on her bed and put my arms around her. I wanted to cry, too, at the thought of leaving Ehmbee and my happy life and going back to my sad, lonely life at the residential school.

After a few minutes, Ehmbee straightened up and said, "Let's go pick some berries." We went far into the bush, going past the snye and up the hill where there were lots of cranberries. When we took a lunch break and sat quietly eating and drinking tea, Ehmbee pointed to a bunch of nearby grouse eating berries, fattening up for the lean winter months. Once in a while, one of them would get up on a log and beat its wings and make a drumming sound. I tried to sneak up on them, but they flew into the trees, making sounds like they were laughing at us. It was nearly dark when we got home.

On my last morning at home, Ehmbee packed up my clothes in

my little bag. Kenneth and Bertha came with us as we walked to the boat. They could tell I felt sad, so they kept joking and doing antics to make me laugh. At the riverbank Ehmbee gave me a long, final hug, and I didn't want to go, but a brother waved his arms and yelled at me to get on the boat. My cousins waved but Ehmbee stood motionless and I knew she was crying. Inside the barge I went to a corner and huddled up, crying.

The water slapped the side of the barge as we left shore and headed upriver. The boat tied up for the night on Green Island, and in the dark we huddled on mattresses. The movement of the waves woke me in the night and I shivered from cold and fear. In the morning Sister shook us awake, pulling the blankets off and yelling for us to kneel for prayers. I knew most of the boys but there were a few new ones, mostly small. My friend Georgie was back, and we stayed close together during the whole trip. We didn't stop at Jean Marie River this time, but we did stop at Browning's farm and sawmill where two boys and a girl got on the barge. After a few days on the river, we arrived back in Providence as the sun was going down.

Chapter 3: Days of Darkness

IT WAS FALL of 1950 when I began my second year in Fort Providence. Sisters Rivard and Lapierre were waiting on the shore with a few boys as we got off the barge. Sister Lapierre led us up the bank to the convent and we went immediately to the dormitory to have our bath and get our hair greased for lice and cut. By the time we were given our coveralls and school clothes, it was dark outside, and we went to bed without eating. I thought mournfully about Ehmbee and all the things I did in the summer and soon fell asleep.

The next day, I went with all the grade ones and twos to class. I was sad to be in Providence, but happy to be back at school. I loved learning. I listened to everything the teacher told us to do. I was no longer the smallest boy and had been put in grade two, even though I had only gone to school for a few months the year before.

During the next few days and weeks, we fell into our routine: picking potatoes, piling wood and going into the bush to set snares for rabbits and squirrels. We went a few times to the boys' shack, and even slept there once. The snye froze and we played on the ice until it was covered with snow. Then we slid on the hills by the barn and at the snye.

One day Johnny, a much older boy, came over while we were sledding and played with me for a while, pulling my sled up the hill for me. He asked if I wanted to come with him to his snares, as he was sure he would have caught some rabbits and he promised to give me one. I thought about the five cents Father would pay me and the candy I would buy with it, and trotted along after Johnny happily when he ran ahead into the bush. We found his snares, but no rabbits. Once we were well into the thick of the bush he abruptly stopped and turned around. Grabbing me by one arm, he quickly took off my parka and pulled down my coveralls. I cried and pushed back at him, but he was much bigger and stronger.

Johnny turned me around, pushed me so that I was bent over and opened up my underwear in the back. I screamed as I felt something hard going into my bum. At first I thought it was his finger, but I realized it couldn't be, as he was holding me with both hands. "Stop, Johnny! Stop!" I cried. Johnny moved back and forth, breathing hard. I had no idea what he was doing, but it hurt, and I was shivering with cold. Suddenly I felt heat in my bum and running down my legs like hot water. Johnny stopped moving, but kept hold of me around the waist. I was crying hard. "Johnny!" I choked out. "You hurt me!"

"Stop crying!" he said sharply. He said that if I told Sister what had happened, he would beat me up. When he let me go, I scrambled back into my clothes, sobbing, and ran back to the hill where boys were sliding. My friend Georgie asked what had happened, but I didn't tell him.

From that time on, I hated and feared Johnny and I tried to stay away from him. Horribly, he did catch me one more time when I was alone in the boys' shack, and he did it to me again. This time it was even worse as it felt like fire in my bum, and when it was over, I wiped blood and cream from my bum and legs. Another time, he grabbed my arm and promised to make me a nice bow and arrow if I went in the bush with him, but I yanked myself away and, crying, threatened to tell Father what he did to me. After that I was careful never to play alone, and I stayed close to Sister when we were at the shack.

I didn't really understand what had happened—all I knew was that it was painful and made me feel bad. I felt sad and ashamed, but I didn't understand why. Sister never told us about things like that, and boys never talked about them. The closest we came to any teaching about sex of any kind was in catechism class, when teacher warned us not to think of girls and have impure thoughts, saying that it was a mortal sin. At seven, I had a vague idea that boys and girls could do something to each other, but I didn't think that boys could do anything with other boys. I was too scared to tell anyone what had happened. During confession I thought about it, but instead I told Father that I thought about girls, and he forgave me my sins. Even though I was able to avoid Johnny, I kept thinking about what he did and wondered if he would try to do it to me again. It made me wonder if all boys did that to each other, and a few times I woke up during the night with nightmares.

Classes and chores continued, and soon it was Christmastime. I was chosen to play Joseph in the Nativity play, and I practised my line over and over: "I am Joseph. There was no room in the inn." On the night of the concert, our class was first on the stage. I was dressed in a long brown coat, sitting by Margaret who was holding a doll and playing Mary. The curtain opened and everyone clapped their hands.

Our teacher, Sister Gallant, stood hidden behind the curtain at the side of the stage. She gave us the signal to start. The boys and girls who played animals mooed and baaed like cows and sheep. The shepherds waved their sticks, and the angels sang "Alleluia." It was my turn. The teacher pointed to me and moved her lips. I froze, forgot my line and started crying. I cried harder when everybody began laughing. After what seemed like forever but was probably just moments, the other children said their lines and sang a song, and the curtain closed.

I was still crying when Sister Rivard came behind the stage. She yelled at me to go upstairs to bed. I felt humiliated and ashamed of myself. For a long time after that, the boys made fun of me, calling me a crybaby and saying that I was stupid for forgetting my line. Only my friend Georgie said that it was okay; he nearly forgot his line, too.

The winter passed quickly. I was a good student and learned easily how to multiply and divide numbers, how to tell time on Sister Rivard's little watch and how to spell words. I read all the books that our teacher gave us. By spring I was almost as big as Georgie, and I was no longer scared to go in the bush by myself.

As had happened the previous year, we waited anxiously for the *Santa Anna* to come to take us home for the summer. Again we climbed aboard and set up camp on the barge's roof. Again we sang "Ave Maris Stella" as we pulled away from shore, happy to be heading home again. Some boys said that they would tell their parents everything that happened and would never come back again.

This time when the boat arrived in Fort Simpson, Ehmbee was with the others waiting on the riverbank. She looked so small as I ran up the hill to her. Gathering me into her arms, she cried and kissed me, exclaiming over how big I had grown. Everything at home was wonderfully the same. My bed was still in the corner across from Ehmbee's and my snowshoes, dogwhip, pack sack and playthings were in their places. Ehmbee put some wood in the kitchen fire and started cooking, not a rabbit this time, but a chicken she had caught in her snare a few days before.

For the next few days, Ehmbee kept me close by her side as we went to visit people living in tents along the river. We went first to the flats, then to the end of the island, going from tent to tent. We even went out to Four-Mile, along the Liard River. That day we started early in the morning, walking up the hill and along the airport road to Go-soa-lia Creek where we stopped for a drink of water. A trail through the bush led to Julie's house at Four-Mile, where we arrived at dinnertime, hot and thirsty. In Dene, the place is called *Eh tow cho*, and it's where all the Deneyoua people live. I had fun playing with Joe and Georgina, who also went to the convent in Providence. We stayed overnight, and the next day Julie and others walked back with us to town to get supplies from the store.

We visited Papa and Ama often. They lived near us in a big house right on the riverbank. Papa liked sitting by the window where he could see people walking on the road and all the boats that travelled on the river. Ama always hugged me and gave me cookies. She talked to me about my mother, Laura, still in the hospital far away. While we visited I played with a girl who lived with them, Bernice, and her little sister, Darlene.

On Treaty Day, Ehmbee and I went uptown to the flats, stopping to visit Ama for tea and bannock. Treaty Day was an important event every year with a big feast and dance. In Dene, they say, "*Samba nah je ah*," meaning that money was going to be paid. Men cleared the bush and set up tents, and in the afternoon we all gathered to sit in the tents or in the shade of tall trees.

Two chiefs, Baptiste Cazon and Louis Norwegian, told how treaty was paid to the people long ago. Baptiste said that when the government people came, our people didn't want to take treaty; they were suspicious and wondered why the government wanted to give them money and have them sign their names on a piece of paper. They knew that white people did not give anything for free. The treaty talk was mostly about hunting and continuing the Dene way of life, about being able to roam and use the land as they had always done. He said the government man pointed to the river and the sun, saying that as long as the river flowed and the sun rose and set, the government would look after them and that they would continue in their way of life. There was no talk about land. Louis said that he was a young boy when his grandfather, "Old Man Norwegian," was a spokesman for the people and involved in treaty talks. He said that the government met with the people for three days and still could not get Old Man Norwegian to sign any papers. One of the government men even promised to buy his grandfather a kitchen stove and carry it on his back to his camp far off in the bush.

Finally they broke off talks, and when they got together again on the following day, the government got another leader, Nakekon, to sign the treaty papers after they promised him a large supply of food. That was the way treaty was signed with the people. Nakekon, believing what had been promised, built a warehouse that winter thinking that in the spring a shipment of food would arrive on the boat. The food never arrived. To this day people still talk about how the government fooled the people into signing the treaty.

That afternoon while Ehmbee and I were attending Treaty Day, some of the people said, "Let's ask the Indian agent for a stove and food," and everyone laughed.

Eventually a truck came down the hill to the flats, trailing a cloud of dust. Two white men and a white woman went into one of the tents. Ehmbee told me that the one dressed in red was a policeman and the man dressed in a black suit was the Indian agent, Mr. Styra. Baptiste came out and told everyone that they could get their treaty money. The woman was sitting at a desk on which there was a stack of money and boxes of shells and fishing nets. When we reached the front of the line, the woman told Ehmbee to sign her name on a paper. Ehmbee laughed and said she didn't know how but took a pencil and made a wiggly cross beside her name. I decided I would teach Ehmbee how to write her name. The Indian agent gave Ehmbee five dollars and a box of shells and shook her hand. Ehmbee laughed again and asked what she was going to do with the shells since she did not have a gun. Mr. Styra replaced the shells with a fishing net. The policeman also shook Ehmbee's hand as she went by. I was scared of the huge white policeman.

Outside, pots were boiling on the campfires and everyone was helping themselves to meat and potatoes. When the sun went behind the hill a tea dance started. Six drummers stood to the side and sang Dene songs while almost everyone else danced round and round in a big circle holding each others' waists. After a while the drummers paused to warm up the drums by the fire, and everyone had a drink of tea or water before the dance started up again. We stayed and watched until I fell asleep sitting by Ehmbee, covered with her shawl. I woke up as the sun was rising across the river, and Ehmbee and I walked back home.

The summer ended when the mission boat arrived. Ehmbee packed my bag and took me to the boat. I cried and tried to hold on to Ehmbee, saying that I didn't want to go to Providence, but Father Lesage pulled me by my arm to the boat. A number of men stood by the barge, and one of them simply picked me up and shoved me aboard. Just before the barge door closed, I looked up the hill and saw Ehmbee, crying.

It was the fall of 1951, and I began grade three that year. Although I was bigger now (I turned eight that November), I was still teased about my brown hair and fair skin and older boys could still make me cry with their teasing.

Just after New Year's, Sister Rivard came to tell me that my grandmother had died. I didn't know a lot about death; I did know that old people died, but it seemed strange that either Ehmbee or Ama would die as they were both alive and well when I left them in the fall. I asked which one, as I told her I had two grandmothers. She didn't know, and it was a few days before a relative, Celine Bouvier, came to the school to visit. She told me that it was Ama who had died. There had been a fire in their house on New Year's Eve, and Ama and her granddaughter, Darlene, had burned to death. As I wept, Celine hugged me and told me to pray for Ama. For weeks afterward I prayed for Ama before I fell asleep. I also prayed for Ehmbee, glad that she was still alive.

The winter passed quickly. We studied, did our chores, set snares, went sliding or went to our shack in the bush. Spring flew by, and then summer arrived with its usual excitement, knowing that we would soon be going home. When the *Santa Anna* finally arrived, we boys all looked through the stacks of suitcases and bags for our belongings. My bag wasn't among them. I went to Sister, who shook her head: "Not you. Your grandmother died; you stay here this summer."

I tried to tell her that it was my other grandmother who had died, not the one who looked after me, but Sister would not listen. When I started crying she sent me upstairs to my bed. From the dorm window, I watched the other boys and girls laughing and shouting happily as they went down to the boat. I couldn't see the boat because Father's house was in the way, but after a while I saw the boat going down the river and disappearing behind the island. I cried until I fell asleep.

Alvin, an older boy, woke me to say it was time to eat supper. Downstairs, I was surprised to see a few other boys who were not going home: Danny, Charlie, Leonard and Alvin. At least I would not spend the summer alone. Alvin told me that he never went home even though he had a mother. Charlie and Leonard wanted to go home, but Sister had told them that their grandmother didn't want them. I learned that Danny had been in the convent since he was a small boy. Alvin said that it was fun staying in Providence in the summer, because the Sisters let us do whatever we wanted. We just had to be at the convent to eat and sleep. We were free to go anywhere we wanted, except town. We could play at the snye or in the bush or go with the brothers when they worked in the fields.

I spent the summer wandering the bush, playing in the snye, and fishing for jackfish down the bank. Sometimes Brother Marcheseau let me help him in the barn. I was scared of the bull, but I liked milking the cows. Sometimes Brother would catch me unawares and squirt milk all over my face. I also liked helping Brother Marcheseau in the root cellar where the potatoes were kept. We sometimes went down there and set mousetraps. It was dark, but Brother lit a candle so we could see to set the traps. We put all the mice we caught in a row, and by the end of the summer we had caught over fifty. Brother also took me into the noisy power house so I could see how the engines worked and where he put oil and gas.

One day Father Denis asked me if I wanted to serve benediction with him. I had never served mass before, so I said yes. I just had to watch everything the older boys did and do the same. I put on a cassock and white vestment and began following the boys around. There were times during benediction when I wasn't sure what I should do so I kept making signs of the cross, one right after another. Afterward, the brothers laughed at me saying that I had made more signs of the cross than Father Denis.

During that summer a boy named Harry arrived by plane. He had been at his parents' camp far away in the bush around Fort Liard, but somehow the Indian agent had found out about him and said that he had to go to the residential school in Providence. The RCMP brought him out by plane to Fort Liard, where he was put in jail for a week. Harry said that they had fed him nothing but lettuce and sardines before taking him to Fort Simpson and eventually flying him to Fort Providence by the mail plane. He was worried because his mother hadn't been around when the police took him away, so she wouldn't know where he was. Harry kept going to the Father Superior to ask if he could go home and return in the fall, but Father would not listen to him. Looking back today, I'm appalled by the fact that a boy could be taken from his family in such a cruelly careless way.

ONE DAY AT the end of summer, Sister told me that I would be able to go home to Fort Simpson for two days while the mission boat took freight to Simpson and returned with the schoolchildren. I was so happy! Ehmbee was waiting on the riverbank when the boat arrived in Simpson. The first thing we did was walk by the big blackened hole where Ama's house used to be. The fire had started at night, and people couldn't get Ama and the little girl out. Papa was trapping down the river at his cabin at the time, and friends went to tell him before he came back to town.

My two days home flew by, but Ehmbee and I crammed a whole summer into them, visiting friends and relatives or her snares, going to Jimmy Cree's store and playing with Kenneth and Bertha. As I got back on the boat with the other children, Ehmbee reached into her sweater and gave me a five-dollar bill from her treaty payment.

Some of the new boys on the barge were crying. Just as Dolphus had consoled me three years earlier, I put my arms around a smaller boy to comfort him. Many girls were sitting at the other end of the barge. A small girl with a blue ribbon in her long, shining hair—she looked just like a doll—smiled shyly at me. I'd never seen her before and I stared until Sister told me not to look at the girls. I wondered why that little girl had smiled at me. Maybe she liked me.

The trip to Providence was rough. We waited a day at Trout River for the wind and waves to die down before we crossed Mills Lake. Brother shot a bear on the shore while we waited, and the crew skinned it and made soup from the meat. Confined to the barge, I felt miserable and sad. My two days home had only been long enough to waken a yearning in me for my mother, Ama and Ehmbee. I wondered when my mother would come back from the hospital.

At supper a few days later, I saw the girl who had smiled at me. Her blue ribbon was gone, as was her long hair, but she still looked like a doll to me. She smiled, and this time I smiled back. The other boys noticed and began teasing me, saying that I had a girlfriend. Sister took notice, too, and made me sit with my back to the girls to help me avoid what she said were "sinful thoughts." Nonetheless, I watched for the girl (Betty, I learned one day), and every time we saw each other, in chapel or in the dining hall, we smiled surreptitiously at each other.

By this time, late 1952, I was nine years old, and it was time to receive my first communion. Ten of us boys and girls would be receiving the small round host on our tongues for the first time. In catechism class we learned that the host was the body of Jesus. I found it hard to believe, so I asked Father Posset. He said it was true and

I had to believe it with my whole heart and soul. Father Posset also explained that before taking our first communion, we had to tell the priest all our sins in confession. On a big piece of paper with pictures of the devil with a fork and a big fire, he showed us what the big and small sins (venial sins) were. Sins made our souls black and dirty and would drop us down to hell, he said, but if we told him all our sins, our souls would become clean and white as snow. Father pointed to the paper where it was bright yellow and said it was heaven. There were angels and saints, people with bright rings around their heads. While I had an idea that in the real world hell was far below in the ground, I didn't know where heaven was, so I asked Father where heaven was. He pointed up. For the next few days, whenever I was outside, I kept looking up to see if I could see heaven.

When I went to confession, I went into a small dark room where I knelt. I heard Father speak from an adjoining room through what looked like a screen, and he asked in a deep voice, "What have you done?" I didn't know what to say. When I remained silent, Father asked if I had stolen anything, said bad words or had impure thoughts. I told him I had taken some carrots from the brothers' garden in the summer. As for impure thoughts, I said I didn't have any but I had smiled at a girl five times. He said that those were just small sins and if I was sorry and promised to not do them again, God would forgive me. He had me say three Hail Marys. Sure that my soul was now white as snow, I avoided looking at the girls' side of the refectory for a long time.

At midnight mass that Christmas we received our first communion. When Father came with the host, I stuck my tongue out as far as I could. I was surprised that the host was just a thin piece of bread and not a big round candy. Sister gave us each a small medal and a card with a picture of Jesus. After mass we went to the refectory for hot chocolate and to watch Father Gote do magic tricks. He made a twenty-five-cent coin disappear from his hand only to find it again in his big beard. He also made rubber balls disappear then discover them under his hat. When the tricks were finished, he frowned and said he had set some traps for a wolf. Wolves were just as smart as a person so he had to use tricks to catch it. Every time he came to visit he told how he had just missed catching the wolf. He made funny faces as he told stories and made us laugh and believe that, with his tricks, he would soon catch the wolf.

BY THE TIME I went home in the summer of 1953, I was almost as tall as Ehmbee. Still, I did much as I had every summer, helping my grandmother with her chores or visiting our friends and relatives.

Ted and Bella Trindell's house was in the middle of the town. Ted was Ehmbee's nephew, but I called him Uncle. Bella brought tea and bannock while Ted asked me about the convent. I told him the sisters were mean and we ate fish almost every day for supper. When I told him I had passed grade four, he said, "You're smarter than me," as he had gone to school for four and a half years but hadn't passed grade four. "I was in there from 1909 to 1914 without going home. Five o'clock you jumped out of bed and prayed, the first bloody thing. Six o'clock you went to mass; seven o'clock, breakfast. You changed your clothes and cut wood with cross-cut saws. They weren't too sharp; you just had to rub it off. We cut wood till nine o'clock, changed clothes again and went to school till twelve o'clock. No recess. You go to school, say the prayers. And if you speak or do anything, you got punished. They wouldn't let you talk to a girl under any circumstance. It was a great big sin. Even to look at them. It was a sin. Twelve o'clock you had dinner. One o'clock you went back to school till three o'clock. After school you cut wood till suppertime. We cut wood, split it, piled it and then filled all the boxes in the place." He rolled his eyes. "I could tell you about fish, but I'll tell you another time." Ted showed me his hands: "We sure worked hard, but at least we left school knowing how to work with our hands."

Bella had also been in the convent when she was a young girl in the 1920s. They had to sleep on the floor. She remembered how the girls curled up on thin mattresses with just one blanket each to keep them warm: "When the stove went out in the middle of the night, it was cold."

I told them that we now had beds to sleep on and didn't have to cut wood and eat fish every day. They were both glad that things had improved since their days in school and, as he said, were "getting smart."

Thinking back, it is amazing to me that the residential school system, founded in 1840 to "educate the Indian out of the child," could have endured so long. In fact, the last didn't close until 1996.

As the summer days got shorter, Ehmbee became sadder and sadder, so on the night before the boat came, I made a plan. Papa had told me that long ago, when he was a boy, his father wanted to take him and his sister south on the last boat in the fall. Papa's mother ran into the bush with him and his sister until Papa's father had gone. He never came back. I figured that if Ehmbee and I were far away in the bush, I wouldn't have to go to Providence. In the morning, I suggested to Ehmbee that we go pick cranberries. She packed a bag with bannock and a tin of meat. We crossed the snye and climbed the hill to where the berries grew. The ground was red with berries so it didn't take long to pick a few lard-pails full. Ehmbee made a fire, boiled water for tea and we ate lunch. I napped on Ehmbee's knees by the fire. When the sun started going down, we walked home. My cousin Kenneth ran up and said that everyone had been looking for me all day. Kenneth and I ran down to the riverbank, and I rejoiced to see the boat going up the river. I had missed it!

Early next morning Father Lesage banged on the door. "Nicholas, you are a very bad boy for missing the boat. You will fly to Providence on next week's mail plane." Ehmbee begged him to let me stay. Father looked furious but didn't say anything, slamming the door as he left.

For the next few days, I helped Ehmbee fill the porch with wood and her drinking barrel with water. On Monday morning, Father arrived in a truck while I was playing outside. I just had time to run inside, grab my bag and give Ehmbee a hug before Father took me to the airport and put me on the mail plane to Providence.

The convent routine was in full swing when I arrived. Before I even had a chance to mix in with the students, Sister told me that I had to go see Father Superior. I didn't know who he was, but I went up to the Father's house and was shown into Father Superior's room. He looked cold and angry as he shut the door. Telling me that I was a bad boy for missing the boat, he pulled me to him, took down my pants and spanked me hard. He told me I should never do that again, and tearfully I agreed.

The sisters who looked after us, Sisters Letourneau and Lapierre, were also angry with me. Every time they had a chance, they twisted my ears or hit me on the fingers with their scissors. Sister Champoux, who taught grade five, was small, but she looked mean and walked around with a long stick in her hand. She made me stand in the front of the class and asked me why I missed the boat. When I said I was picking berries with my grandmother, she hit me across the back with the stick. I started crying and said I missed Ehmbee and my mother. Sister put me in the corner of the class, where I stood and cried. For the next few days, whenever I cried, Sister put a sardine can on my desk for my tears.

That year and the next, grades five and six, were my final two years at Providence. I became great friends with Alvin and Ernest, and on weekends we often went together to set snares, cooking and eating any rabbits we caught. Often, after we finished eating, Alvin would take a shiny mouth organ out of his pocket and play songs that we liked, such as "Ave Maris Stella," which was the song everyone sang when the *Santa Anna* took us home every summer. While he played, we would say "chug, chug" like the sound of the motor as the boat left Providence. He also played "Frère Jacques" which Sister had taught us in class. We also set snares for squirrels, and one day Alvin caught a big black fox, which made him proud. He took the skin to the HBC store and got two dollars which he used to buy snare wire, another trap and some candy.

Halfway through my final winter, 1954–55, Alvin got a letter from his mother with money to buy a ticket on the plane for home. Alvin hadn't been home in seven years. Later, we got a letter from him saying that he was in Calgary with his mother and that he missed all of us at the convent. He didn't like the city. One time when he was in a café and ordered rabbit, they laughed at him and said they only had cow and pig meat.

During that same winter my mother wrote to me from the hospital in Edmonton telling me that she was getting better and would return to Fort Simpson the following summer, at long last. When we all climbed aboard the mission boat to go home, the usually joyful day was marred by an event that had occurred several days earlier. We were crowded in the back of a truck on our way back to the convent after a picnic when one of the gates fell off. Several students tumbled out, and Emma, a girl from Fort Liard, was crushed at the bottom of the pile. A few days later she died and was buried in the cemetery at the convent.

Sister Champoux, for all her sternness, showed some kindness when Margaret and I finished the year as her top students in grade six, giving each of us a pen. Despite its hardships, Fort Providence had taught me much. I could read and write and do arithmetic. I knew the catechism by heart and could serve at mass. I could carve a bow from a diamond willow and pick straight red willows for arrows. I could spot birds' nests and knew which kinds of birds made certain types of nests. I knew how to set snares and catch rabbits, and I knew the best ways to trap squirrels. I was now eleven years old and thankful to be going home to Ehmbee and my mother.

THAT SUMMER EHMBEE and I waited expectantly each week after we heard the mail plane from Edmonton arrive. Would my mother be on this one? Finally the day came when she stepped through our door. Except for some grey hair, she looked much the same as I remembered. I felt shy with her—I hadn't seen her in six years—but we hugged long and hard.

Life at home settled into a familiar rhythm. Ehmbee went to her snares and carried wood in her big pack sack. I went every day with my cousin, Kenneth, joining other boys and sometimes Bertha. The Fort Simpson mission, with its barns and warehouses, fields and gardens, was our playground. When we tired of that, we went to the end of the island to climb the high towers, swim at the snye or fish for chubs. On July 1st, we had a sports day with races, pop and hot dogs, ending the day with a show. When barges arrived full of freight, Johnny Goodall's trucks hauled it to town. We chased them and hitched rides, sometimes far into the night. On hot days, we spent all day swimming in the snye. I often forgot about eating and came home hungry, ending the day with a meal of porridge and bannock.

We all had bicycles. I found mine at the dump and fixed it up with hay wire. It didn't have a seat, so I made one with a board and covered it with moosehide. We became expert in fixing our bicycles, and on days when it rained and we couldn't play outside, we painted them, a different colour every time.

In fall, the snye, from the southern tip of the island to the north, became our skating rink. I don't remember learning, only putting on an old pair of skates, which I bought from one of my friends for twenty-five cents, and skating like the wind. When the snow covered the snye we cleared a space on the river and played hockey. At the mission, Father had a small rink by St. Margaret's Hall, so during re-cesses and after school we played there, too. A second rink was by the Hudson's Bay store and we used it at every opportunity. Skating and hockey were our twin passions; even if there was a big storm, we cleared the ice with shovels and played till it was dark.

For the next few years I went to St. Margaret's Hall, a one-room Catholic schoolhouse with about thirty students from grades one to eight. It was in an old building, but during my grade seven year we moved to a new classroom attached to the public school. With the move, Sister Mack was replaced as our teacher by Mr. Gallant, who was assisted by Miss LaFleur to help the young students. Gabe Sabourin taught woodwork in a small room to the side. He was pa-tient with us and made the class enjoyable.

When Mr. Gallant arrived, I asked him to call me George. I didn't like the name Nicholas. It was not a common name; no one else in Simpson had it. Outside the classroom, however, I was still known as Walkie, for a Sergeant Walker of the US Army suspected of being my father. Henry Lafferty, an uncle, had started calling me Walker when I was a baby, but Ehmbee couldn't pronounce the name properly and called me Walkie, and the name stuck. My formal name, given to me by Mother at my baptism, was Nicholas George Frederick Alfred Sib-beston. Nicholas came from my godparents, the Shagarrys, who were of Russian descent. She may have named me George after my real father, George Dalziel, though I wouldn't know that for many years. Frederick was the name of my uncle. Why Alfred? I never did figure that out. Perhaps a priest liked the name. As a child I often wondered why I wasn't given a common name like John, Joseph, Albert, Jimmy or Charlie like everyone else. My attempt to change my name lasted less than a year, as Miss McEachern, who began grade eight, wouldn't call me George. So Nicholas, or later Nick, it was for the rest of my life.

Miss McGuiness taught me most of grade eight. She was a spirited Irish lady with a temper who demanded obedience in all things. On one occasion she reprimanded me severely, and I ran away down to Charlie Hansen's hotel, where I was staying and working part-time. I was determined to quit school, but Charlie talked me into going back, telling me that women were emotional and, as boys and men, we had to give them some leeway.

In my last two years in Simpson, Marie Lafferty, Marian Bailey and I took grade nine by correspondence courses from Alberta. The girls studied in a room on the Anglican side of the school and I studied on the Catholic side. Mr. Allen Cooke was our teacher. Doctor Cass, an optometrist, lived in the other side of the house. She was interested in Dene stories and learning Dene and would often ask me to get stories from my grandmother and write them down, which I did as often as I could.

Mr. Cooke tried to help me study, but he didn't know the subject material well, particularly math. When I finally wrote the departmental exams, I failed. Despite this, Mr. Cooke thought I had potential and encouraged me to continue in school. He had friends in Fairview, Alberta, who would let me stay with them and attend school in the fall. The family wrote suggesting that I travel to Hay River and take the bus south from there, but there were no roads or plane schedules to Hay River, and in any case I didn't have any money to get there, so the plan never materialized.

During those years I learned how to play guitar, inspired by watching the Lafferty brothers playing at Andy Whittington's dance hall. I would sit up close watching Morris and Peter play and examining where they placed their fingers on the guitar. I gazed longingly at the guitars in the Eaton's and Simpson Sears catalogues. With Ehmbee's help, I eventually ordered a Palm Beach model that cost fourteen dollars and ninety-nine cents. When it came in the mail, I practised the chords for hours. Johnny Cash was one of the popular singers at the time, so I tried singing all his songs starting with "I Walk the Line."

At home, I had become the man of the house, at least for cutting wood and fetching water. I was too young to go out in the bush to hunt or trap, but relatives gave us meat and fish to live on. Ehmbee still had her snare line and I would run up to the mainland and catch the odd squirrel, which I sold to the stores for twenty-five cents.

My mother had a small gun with "Ace" and "22 Short" written on it. It was kept upstairs in a big wooden box. I asked her if I could use it when we went in the bush but she was worried I might shoot myself. One day Ehmbee let me take it with her when we went to visit her snares. At the snye, she let me practise by shooting at a tin can far away in the sand. On the way home as I walked ahead of her I saw a chicken fly up into a tree. I ran back and asked Ehmbee for a shell. I was excited and I aimed at the chicken while Ehmbee was standing behind me. I shot once and missed, but the bird kept sitting there, so I got another shell and missed again. Ehmbee smiled as she gave me a third shell. This time the chicken flopped to the ground flapping its wings. I wanted another shell to kill it, but Ehmbee just grabbed the bird and wrung its neck. I was proud that I had shot my first chicken.

In addition to what we caught, we lived on Ehmbee's old age pension, twenty-five dollars a month. My mother went to the police for a ration voucher whenever we were short of food. Unfortunately, not all the money went for food. Mother continued drinking on weekends, ignoring Ehmbee's scolding. One winter night when she did not come home, I found her sleeping on the road by the Imperial Oil tanks and helped her walk home.

Drinking was part of life in Fort Simpson, even though there was no liquor store and no public place where people could gather to drink. Ehmbee did not allow any liquor in her house, so my mother had to go out to friends' homes to drink. Even as children we knew which homes had drinking going on. We were curious and sometimes watched as the partiers staggered out.

People made brew in their homes, always careful not to let the police catch them as it was illegal. If the police found a pot they would spill its contents on the ground and charge the brew-makers. During the summer, people hid brew pots in the bush. One person was surprised when he went to his pot and found that a bear had gotten into his brew and was thrashing around in the bush, drunk. Brew was made early in the week and hidden away until the weekend. It was not potent and one had to make at least five gallons to have enough for a party.

My cousin Bertha knew the recipe from watching her mother, and, one time in the summer a bunch of us went into the bush with a pot and some raisins, sugar and yeast and made brew. A few days later, we had a party. We drank a lot before we felt anything, but nonetheless, we were soon running around, yelling, laughing and acting like the drunken adults we had watched. Fortunately, nothing bad came from it other than throwing up and getting some scratches and bruises.

My mother eventually left to move to Hay River. She found it hard to live with us after so many years in a hospital where it was always warm and had indoor toilets and southern-style food unavailable in Fort Simpson stores.

One winter, Charlie Hansen came to town with my aunt Edna and their daughter, May, to fix up Andy Whittington's hotel. Andy had retired south and Charlie bought the place for a hotel and café. I began working for them when I was thirteen, doing everything from bringing in wood and ice to working as a waiter in the café. After a few months, I began staying with Edna and Charlie so I could work early in the morning or late at night, and they even took me to Edmonton for a month one spring. I liked the city and seeing all the different sights. It was the first time I really understood that there was a big world beyond Forts Simpson and Providence.

Chapter 4: A Northern Education

WHEN FALL OF 1959 came, I decided to go to Sir Alexander Mackenzie School in Inuvik to finish my schooling. I was fifteen years old (I would turn sixteen that November) and I made the decision by myself; my mother was in Hay River and my grandmother would probably have rather had me stay home. Grade nine was not offered in Fort Simpson, and I had failed the correspondence course I took the previous year. I could have stayed and worked for my uncle at the hotel or simply lived with Ehmbee and looked after her, but it didn't seem like enough. I knew I had to continue my education, even though leaving Ehmbee by herself to get wood and ice in the winter was difficult.

The afternoon I left was a beautiful fall day. Ehmbee walked with me down to the river where a single-engine floatplane was docked and a dozen of us students clambered on board. In theory, a single Otter plane could carry only about ten passengers, but they jammed us in wherever they could with little concern about safety. Other students from further up the river were already aboard, and once more, as the plane propelled its way away from the shore into the river current, Ehmbee stood on the riverbank, hands wiping away tears from her eyes. The image of her on the bank, filled with grief, haunts me to this day. The plane rose and headed north, stopping at communities to pick up more students. When we got to Inuvik, twenty-five of us climbed out into the swirling snow.

I immediately regretted my decision. All the Catholic students were brought to Grolier Hall, the Catholic residence. I was separated from my friend Richard Hancock who went to the Anglican hostel for the year. Also, I had been away from residential school life for four years, looking after myself, eating when I was hungry, sleeping when I was tired and doing what I wanted to do. Now I had returned to a strict routine and to the hands of sisters, brothers and priests.

At least the arrival ritual was not as traumatic as in Fort Providence. They did not delouse us, bathe us, shave off our hair or take our clothes away. I guess they realized that, as teens, we would not have put up with such treatment. We did shower and were given haircuts, but we kept our own clothes. Nevertheless, the routine at Grolier Hall was very much Providence all over again, albeit with more modern and comfortable surroundings.

By Providence standards, Grolier Hall was a palace. Everything in it was new, clean and huge. We didn't have to pick potatoes or haul and pile wood or go outside to the toilets. The boys' and girls' sides were separated by a large central refectory for eating, a chapel and administration offices. The priests, brothers and sisters ate their meals in a small room off to the side. Our dormitory held approximately sixty beds all lined up in rows and the hall had a gymnasium and play area. The food was better, too. I wrote my mother to tell her we ate just like in a café. In the morning, we had eggs, toast, porridge or beans; at lunch we had soup and sandwiches, at supper, reindeer meat. At least we didn't have boiled cabbage, cooked blood and fish, which were the main foods in Providence.

One notable change was that we older boys did not have sisters looking after us. Instead, we had Brother Morin and Mr. Roger Moore. (The smaller boys and all the girls still had sisters as their supervisors.) The little boys, as young as five and six were under the care of Sister Hébert, a stout woman who ordered them about brusquely. We called her The General. It reminded me of my Providence days, and I wondered why the sisters had to be so harsh. Couldn't they show kindness with children? Things hadn't really changed despite the more lavish surroundings.

Brother Morin and Mr. Moore were rigid and authoritarian in their own way. One issue was their insistence on coveralls. At first, as in Providence, whenever we were not in mass or class we were made to wear coveralls. We were in and out of them throughout the day. It didn't make any sense and it made us feel like small boys unable to keep our regular clothes clean. We reluctantly complied, except Kenny Hodgson. He was big enough that neither Brother Morin nor Mr. Moore could do much about it when Kenny refused to wear the coveralls. We all quietly admired him and wished we could do the same. Still, we complained to Father France, the Superior and, after Christmas he changed the policy, at least for the older boys.

Brother Morin caught me smoking on the way back to the dormitory after school one day. He reprimanded me as if I had committed a great offence, and on the following Sunday, immediately after church and lunch, I was sent to bed for the rest of the day. I could see boys and girls skating on the rink and having fun. I went without supper and missed the Sunday evening show. I thought that my punishment was overly severe and inappropriate for my age, and I resented the way Brother Morin treated me. Later in the year, he was replaced by a young man named Cliff Winniandy, with whom I got along quite well.

Our classes were in Sir Alexander Mackenzie School, which had hundreds of students from both the residences and the town. Grades one to nine were segregated by religion into the Catholic and Anglican wings. My grade nine class held about twenty-five students from Grolier Hall and a few from town.

I immersed myself in my classes, though I sometimes wondered about the value of what I was learning. Why, for example, did I need to know about the different soil types across Alberta and the different grains that grew there? With the wind raging outside in minus-forty-degree weather, it didn't seem relevant. At Grolier Hall, I played hockey and learned to play basketball. We built a skating rink with boards and lights near the residence, which we flooded every day from a barrel filled with hot water. Hockey was our main activity, and we were organized into teams. I was on the Black Hawks, and when our team won in the finals, we were awarded a trip with Father France in a Bombardier to Reindeer Station. Kenny Hodgson was one of our better players, and Arthur Jumbo from Trout Lake, who had never played hockey before, was an excellent goaltender.

My best friend there was Billy Bourque; we were inseparable and even shared some of the same girlfriends. I had a few puppy-love girlfriends—Elsie, Wilhelmina and JoAnne were three I remember.

Groups of us went into town on Saturday afternoons to see movies at Peffer's and shop in the stores. It was common for us to go the HBC store and steal things like hair cream and toothpaste. One boy, Jamie, perfected the art of concealing things under his coat, coming out of the store with jeans and shirts.

There were strictly enforced curfews on our town "leave." We passed over the utilidor (the above-ground water and sewer system) on our way to and from town, and near it were some sheds that provided privacy. We would time our trip home such that we could spend a few moments in this "kissing" area with our girlfriends.

Everyday chores included keeping the dorm, washrooms, hallways and entrances clean and keeping the rink free of snow and flooded. We helped Father Ruyant haul cases of food from the warehouse or cart laundry to and from the laundromat in town. Father Ruyant even let us drive the truck occasionally. During the winter a few of the boys decided to try the test for a driver's licence. Even though I had only driven a few times, I decided to try too. My test took place on a back road that led to town. The examiner was sitting by me in the front and Father and the boys were in the back urging me on. I was nervous as I put the truck into first gear, releasing the clutch and starting down the road. So far, so good, but I couldn't go forever in first gear. I pressed the clutch in but I had a hard time finding second gear. I looked down, and in that brief moment, I drove off the road into a snowbank. Once everyone recovered from the shock, they howled with laughter. Needless to say, I didn't get my driver's licence and was the brunt of lot of teasing. It was years before I tried again.

Playing guitar with friends was a constant pastime. Billy also played guitar and sang, while Richard Lafferty played the violin. We whiled away many hours of our free time. Towards the end of the year, Mr. Frank Frey, the principal, called me into his office and warned me to play less guitar and to concentrate on preparing for the Alberta departmental exams. I don't know where he got information about my playing, but I didn't pay much attention to his advice. As the river ice began breaking up at the end of June, we boarded a DC3 and were dropped back to our home communities as the plane made its way south. I was happy to get back home.

That summer I stayed with Ehmbee and worked on the new school and residences they were building in Fort Simpson, Bompas and Lapointe Halls. One of my jobs was helping to tile the ceilings. I would put five dabs of glue on each tile and throw it up to Jonas Antoine on a high scaffold. He, in turn, handed the tile to another man, who placed it on the ceiling. Once in a while my aim in throwing the tile was a bit off, and glue would spatter all over the two men, who would curse and threaten to fire me. With my first paycheque I bought a carton of Black Cat cigarettes because "a working man should smoke." Later I bought a radio, ordering it from Eaton's catalogue; all of my young life I had envied people who could listen to music at nights when the reception from the southern stations was good.

Midway through that summer of 1960, the results of my exams came. No one was more surprised than me to learn that I had passed the grade nine departmental exams. I had not been giving much thought to school, content to work, make money and enjoy being with Ehmbee. But toward the end of that summer I worked with Joe Wager, an electrician. He was a kind man, good to work with, and because of him I decided to become an electrician. Thus, as fall approached, I applied to the industrial trades program at Sir John Franklin School in Yellowknife.

Everything was arranged, but the day we were to fly to Yellowknife, Sid Hancock, the school principal and administrator for the government in Fort Simpson, said that I and his son Richard were to go to Inuvik, as there was no room for us in the residence in Yellowknife (Akaitcho Hall). I declared that I would rather quit school than go back to Inuvik, and Richard agreed. For a few weeks, we just hung around town doing nothing. One day Mr. Hancock came to my house to say that there was still no room in Akaitcho Hall, but there was in Breynat Hall in Fort Smith. I could take regular classes for my grade ten. By this time, my enthusiasm for a career as an electrician had waned and I was bored, so I agreed to go to Breynat Hall. I felt bad leaving Ehmbee again, but knew that I had to continue my education.

I flew into Fort Smith at night. No one picked me up, so I caught a ride into town and stayed at the Pinecrest Hotel, walking over to Breynat Hall in the morning. Father Mokwa was the Superintendent and

Brother Klaus was our supervisor. Breynat Hall was a typical Catholic residential school. Except for the superintendent, Father Mokwa, and the supervisor, Brother Klaus, all the staff were Grey Nun sisters, plus a few local women who worked in the laundry and kitchen. The dormitory, playroom and refectory were organized in the usual residential school manner, and the daily routine of praying, eating, doing chores and attending school was similar to Inuvik. On weekends, particularly in the fall, we went out to the boys' cabin in the bush, a few miles out of town. The rules were not as strict as what I experienced in Inuvik though we were largely confined to the yard and area around the school. Brother Klaus was an easy-going older man who didn't keep too close a watch on us. We could occasionally make evening forays into town, getting back just in time for bed.

I was the only one in grade ten staying at Breynat Hall. I longed to have other students in the same grade to talk about classwork and help each other if needed. I soon discovered that three boys in my grade ten class—Robert Beaulieu, Isidore Tourangeau and Leon Sambele—lived at Grandin Home just across the road. Partway through the year I asked Father Pochat, the head of Grandin, if I could transfer, and he agreed so I packed up and moved in. It was a good move. We each had our own room where we could study. In all my previous years in residential schools in Providence, Inuvik and now Fort Smith, I had never had a private room. Living in Grandin Home, away from a dormitory atmosphere, was a pleasant change.

Grandin was primarily home to young boys (such as James Wah-Shee, Freddy Zoe, Wilbert Antoine, Barney Masazumi and Charlie Charlo) who had been chosen from throughout the north for their academic ability. At Grandin they took grades six to eight but were also being groomed to become brothers and priests. A similar program operated at the hospital in town for young girls interested in becoming nuns. One of the girls there, Phoebe Nahanni, was my girlfriend that winter, and I teased her that if she kissed me, she couldn't become a nun.

We older boys followed the rules of the house as far as the meal schedules and study periods were concerned, but apart from that we were pretty well free to do as we wished. We were all mature and determined to do well in our courses. We didn't drink and kept ourselves busy studying and taking part in the sports programs at school. All four of us played basketball with Mr. Daryl Clarkson as our coach. I hadn't played basketball seriously before but I learned quickly. I was not very tall so I played guard and became a rough-and-tumble guy in that position. We travelled to Edmonton a few times to compete against city high schools. We played a lot of hockey, too.

The high school had many excellent teachers, such as Mr. Muse, our homeroom teacher, and Mr. Bob Shone, who taught science. With its quiet atmosphere and solid programs, I got a good grounding in all the academic subjects I would need to go to university. The two years at Grandin Home went fast, and I soon finished grades ten and eleven. Father Pochat told Robert, Leon, Isidore and me that they could not accommodate us any longer as they needed the space for younger students. I was disappointed, as I liked the high school, the teachers and the friends that I had made there, and I'd come to like the town as well. But I couldn't stay, so in the summer of 1962 I went back home again to Fort Simpson.

By this time, Ehmbee was quite old, close to one hundred. She was having a difficult time going into the bush and packing wood as she had done all her life. She would look to the river and say, "I wonder if I'll live to see the ice go away next spring."

I had gone well beyond anyone from the community by finishing grade eleven, and I pondered whether to take the next step and go on to grade twelve and finishing high school. In the end, I decided to go, and to do that my only real option was Sir John Franklin High School in Yellowknife, where Akaitcho Hall was the residence.

It was like going from church to a square dance. Whereas Grandin Home had an atmosphere of quiet study and academic performance, Akaitcho Hall was a great big social zoo. Hundreds of young people of both sexes from all over the North stayed at Akaitcho, taking academic programs as well as basic vocational ones. It was a territorial melting pot. If we weren't doing chores, attending school or sleeping, we were socializing, making it difficult to study and take our courses seriously. There were dances every weekend and opportunities to go uptown almost every day. Quiet time was scheduled each night for study, but it was difficult to work with four roommates close at hand. I was serious about my courses but I often felt that I was going against the grain trying to be a good student.

Bert Boxer was the Superintendent of Akaitcho Hall; Miss Fairfull the matron. John Radcliffe oversaw the boys; Miss Stoby, the girls. A few boys were chosen to be monitors to help Mr. Radcliffe supervise and enforce the rules. Though I was newly arrived, I was placed in one of these privileged positions. We made sure that the boys got up in the morning, went to bed at night and did their chores according to the schedule set by Mr. Radcliffe. Disobedience was punished by the loss of town leave. Monitors were given extra privileges such as movies on Sunday night.

A number of us had musical instruments and would get together and play music in the common room. With Mr. Radcliffe's encouragement, we formed a band called the Arctic Ramblers and played for all the Friday night dances. As we got better we played other places, including Fort Providence and Hay River. Members of the band included Gordie Cardinal, Billy Bourque and Albert Canadian as singers; Alfred Lockhart, Isidore Tourangeau and myself playing guitar; and Richard Lafferty on the fiddle. We laughed and said we were like the Thousand Strings orchestra; once we got into a certain rhythm, we could go on endlessly and were hard to stop.

Throughout my stay in Akaitcho, I played juvenile hockey, and at one point I played briefly with the Giant Grizzlies men's hockey team. Earlier, I had started smoking Matinee cigarettes, which were not too strong, but I quit when I started playing men's hockey. After that, I smoked only when I drank, which in those days was seldom as I was focused on my studies. In any case, there were few opportunities to drink and we were never free to go uptown for more than a few hours at a time. My friends in those days were Gordie Cardinal, Alfred Lockhart and Ron Holtorf. Girls were ever present, and, like everyone else, I had various casual girlfriends—Margaret, Ellen and Lily come to mind—but nothing too serious.

My first year at Sir John, 1962–63, was successful, though I often had to go over to the school in the evenings to study by myself away from the activities in Akaitcho Hall. I had excellent teachers like Mr.

Audie Dyer, who taught social studies and was my homeroom teacher. At one point, I had a crisis when my mother, still drinking, arrived in town without a place to stay. I considered leaving school and working to help her, but Audie and his wife, Vera, came to the rescue and took my mother in; she worked for them for a time doing housework and looking after their young children.

I passed all of my grade twelve courses except English, so after a summer working with the Department of Public Works in the bush I returned to Akaitcho Hall in the fall of 1963. I would repeat English 30 and one other course to upgrade my marks with a view to going to university.

By the end of January 1964 I had finished high school, though I had failed English 30 again. I was offered a job at Giant Mines and played hockey with their team. My main task was to keep the rail tracks which ran between buildings clear of snow. Often I would take a break in the utilidor that snaked through the mine site and catch some extra sleep. Those of us who played hockey for the mine were given special treatment, and as long as I kept out of sight, I was fine. When spring arrived and the hockey season was over, I went to Edmonton and stayed at my aunt and uncle's place while I took an English 30 correspondence course. I wrote the exam in June but failed once again. I returned to Yellowknife to work for the rest of that summer and made arrangements to write the supplementary exam in the fall. This time I took a different approach. I didn't study before the exam and decided to be very creative in my writing. I focused on the essay portion and passed with a 60 percent grade. At last! It was good enough to get me into university.

It was during my time working in Yellowknife that I began my drinking career. I thought I was just being one of the guys, enjoying a few drinks and chasing girls and, on a few occasions, sleeping with them. I enjoyed drinking, and liked the taste of beer and various stronger drinks. I often went to extremes in doing ridiculous things to have fun. One time, my friend Ron Holtorf and I were flying to Fort Simpson for a spring visit. We were the only passengers on the DC3; the rest of the space was filled with freight. We opened up the bottles of whiskey in our pack and began drinking; before long we were feeling good. We found a case of ice cream in the cargo and thought: why not? By the time we landed in Simpson we were very high and as the plane door opened we stood singing with a bottle in one hand and an ice cream in the other. We made a nuisance of ourselves, running through the bush and slipping around in the mud. This was before Fort Simpson had a liquor store, and whiskey bottles were scarce. I quietly left town after staying low for a few days, as I had made quite a fool of myself. By this time Ehmbee was confined to a hospital, and I was thankful she didn't know about my bad behaviour. Another time, after my friend Gordie Cardinal and I had drunk quite a bit, we decided that we would cut down our boozing by drinking one less bottle each weekend until we had it under control. Of course, that didn't work, and we continued our carousing every weekend.

Chapter 5: University and Marriage

IN THE FALL of 1964 I went off to the bright lights of Edmonton to enrol in the Faculty of Education at the University of Alberta. The thought of a big university was exciting for a northern boy whose high school had held only a few hundred students.

I never had aspirations to any particular profession. I kept going to school just because I knew I didn't want to be a labourer and work hard physically, and I intuitively knew that education would be useful in whatever I did in life. I just went grade by grade and was always surprised when I did well.

Throughout high school teachers had been my main influence and inspiration. Allen Cooke had helped and encouraged me through grade nine in Fort Simpson. Fort Smith was full of good teachers like Mr. Muse, Mr. Shone and Daryl Clarkson, our basketball coach. At Sir John Franklin, by far the most influential person was Audie Dyer, who took a personal interest in me and assisted my mother when she was in need of help. So when it came to choosing a faculty, it seemed natural that I should become a teacher.

During my first year I stayed at St. Joseph's College, a residence in the middle of campus where, like Grandin Home, there was a studious atmosphere. I had a room to myself and all around me were serious students. While I was comfortable at St. Joe's and engrossed in my courses, as a northern Aboriginal I was uneasy and intimidated by the south, by the big city and by the enormity of the campus. The students in the south all seemed much smarter than me and English was still difficult. As long as I attended classes and studied, the feeling of insecurity remained latent. Still, I was shy amongst southern students and preferred the company of northerners, particularly Aboriginal people. With them I was in my element, joking and having fun. And when I had had a few drinks, there wasn't a happier and more fun-loving person than me.

The social activities on campus didn't interest me much. I visited a couple of fraternities but I didn't fit into that crowd. I dated a bit, including a few white girls, though I was mostly attracted to northern girls who had the same cultural outlook as me. All my high school girlfriends had been Dene or Métis. On weekends I often went downtown to places where I could find people from the North. Hotels and bars like the Cecil, Mayfair and Corona along Jasper Avenue and many along 97th Street were known to be "northern" hangouts. Far too many Sundays were spent feeling hungover and regretting the loss of valuable study time.

A number of us decided that it would be good to have a northern students' organization to provide a social network and help other northerners adjust to city life. We were getting together practically every weekend and it wasn't hard to corral everyone for a few hours of sobriety to do something good. Maybe we were seeking a way that would help save others from the sins of life in the city and keep them focused on their studies. We informed the government educational officials who were responsible for directing and monitoring students, and they were supportive.

For any student, the transition from high school to university or college is difficult, but for northerners it presented additional cultural shocks. A small group of us sought out northern students attending the university, the Northern Alberta Institute of Technology, Grant MacEwan College, McTavish Business School and Marvel Hair Dressing School and invited every one of them we could find to a gathering at a downtown hotel. About fifty turned up, and reporter Ralph Armstrong from the *Edmonton Journal* wrote an article about the organization, extolling all the good things we planned to do. That day we formulated a constitution and bylaws; I was the first president, with Ron Holtorf and Jake Heron as vice president and treasurer. When all the formalities were done, out came the beer, and eventually we were politely asked to leave the hotel due to the traffic and noise. Back in Yellowknife, we organized dances to raise money and received a little financial assistance from the government. The following fall, we brought two high school students along with a chaperone from Yellowknife to Edmonton to tour a number of academic campuses. We made sure that we impressed on them that academic life was nothing but gruelling hard work, study and little or no social life.

In my very first year at university I met Karen Benoit, a beautiful girl from Lloydminster, Alberta. In the four classes we shared, she sat near the front, and from my usual seat at the back of the class I admired her flowing blond hair. I sometimes saw her at the Newman Centre in the basement of St. Joe's, where many Catholic students gathered to eat and socialize, but I was too shy to ask for a date. In fact, I saw her picture sitting on the desk of a boy named Dennis, whose room was next to mine, and thought she was already taken.

Nonetheless, when I was invited to a keg party at the end of the year for the few students and staff remaining at the college, I called Karen on the off chance that she was still in the city. She had just come out of the hospital with mononucleosis and was hesitant to go out, but I persisted, telling her that it was a St. Joe's function and that the priests and brothers in attendance would keep it a mild affair. I even told her that she was the thirteenth girl I had called without success. After more of the hemming and hawing that girls do when they don't really want to go out with you, she agreed, on the condition that I take her home early.

The party was well underway when we arrived; beer was flowing freely and the whole hillside was covered with guys and girls and college staff. I had a few drinks, and then a few too many, and it wasn't long before Karen wanted to go home. I could tell that she wasn't too impressed with me or the antics of the supposedly saintly St. Joe's gathering. A friend drove us back home, and as we sat in the back seat Karen had to repeatedly slap my wandering hands. The next day, remorseful, I was sure that she would never go on a date with me again.

When first year ended, I worked for the Department of Public Works (DPW) on a land survey crew in Inuvik and Fort Smith. The results from my exams reached me while I was in the bush at the

DPW highway survey camp. I was overjoyed to find I had passed all of my courses except English, which I would have to repeat during my second year.

I think I was caught up in the notion that once you passed first year, it was clear sailing, so I decided to live off-campus and got a room in a boarding house. I had cash from my summer's work and money from the student grant program. The first few weeks were fine but soon I began partying again, and within a month or so, I was missing more classes than I attended. By Christmas I realized that I was failing and made the decision to move into Lister Hall, a men's residence on campus.

I reconnected with Karen at the Halloween dance at the Newman Centre. Looking cute as Raggedy Ann, freckles and all, she danced non-stop. When I finally got bold enough to ask her for a dance, she said she didn't want to be limited to any one suitor. She went to dances for the sheer enjoyment of dancing, not for the benefit of boys. Still, by the end of the evening, she had agreed to a date with me for the following weekend.

Karen was different from other girls I knew. For one thing, she didn't drink. All my socializing with girls until then had included alcohol of some sort, but Karen enjoyed things that didn't involve liquor such as ping-pong, skating, cross-country skiing, going to movies and, most of all, dancing. We went often to the discotheque Outer Limits on Whyte Avenue. Karen was serious about her studies, and she also said no to my advances.

Despite Karen's good influence, I continued to drink and skip classes, with the predictable result that I failed most of my courses that year, including English. During a break from my summer job as a telephone lineman at Fort Smith, I went to see Dr. Pilkington, the Dean of Education, and pled with him to give me another chance. He said he would consider my situation, and in a few weeks I received a letter agreeing to let me repeat my second year.

It was while I was in Fort Smith that summer of 1966 that Ehmbee died. It was impossible to make the journey from Fort Smith to Fort Simpson in time for the funeral, so I grieved alone.

BACK IN EDMONTON that fall, I moved in with my aunt and uncle, Charlie and Edna Hansen, renting a basement apartment in their home. I bought a car from my friend Jake Browning, and during one of the fall breaks I hitchhiked north to pick it up. My mother came back with me, as I thought it would provide some stability to my life to have her with me. Unfortunately, both the car and my mother ended up being troublesome. The car was costly to operate and to park at the university, and my mother went out drinking every weekend. I hadn't lived with my mother since I was a young teenager when she returned home to Simpson from the hospital, so I didn't realize the extent to which drinking was part of her life. During the week she was a perfect mom caring for me, cooking and looking after my clothes. Come Friday night, she paced the floor wanting to go downtown, driven to drink as strongly as ducks wanting to fly south in the fall. Sometimes I physically tried to stop her from going, but all attempts failed. On many a Sunday night I received a phone call from the 97th Street area asking me to pick her up.

Karen and I went steady all that fall and winter. When I felt assured that the relationship was real, I took her home to meet my aunt, uncle and mother. Charlie and Edna took an immediate liking to Karen, but my mother took one look at Karen's fashionable hairstyle and put up her nose. She turned away from Karen's proffered hand and left the room. Later, alone with my mother, I scolded her for her behaviour and asked her who she thought was more suitable for me in Simpson. She didn't answer. Fortunately, Mother's reaction was short-lived, as she came to like Karen very much once she got to know her—a nice, down-to-earth country girl and not the uppity city girl of her initial impression.

My mother returned north at Christmas. Her drinking in the dangerous 97th Street area had caused me endless anxiety, so I wasn't sad to see her go. I ploughed into my studies, but for some reason I wasn't doing well. A lot of the time I felt restless and unhappy. I still drank a lot on weekends, and I missed classes during the week. I had none of the focus or enthusiasm of my first year. When I missed a few of my practice teaching placements in city high schools, my professor, who knew that I was from the North, told me, "You can't just go shooting squirrels any time you feel like it," and failed me. With that, my hopes of becoming a teacher ended. In fact, I ended up failing most of my courses, again including English. It was the second time I had failed my second-year courses in the Faculty of Education, and I knew there was no chance I could persuade the dean to let me try again. After three years in university, I had less than one year of courses to show for it.

Karen, of course, had passed all her courses and was eligible to go into her fourth and final year of education studies. She came with me to Yellowknife for the summer. Her parents were concerned, her dad saying, "What do you want to go to that Godforsaken country for?" She stayed at Hugh Arden's house initially, then at the YWCA, while working as a bank teller. This was during the time when Yellowknife was strictly a mining town and there were something like nine men to every girl. I knew that Karen had many admirers and I used to make frequent deposits at the bank to keep an eye on her. To my delight, Karen liked the North, the long days and the rocky environment. We spent a lot of our spare time exploring and walking on the rocks along the lakeshore.

The thought of Karen going south to university without me was painful. She was attractive and sociable, and I knew she would be pursued by other men. I was in love with Karen and couldn't endure the thought of letting her go back south while I was stuck in the North with no future. Fortunately she liked me too and wanted to stay in the North.

Late that summer I had to go to Fort Smith. During the previous summer I had a relationship with a woman that resulted in a child being born. I had to deal with the issue and Karen agreed to come with me. I arranged to see my son and speak to the mother. I did not see him again for many years. I also visited Father Pochat in Fort Smith, and he offered Karen a job as a supervisor at Grandin College. I went next door to Breynat Hall to see Father Felix Labatt and was surprised to find that they needed two supervisors for the coming school year, one for the boys and one for the girls, so I applied for and got the boys' supervisory job. A few weeks later Father Pochat advised Karen that their plans to expand had fallen through so couldn't hire her, but Karen applied for the girls' supervisor job at Breynat and was accepted. Thus we had easy landings with good jobs for the fall and winter of 1967–68. Father Labatt was soon replaced by Father Camille Piche, who turned out to be a great administrator and friend.

There were approximately two hundred students staying at Breynat Hall at the time, broken down into about thirty-six senior boys, thirty-six senior girls, sixty junior boys and sixty junior girls. Robert Beaulieu and I looked after the senior boys, and Sister Drolet and Karen, the senior girls. We immersed ourselves in our jobs, engaging with the students and working hard on every aspect of the students' lives. Two things we did early on improved the living and study situation of the students. Breynat Hall, which was built in the fifties, had large open dormitories for the students. We undertook to have these large open spaces broken down into smaller rooms to give our older students privacy. We then turned the chapel, which took up a large area in the centre of the hostel, into a study room for the students. We joked that from now on students were going to work for their marks, instead of praying for them.

Robert and I worked together very well. We shared the responsibilities for the boys; he was in charge of sports, while I focused on helping students with their studies. Karen, paired with Sister Drolet, had a harder time. Sister was stern in her handling of the girls and seemed to relish making life as miserable as possible for them. For instance, after the smaller sleeping areas were made, she intentionally put girls from different communities together in the same room, even though they spoke different languages and she knew that the girls preferred to stay with their relatives and friends from the same community. Sister was also unduly restrictive about granting free time to the girls to go to town, and unreasonable in insisting that they not go into the café, ostensibly lest the place catch fire and burn down. Karen disagreed with many of Sister's strictures and tried unsuccessfully to get her to be more reasonable in her approach. When their differences were brought up in our staff meetings, Father Piche would invariably agree with Karen and query Sister's stubborn, negative approach. By Christmas, Sister had had a nervous breakdown and left Breynat Hall, leaving Karen (or Miss Karen, as her students called her) with thirty-six girls aged from twelve to twenty-one for about three months until another supervisor was hired. Karen and I worked throughout the week, with weekends the busiest and only Mondays off. It was hard to take even a day off as the students were so attached to us and us to them.

By the end of the year, Karen and I were pleased that many of our students were on par academically with those from Grandin College, which had the reputation of having the best students from across the North. In sports, particularly in hockey, because of Robert's coaching ability, we usually beat them. We prided ourselves on treating the students reasonably and they in turn responded positively. Having spent eleven years in residential school, I was sensitive to treating students as I would have liked to be treated. There was no way that I was going to mistreat students the way I had been.

The year away from university was good for me. I got some ground under my feet and settled down. At Easter 1968, I took the next big step.

I had bought an engagement ring a few weeks earlier while I attended a Liberal convention in Ottawa. On Easter Saturday, before midnight mass, I borrowed the hostel vehicle and I drove with Karen to the Slave River. I planned to find a nice setting along the river in the moonlight and propose to her, but as we approached the river our van became thoroughly stuck. I had started shovelling snow when an RCMP vehicle came and stopped behind us. Two big policemen came alongside the vehicle, shone their flashlights on Karen and looked around suspiciously. They asked what we were doing down here, and I said we were on our way to church. Given that the church was nowhere near us it wasn't much of an answer, but they didn't say much, except "It serves you right!" and just pushed us out of the ditch. Alone at last. With a full moon shining across the river, I eased over to Karen and kissed her. After some passionate moments and catching my breath, I asked Karen if she would marry me. She agreed at once. I had gotten her size and the diamond ring slipped perfectly onto her finger. In my excitement, I just about went into the ditch again, but I managed to stay on the road until we reached the cathedral where mass was well underway. We sat in one of the back pews and held hands all through the service, enthralled by our engagement. When mass ended we returned to the hostel for the Easter meal, where Karen broke the news.

The next day we phoned Karen's parents, and I told my mother. Being an only child, one might think that I would be somewhat intimidated by Karen's family, but I wasn't. Maybe the experience of being amongst so many children at residential school had one positive side effect. When Karen brought me home to her family in Lloydminster for the first time, I instantly felt comfortable with her parents and siblings. She had nine brothers and seven sisters; she was the fifth eldest child and the second oldest daughter. They lived in a large, two-storey house and their farm included grain crops, cattle and a huge vegetable garden. The farm setting and their simple lifestyle appealed to me and reminded me of the mission farm I roamed in my childhood. Not coming from a normal family, having only my grandmother and mother, I relished the idea that I would be part of a large family.

Her dad, Art, an uprooted Acadian farmer, was very down-to-earth, interested in hunting moose and curious about the North. I immediately hit it off with Karen's mom, Norah, who had a British background. I reminded her about all the British explorers who came north and perished. Those who survived only did so because of the kindness and skills of the Natives. I teased her that we in the North were tough, lived in teepees and igloos, ate wild animal meat and dressed in furs and suggested that her daughter would do well in that environment, coming as she did from the Benoit tribe. Through the years, I think that I became her favourite son-in-law. As for Karen's brothers and sisters, I got along well with them, threatening those my age and younger that I would take them outside and wrestle them to the ground.

Meal times were a sight with twenty or so people around a table, reaching and jostling for their fair share of food. When meals were done everyone moved to the living room, where there were never enough chairs and couches for all. One had to be quick, smart or devious to get a seat. I would tell the person who had the best chair that their mother wanted them in the kitchen. Joe, Karen's younger brother, was the first to fall for this ploy, though with time, everyone knew that if their mother wanted them, she would call herself. In this household it was survival of the fittest.

I'm sure Karen's mom and dad wondered what made their daughters attracted to men of other nationalities. Couldn't they just bring home the neighbourhood guys? Joan, their first and eldest daughter, had married a black man from Barbados, and now their next daughter had brought a Native guy from the North. Good thing they were not prejudiced.

As the year at Breynat Hall was coming to an end, I went to Edmonton to see about getting back into university. Student Services interviewed me thoroughly, trying to uncover the reasons for my previous failures. My drinking habits were closely examined, and I promised them I had nearly quit. I was a new man with a new attitude, soon to be married and ready to start university again.

They gave me extensive written tests to assess my psychological and mental capacity. The tests showed that I was in the top one-quarter percentile and capable of performing at the university level, so they suggested that I see the Dean of Arts about my re-entry. By this time I was no longer interested in continuing in education and had decided that political science would be more suitable. The dean was an elderly man with a scholarly demeanor. We talked at length about possible fields of study, and I felt that I had aroused his sympathy, particularly since I was Native and from the North. But after looking through my university records, he said, "Young man, I don't think you're ready. You have a terrible record and you're having trouble passing English, aren't you?" I felt like a criminal sitting before a judge. I agreed with his assessment but argued that English wasn't my first language. I was practically pleading with him by this stage to admit me to his faculty. He opened the university calendar and pointed at English 200, the most difficult of all the first-year English courses. "If you pass this course with a good mark, you can come back and see me." I'm sure he thought he'd never see me again, but I left the dean's office feeling relieved that I had at least gotten a foot in the door.

Nothing focuses the mind like a woman and an impending marriage. I was determined to put aside my past failures and look to the future. While I studied English in Edmonton that summer, Karen stayed with her family in Lloydminster, making her wedding dress and dealing with the other wedding preparations. My English professor was an amiable person, and I felt at ease in the small class and took part in the discussions. As I got into the heart of the course, I wondered why I had so much difficulty with English in the past. I grew to enjoy reading and came out of the course with an appreciation for English literature. Whether the satire of Jonathan Swift, the tales of social injustice by Charles Dickens or some more modern fare, they all opened up new worlds for me, worlds that I continue to explore to this day. I felt confident that I had a good grasp of the subject matter and would do well in the exam. I wrote the exam on a Thursday in mid-August, and the next day I was on my way to Lloydminster to see my bride-to-be and get married.

The wedding that Saturday, August 17, was wonderful. Karen was beautiful in her hand-sewn dress. Despite working late into the night on the final stitches, she looked fresh and glowing with happiness. All the preparations that Karen had worked so hard on during the summer made the wedding flow like a fine-tuned clock. Karen's oldest brother, Ray, a mechanic, and a few of the boys helped us buy a small red Ford Falcon, which he fixed up for us. We paid two hundred dollars for the car and it lasted for many years. My mother, other relatives and friends came from up north and elsewhere and were warmly received. Father Piche performed the marriage ceremony in the church, and a banquet and dance were held in a country hall. A band, consisting of Robert Beaulieu, Tony Buggins, Rick Mandeville, Donald Beaulieu and Philip Constant, all boys from the hostel, played at our wedding dance. Folks around Lloydminster had never seen an Aboriginal group play so well. All the Benoits and their hundreds of friends attended, making it a truly memorable wedding. After midnight, Karen and I made our escape down the highway towards Edmonton, Banff and ultimately to Campbell River on Vancouver Island where we honeymooned.

We returned to Edmonton in early September. I had achieved Stanine 7 in my English course, equivalent to the high seventies. I had not forgotten the dean's invitation, so with the result in hand, I went to talk to him about enrolling in the Arts Faculty. The dean was surprised but all smiles; I registered in the honours program, selecting mostly political science courses. Karen also registered in a full complement of courses to complete her degree in education.

I was now a married man. Gone was the weekend drinking and partying with a variety of friends. Our life now involved visiting non-drinking friends, attending church services and doing a lot of studying. It all came home to me when my friend Ron Holtorf came from the North, loaded with money and looking to party. A party was in full swing at his downtown hotel room when we arrived to see him. Ron was entertaining as he talked about his work prospecting in the Barren Lands and showed us dozens of carvings he had bought from the Inuk guys who worked at the camp. I had not drunk any liquor for a long time, and for a while I sat with Karen on a sofa on the edge of the party. At Ron's urging, I finally had a drink. Inevitably for me, that first drink wasn't enough, and before long I was feeling good. As I was edging into the midst of the party, Karen said she wanted to go home. I didn't want to leave, but Karen became impatient with me and insisted. It was then that the reality of being a married man struck me. Married couples go home at reasonable hours, particularly when their wives say so; single people party without limits. For the first time in my life, I left a party while it was at its height. The next morning, when I woke up sober and invigorated from a good sleep, I appreciated Karen's insistence on leaving. Otherwise I probably would have stayed until there was no more booze or everyone was gone or passed out.

I CALL IT a phenomenon, the getting together of an Aboriginal person and a white person. Each comes from a different background, culture and geography and often they have different values and notions of what is right or wrong. Is it that opposites attract? Or does each want something different from the norm? Are they conscious of their differences yet decide to get together anyway? Or, is it merely a matter of chance?

The natural tendency is to end up with someone of the same type. If you marry someone from your hometown or neighbourhood you increase the likelihood of success as you eliminate any social and cultural differences that might lead to conflict. So why does this phenomenon occur so often in northern society? Travelling to other parts of the country can have a lot to do with who you end up choosing to live with. To an extent, that's the story of many people in the North, from local people visiting other communities or people from the South venturing north, not intending to stay, but ending up here all their lives. While they are in the new community someone tickles their fancy and boom! Sparks go off, loves sets in, and a meteoric explosion sets people's lives on a new course. It certainly stirs the gene pool and creates a good breed of people.

IT WAS A happy time for me, for us. Karen became pregnant, and we both did well in our courses. For me, there was never any question about my mental ability, just my work habits and partying. In the summer of 1969 our first son, Glen, was born. By the end of the following April, I had finally finished my university program and received my Bachelor of Arts.

I had the opportunity that spring to go to Ottawa to work for Robert "Bud" Orange, the Member of Parliament for the Northwest Territories and parliamentary secretary to J.J. Greene, Minster of Energy, Mines and Resources. Karen and I had come to know Bud as young Liberals during his election. I worked on an assignment dealing with changes to the Indian Act that the federal government was contemplating. Our young family experienced the hot, muggy weather of Ottawa for a few months, then returned north so I could take on the job of secretary manager of the hamlet of Fort Simpson.

Father Posset had phoned to tell me of the job opening, which he thought would be perfect for me. Getting the job wasn't without controversy. When the hamlet council members considered the different applicants, including me, they were split on whether to hire me or someone with more experience. My uncle Ted Trindell was one of the council members, and he laid it on the line: "We encourage young people to get an education, and when they do, we turn around and say they're not experienced." Ted told me later that if the council had not hired me, he was going to resign on principle.

In many respects Ted had been like a father to me. He was a critical influence in my life until the day he died in 1984. I still have a large portrait of him, painted by my son Randy, hanging on my wall at home.

I began my job as the secretary manager in late summer 1970. I was the first paid administrator of the community and was responsible for all public works: roads, signs, dogs, garbage, water delivery and a few other things. I was the only employee and had to do everything myself. I launched into the work with enthusiasm, setting up an office and hiring a secretary. I spent many days with a shovel putting up road signs and wondering which way and where the ditches were to drain. I stopped at having to build a dog pound and hired Albert Norwegian to build one for me, but I still had to go out myself to chase dogs and put them in the pound. Mark Fairbrother, the chairman of the council, often remarked to me that the administrator before they hired me ran the community out of a shoebox. I think Mark resented the changing times and increased reporting requirements placed on the hamlet by government; he never missed a chance to cast negative aspersions on my work. It was a tough job—especially the accounting side as I had never had financial training—but I threw myself into it and learned as I went on. Those lessons stood me in good stead later in life as a politician and businessman. I did that for the summer of 1970, through the fall and into the early winter, and then there was a territorial election.

Part Two:

TERRITORIAL POLITICS

Chapter 6: My Political Life Begins

TERRITORIAL POLITICS DIFFERED from federal and provincial politics in a number of important ways. First of all there were no political parties, a practice that continues to the present day. Instead, members were elected as independents to the legislative council, as it was called in 1970, to represent different regions of the Northwest Territories. The fourteen-member council served to advise the commissioner, a federal bureaucrat who held all executive power in the territorial government. In effect, he was the government. The process to replace the commissioner with a fully responsible government was a long one that was not completed until 1986.

The NWT Council, unlike that in the Yukon, which had been fully elected since 1909, consisted of both elected and appointed members. In 1966, the elected members had formed the majority for the first time, outnumbering the appointed ones seven to five. In 1970 that ratio was changing to ten to four. In most respects the council operated like other Westminster-style legislatures, debating and approving laws, questioning senior officials and discussing matters of importance. Many decisions were reached through a process of consensus, though formal votes were held and on some matters there were sharp divisions.

The twelfth general election of the Northwest Territories was scheduled for December 21, 1970, and I was considering running to become a member of the territorial council. Karen was not enthusiastic about the prospect. We had just moved to Fort Simpson and were living in Jimmy Cree's comfortable old home. I'd been on my job for barely six months. As well, our second child was due in November.

Bud Orange phoned me at one point and suggested that I delay my candidacy until the next election. (Later, I learned through the grapevine that my opponent Don Stewart had asked him to discourage me so I wouldn't mess with his chance of being re-elected.)

I was cautious. Over the last few years I had come to believe that I would someday be a spokesman for the people, but I was uncertain if this was the right moment. Still, I had laid some groundwork. In addition to studying political science at university, I had attended a Liberal convention as a young Liberal in 1968 when Pierre Trudeau won the leadership. I had worked briefly for Gordon Hornby years earlier during a territorial election campaign in Yellowknife, and was involved along with Ron Holtorf and Bob Overvold with Bud Orange in his federal campaign. I had also come to know territorial council member Duncan Pryde, a colourful Scotsman who amused me with stories about the Arctic and his many political and personal adventures.

Growing up poor with my mother and grandmother in a small town, I was aware of the distinction between the Dene people who had just the basics to live on and the white people who had more. We were not the poorest of the poor; my grandmother had a nice log house that was one of the finest Dene homes in the village. Ehmbee, who was several times a widow, had married the local chief, Joe Hope, in the 1930s. Before he died in the big flu epidemic, he had built Ehmbee a house with an upstairs, hardwood floors and beaverboard interior walls. But the best Native house was nothing compared to the houses where the few white people in the community lived.

The distinction wasn't just about having things. It was about having power, being able to control people, things or events. Every day and in every way, this was demonstrated to us. The HBC manager, Mr. Craig, had the keys to the show hall and could charge us twenty-five cents for a movie. The RCMP officers and the Indian agent all had big houses with well-kept lawns and Native people—prisoners or low-paid labourers—at their beck and call. The few vehicles in town were owned by white people. My grandmother went to the Indian agent's place every month with her bag in hand asking for tea, bacon and rolled oats—charity for elderly and destitute people. I recall a story of an old woman who had walked from the far end of town to buy a small bag of beads; when she arrived at the government office the woman at the counter told her she had come a few minutes too late and would have to come back another day. This kind of incident made me realize how poorly people were treated. Subconsciously, a determination had grown in me to someday do something about it. Maybe, I thought, the time had arrived; with the education I had, I could make changes in people's lives.

That fall I decided to make a road trip to Kakisa and possibly Hay River, depending on construction on the unfinished highway, to see how people felt about me running. One Friday after work, Ted Trindell and I set off in my red Falcon. About sixty miles out the car broke down and the motor caught on fire. We scrambled to put it out and then, stranded, we set up camp along the highway in the bush.

The highway from Fort Simpson was still under construction, so we didn't expect anyone to come along any time soon to help us out. In the morning, to our surprise, a truck came barrelling up the highway from the south. We waved it down. Of the two men in the cab, one was Don Stewart, who would be my opponent if I decided to run in the upcoming election. I had seen pictures of him but knew him only from his public profile as mayor of Hay River. He, of course, didn't know who I was. After we squeezed into the cab and were on our way to Fort Simpson, Stewart chatted about the coming election, mentioning that some young guy from Simpson was planning to run against him. He rambled on about how he was such a good representative and that he would win handily. Ted and I were amused by his brashness and didn't let on that the person he spoke about was sitting next to him.

When we got home, we went straight to a dance at the community hall. It didn't take long for Ted to get feeling high. Later on I noticed a commotion at the door, and I was surprised to see that Ted was being pushed out the door by a couple of burly men. In the process of trying to stop them, I was also pushed out the door into the cold. A few days later Ted and I received a letter from a Mr. Hanrahan, the president of the community club, stating that we were both suspended from the hall for six months. Was there a message to my car burning on the way to my first campaign visit, being picked up by my opposition and then being kicked out of the community club?

Karen had to go 1500 kilometres to Edmonton to have our second child. As I drove her out, we decided I would not run in the election. We rationalized that it wasn't the right time because of our young family, my starting a new job and our getting settled in our home. But on my way back north alone, I began rethinking our decision. As I got closer to Hay River, I thought that I should at least check out the sentiments of people. I visited people across the river at the Indian Village and the people living in West Channel and Old Town. To my surprise, I found that people were glad that I was interested in the election and said that they would vote for me. Leaders like Edward Fabian and Daniel Sonfrere from across the river and Alex Morin, Len Cardinal and Ed Studney from West Channel were particularly enthusiastic about the prospect. Don Taylor, the owner and editor of *The Hub* newspaper, was also supportive and offered to help in drafting my platform and to provide advertising. I sensed a real desire from them to have someone other than Don Stewart as their representative. Hay River was ripe for a serious contender and genuine change.

I phoned Karen in Edmonton and told her of my visit and people's positive response. Karen was preoccupied with the imminent birth of our second son while contending with our first son Glen, who was sick with epiglottitis and had to have a tracheotomy done on very short notice. I let the matter lie for the moment, but on the way home I stopped at Kakisa Lake and visited the chief, Philip Simba, and the rest of the people living there. All expressed support and promised to vote for me if I ran in the election.

Back in Fort Simpson I tended to my job. Over the following few weeks, Karen and I discussed the situation by phone. When Karen saw how interested I was, she agreed, knowing it could mean yet more changes.

I quickly filed my nomination papers. Don Stewart and Bobby Porritt, both of Hay River, were also candidates. Peter Cowie, a local pilot, agreed to be my official agent, and I started my campaign by visiting all the small communities around Simpson. During the early part of the campaign the candidates were interviewed by CBC Radio in a hotel in Hay River. As I was going into the interview room, I met Don Stewart on the way out. He said, "We have a file on you that thick," spreading his fingers to show two inches. Obviously he was trying to intimidate me, but I wasn't afraid at all, merely amused. I thought, "I don't need a file on you; your reputation precedes you." In Hay River, Don was a feared politician, scaring off many opponents, but I was young, fearless and motivated by my desire to do good and help people.

By the end of November I had visited all of the small communities in the Simpson area and was getting ready to travel to Hay River to campaign there. I asked Baptiste Cazon, the chief, to come with me. I knew he was respected amongst the Dene people. As we were leaving town, a small plane flew into the town airstrip from the south: Don Stewart coming to campaign in Simpson and the outlying communities. As luck would have it, the weather turned bad and he wasn't able to travel to any of the communities. He ended up spending a lot of time hanging out at Mark Fairbrother's gas station. He made no effort to go amongst the people in Simpson to garner support, counting on Mark to deliver votes his way. So while Don was stuck in Simpson and not doing much, Baptiste and I campaigned ferociously in Hay River, making a lot of political hay.

People seemed sincerely interested in what I had to say and were excited about having me represent them and their concerns. Baptiste was a terrific campaigner, a flamboyant and charming man, and we made a terrific team. We campaigned in Hay River for one week, going house to house in all parts of the town. We often ended the day by going into the bars, and it was fun and interesting to see friends and relatives. When we had covered the whole town and were exhausted, we headed home to finish the campaign in Simpson and the surrounding communities, satisfied that we would get a fair share of the votes from Hay River. I was thrilled to find Karen there to greet me, with our new baby son, Randy, born November 24.

On election day, December 21, I worked hard driving people to the polls. That night, we gathered at the hotel and waited by the radio to hear the results. It was a new experience for many, especially Native people, and there was a sense of anticipation. The first result came in from Kakisa, where the vote count was twenty-three votes for me and one vote for Don Stewart. I was surprised that I would get such overwhelming support, thinking that there must be a mistake. There were two polls in Simpson, the north and south. When all the votes were counted I had received all the votes in the south poll except fifteen and all the votes in the north poll except two. John Goodall, a former councillor, dropped into the hotel exclaiming that it was like Trudeaumania. The results from Hay River were similar. I had won majorities in the Indian Village, West Channel and Old Town and got a good portion of the New Town where Don Stewart lived.

I had won the election. Don may have been feared, but when given an opportunity by secret ballot, people expressed their will clearly. I was the most surprised guy there when the CBC commentators announced my victory as "out with the old and in with the new." The vote tally was Sibbeston 644, Stewart 370 and Porritt 163.

Although I was young and enthusiastic, I didn't know much about the government in place at the time, other than that the federally appointed commissioner, Stu Hodgson, dominated it. I had studied political science and written research papers on government in the North, but I had never had many dealings with the government in Yellowknife. With the victory, I had a mandate to speak on behalf of people, and I was conscientious about doing a good job. What I did know was that I would work furiously for better housing, highways and schools. I also wanted to protect Native cultures and language and make the government more responsive and responsible.

Status Indians had only been granted the vote in federal (and as a consequence, territorial) elections in 1961, though they were not excluded from provincial legislatures. Métis had served in the first provincial government in Manitoba in 1870 and Louis Riel had been elected to the federal parliament, though he was never allowed to take his seat. An Aboriginal MLA served briefly in Quebec in the 1920s; and Frank Calder, whose name is attached to one of the landmark Supreme Court decisions on Aboriginal rights, was first elected as a British Columbia MLA in 1949 and served for nearly thirty years. More recently an Inuk member had been elected to the territorial council in 1967 and Len Marchand from British Columbia was elected in 1968 as a member of the Trudeau government. Still, I knew that I and the handful of other Native people elected in 1970 were a pioneering group.

IN THE WEEKS after Christmas, Karen and I had to leave the hamlet staff house. Moving didn't make her too happy, especially with a baby and a small child. My grandfather had a small shack which had been sitting empty since he died, so I got permission from the family to use it. I took out the old cupboards, ripped up the old flooring and made a small bedroom, and the rest of the space became our kitchen, dining room and living room. We put in a new oil stove, cupboards and flooring and painted all the walls.

In late January, we set off with our two young children for Yellowknife to attend my first territorial council. That first session we were put up at a hotel, a fairly new experience for me, as was all the deference shown me as an elected politician. Later, we were given the option of staying in an unused government staff house. In those days the government provided housing for most of its employees, and there were always a few vacant houses. We brought foamies, dishes and blankets and bunked down using cardboard boxes for furniture for the month to six weeks of the session. A few sessions on, Stu Hodgson offered us the use of an apartment on the top of Fraser Towers. This was called the Royal Suite, a lavishly furnished suite set aside for VIPs who visited the North. Queen Elizabeth had stayed there on her recent visit, as had the governor general and the prime minister on earlier visits. Stu was politically crafty and, I believe, offered me this opulent suite to temper my frequent criticisms. Karen and I enjoyed the comfort, though with all the intricate carvings and fancy furnishings we were always on edge, watching our children lest they break or scratch things. When that session was finished, we were relieved to get back into our plain shack in Fort Simpson.

THE POLITICAL SYSTEM in the North was evolving rapidly. The seat of government had only been moved to Yellowknife in 1967; previously everything had been run out of Ottawa. Stu Hodgson was the commissioner of the Northwest Territories appointed by the federal government. The territorial council, we were constantly reminded, was only advisory. It consisted of ten elected members and five appointed members from the south. Appointed members were there, we were told, to advise and help northern elected members, who were deemed by Ottawa not to be experienced and educated enough to make decisions on their own.

The council table was arranged with the commissioner at the head and the fourteen members sitting in a horseshoe shape, with the appointed members interspersed amongst the elected ones. I had Air Marshall Hugh Campbell (appointed), a retired member of the Armed Forces, sitting to my right and Willie Adams (later Senator Adams), elected from Rankin Inlet, to my left. We were gathered as people's representatives from all parts of the North and were to express the views of the people to the government. The government, in turn, was to respond and try its best to provide needed services to the people.

Democracy was a new experience for most people in the Northwest Territories. In the initial years of Fort Simpson's settlement, the Catholic Church was the most dominant institution. They were in many ways the acting government, providing religious services, a hospital and education to the people. Later on the Indian agent provided houses, food for the destitute and support for the chief and council. Prior to 1960 the Dene people did not have the right to vote in federal elections. The Government of the Northwest Territories (GNWT) arrived in the North only in 1967. Before that, they were just as far and remote as the federal government. Any government official who wandered into the North and visited a community was likely never seen again.

Elected representatives before me in our area, John Goodall, Bill Berg and Mark Fairbrother, had tried their best, but didn't have the kind of rapport, communication or effect that I would have. Nothing can be better than coming from the people, being steeped in their culture and language and giving voice to their hopes and aspirations. John Goodall used to say, disparagingly, "Give the Native people a pot of brew and they're as happy as could be." I knew that I would be able to provide more than that.

This was the era in the North when Native people had little voice. They did not dare speak up to criticize the government or white people. Aboriginal people had only just begun to realize the power they could wield through organization. The Indian Brotherhood (later the Dene Nation) formed in 1970, as did the Committee for Original Peoples Entitlement (COPE) up in the Delta, partly in response to the white paper the Trudeau government had issued and partly because of the proposal to build a gas pipeline. Many Native people were used to operating on the agenda of Indian Affairs and were nervous about openly criticizing white people. There were only a few Native people on the Territorial Council—Jimmy Rabesca from the Dogrib (Tli'cho) area; Lena Pedersen, an Inuk woman from Coppermine; and me—but along with a number of non-Native allies we were soon playing a major role in criticizing how government was done in the North.

In 1970 the commissioner, Stu Hodgson, was the central figure. He controlled the public service and determined the budget and the legislation the council would consider. We could pass motions but, in reality, he could pick and choose what he acted on and what he ignored. One of the traditions that Commissioner Hodgson initiated was to hold a ball each winter, usually in January or early February to mark the opening of the winter session. People were invited from all regions of the North and, in addition to the commissioner's guest list, each council member could invite two guests and their spouses. It was the biggest social event on the northern calendar and no expense was spared. He brought in chefs, special foods and orchestras from Edmonton. The hall where the ball was held was decorated with themes related to the military or police. All the men dressed in formal suits or military uniforms, while the ladies wore long evening dresses. Cooked foods of all kinds from Arctic char to pork were spread out on long decorated tables. There were pastries galore and every imaginable fruit and exotic treat. A striking figure carved from ice sat in the middle of the table.

The orchestra played southern-style dance music while people swirled across the vast floors. Inuit and Dene people, more attuned to square dancing or drum dances, did their best to copy the intricate steps of the Viennese waltzes and lively swing numbers. Liquor flowed freely, and before long, a few people, those not used to drink or the heat, began falling by the wayside, quickly helped outside into the cold Arctic wind by large men hired especially for the occasion. This tradition continued for a number of years, even after Hodgson's departure, though gradually it became more focused on northern dancing and charitable activities.

TODAY, THE LEGISLATIVE assembly reflects the diversity of cultures and people of the North and its traditions have adapted to reflect northern realities. Contrast that with my experience at the opening of the June session in 1970. The Elks Hall was crowded with people curious at the start of the council session. A booming voice yelled "Order!" and everyone fell silent, rising as a procession entered from the front of the hall and wound to where we waited for the proceedings to begin. A scarlet-clad RCMP officer led the parade, followed by Binx Remnant, the clerk, in his long black sweeping robe. Several more black-robed assistants arrived, then the sergeant-at-arms, decked out in medals and carrying a five-foot mace on his shoulder. Finally, Stu Hodgson, the commissioner, in a formal suit, marched in and took his place at the head of the table, like a father before his children. Hodgson said a prayer and we all listened to his opening address, which told us the work we would do in the ensuing few weeks.

I had taken a degree in political science and even worked briefly in Ottawa for MP Bud Orange but to actually be at the table, with the responsibility of representing so many people, was entirely different.

Commissioner Hodgson opened this first session before a full house including the Minister of Indian Affairs, Jean Chrétien. His lengthy speech reviewed the events of 1970, the centennial year of the Northwest Territories. The year was highlighted by the visit of the queen and the royal family as well as tours by Governor General Roland Michener and Prime Minister Pierre Trudeau. Hodgson lauded the progress that had been made since the arrival of the government in Yellowknife in September 1967 and the establishment of a civil service with government offices and personnel in Yellowknife and throughout all regions of the North. The territorial government took over the Mackenzie District in 1969 and the whole of the Keewatin and the eastern Arctic areas in 1970. The territorial government now had responsibility for all of the Northwest Territories.

The territories would never be divided, said the commissioner, nor given over to the provinces (as it turned out, he was only half right). With the public service now at 1,734 positions, including 490 teachers, decentralization into regions and communities would proceed along with the establishment of settlement councils. He listed the activities of the government during the past year and plans for the coming year, some of which, in retrospect, have an oddly modern ring. An independent study had been done of a bridge over the Mackenzie River at Fort Providence (which only took another thirty years to bring to completion), and an internal committee had been set up to look into increasing the ratio of Native northerners in government. Devolution was also in the air. Territorial Medicare became effective on April 1, and the transfer of many programs to the territorial government was complete or in progress, including the Magistrate and Justice of the Peace program and the Northern Rental Housing Program.

New initiatives included the introduction of a three-year program to train game management officers and a program whereby trappers got money in advance of the auctions of their furs. In areas of economic activity, polar bear and buffalo sports hunting were to begin as an endeavour by local peoples, the arts and craft industry were to be bolstered by craft stores in a number of centres and a knitting plant would be established in Frobisher Bay (later Iqaluit), with a weaving shop in Pangnirtung and a fibreglass plant in Fort Providence. The fishing industry on Great Slave Lake and elsewhere and the forestry industry, which produced five million board feet of lumber a year, were growing.

Schools throughout the North held 10,311 students, and the rate of growth was the highest in Canada. In the area of social services, the government was to increase social assistance to be in line with current costs, and alcohol education programs were to be carried out in the larger centres in the North. A Liquor Control Board was formed to control all aspects of distribution and sale of alcohol in the North, and John Tetlichi and Simonie Alainga were appointed as special advisors to the board. The maintenance of band lists and the payment of treaty monies were also transferred to the territorial government.

Stu finished by announcing that the Committee of Finance would continue and that a new Committee of Legislation would be established with membership by elected councillors.

The first day of the session was dominated by ritual and by the commissioner's speech, but many of the council members, especially the elected ones, were eager to have their say. Debates that first year, covering a couple of sessions, were wide-ranging. Some issues were particular to that time and space but other matters discussed laid the groundwork for the many changes that would come over the years. Of particular interest was the future development of the territorial government and of the economy of the North. However, we also had lots to say about social issues, including the effects of alcohol and needed changes to the provision of education and housing in communities.

The commissioner's speech was our equivalent to the speech from the throne given by the lieutenant governor in a provincial legislature and was followed on subsequent days by replies by individual members. Some members spoke briefly on specific issues of concern to them; others waxed eloquent on a range of issues—sometimes to make specific suggestions for programs or actions but often speaking quite philosophically about the direction of government and its future development.

Lyle Trimble, the council member for the Delta, was often the first on his feet to make his reply. Lyle, a former RCMP officer, was a pilot and owner of a charter airline in Aklavik. He was first elected in 1964, one of four elected members from the Mackenzie area in the days when there were none from the eastern Arctic and the five appointed members had a majority. He began gently by recognizing the "dynamic drive, ability and initiative" of the commissioner and deputy commissioner and the contributions of the appointed members. The transfer of programs from the federal government had brought many improvements: local government in the communities, the expansion of tourism, assistance to trappers and an improving education system.

Having said that, Lyle went on to criticize the continued growth of the public service, despite the previous council's resolution calling for a freeze, especially in headquarters and regional centres. He was also concerned that proposed decentralizations to local communities didn't represent real change; previous initiatives had actually weakened the power of local councils. He wondered if the proposed addition to the sixth floor of the Laing Building (where senior officials were housed) was "for recreation facilities to expend idle time, or is the government pessimistic of the success to be achieved in its employee freeze or decentralization policies?"

He urged the council to learn from the past and to be more unified in dealing with the executive by creating a caucus system, together with meaningful and forceful special committees, in order to better represent the interests of the people. He finished his speech by saying he would be like the Mad Trapper, who, surrounded by RCMP, looked out on his foes and said: "Okay, that's it. No more Mister Nice Guy."

Newly elected James Rabesca from Fort Rae took a strong position on his role as an "Indian" on the council, reflecting the growing strength of the Indian Brotherhood (which eventually became the Dene Nation). "Our people will be coming to the council table with big questions about why they have not been treated with respect. They will be asking why they are not holding the top jobs[,] ... why they are dying earlier and why their kids end up in jail." James believed it was the chiefs and the Indian Brotherhood who spoke for the people, not the territorial council.

In contrast, Tom Butters from Inuvik wanted an expanded and strengthened council. Quoting Prime Minister Trudeau that "the first responsibility of government is to govern," he then referred to a CBC report that stated "Territorial councillors are political eunuchs ... and the council a debating society." Tom then launched into a long speech on the history and development of the Northwest Territories, beginning in 1885 when it included all western and northern territories from Manitoba to the North Pole. Through the struggle for responsible government, Alberta and Saskatchewan were created in 1905 and the remainder of northern lands reverted to control of the federal government. The present Northwest Territories was now undergoing that same struggle for responsible government. Tom argued that it was time for an extension of self-government. In the Yukon, elected council members were part of the executive, responsible for the departments of education, health and welfare. He urged similar changes in our executive council. "Responsible government is working in the Yukon; responsible government can work in the Northwest Territories."

Along a similar line, and echoing a concern that would resurface some fifteen years later in the Meech Lake Accord, Trimble made a motion regarding provincial involvement in present or future affairs of the Northwest Territories. The motion was in response to the premier of Nova Scotia, Gerald Regan, urging his provincial colleagues to become involved in decisions relating to the North with an eye to sharing its vast resources. "The people of the Northwest Territories look forward to the day when, with an increased population and an increased means within the territories to support ourselves, all of the Northwest Territories will become a province or possibly several provinces."

David Searle reminded members of motions that had been made by council in the past urging the federal government to hold the natural resources in trust for northerners.

Not all the debate was at the theoretical or constitutional level. Members were also concerned about the day-to-day operations of government. The civil service was a favourite topic for Lyle, particularly their non-availability in the summer. "I am inclined to think that in this, the busiest time of the year in the North, if much of our public service can disappear for a month or so, it suggests to me that a good deal of this public service was not required in the first place."

I had my own views on the public service and made them known early in the session. "The number one problem was the lack of communications between government and the people.... In almost all cases, the area service officers, welfare workers, industrial development officers go through the motion of visiting these communities, but this is all, no more is done. The civil servants visit the civil servants residing in the communities and immediately take off home." The idea that the government was providing some service to the people was an illusion. If the civil servants did nothing else but communicate with the people, they would have done a good thing. "Get interpreters and tell the people about the services and programs that the government has available." If they didn't want to build rapport with the people, I said, maybe they should leave and let some other people do their job. To drive home the point, a few days later I proposed the following motion:

> Whereas there is little communication between the people and the civil servants in the communities, and the local people, especially those in smaller Native communities need to know what government is, what services they have available, and what programs the government is proposing. Therefore I move that assistance for better communications be established whereby hundreds of buttons or sticks be distributed throughout the community to the people and that the civil servants visiting the community be required to pick up ten or twenty of these each time they go there. This way we would be assured that the Territorial Government representatives meet with the people.

I was not serious about having this motion proceed further, but I was very serious about the problem of communication. Stu Hodgson said that he would encourage his staff to better communicate when they were in the communities.

The economy, as always, was of great concern to council members. David Searle, for example, called for the transfer of mineral, fishing, timber and water resources to the territorial government so they could be developed for the benefit of northerners. Some of this has been accomplished over the years but others are still being negotiated to this day. He also proposed the creation of an economic development corporation for the Northwest Territories to stimulate the creation of business.

Lena Pedersen, a new member from Coppermine, wanted more direct and immediate government action, specifically, to have all available jobs in the settlements go to local people. Moreover, with unemployment in her communities in the range of 90 percent, the emphasis of the government must be the creation of jobs. Government projects, such as duffel hat production, were stop-gap measures that would not satisfy the one thousand or so jobs that would be required over the next few years. Education had to be more effective and broad-ranging, considering that the Inuit were making a transition from "primitive camp existence" to living in "sophisticated" communities. Paul Kaeser of Fort Smith chipped in with a proposal to develop the hydro potential of the Slave River.

Bryan Pearson of Frobisher Bay suggested that instead of merely building a new school in Frobisher Bay using fibreglass, the government work with the contractor to move the fibreglass plant to Frobisher Bay and fabricate schools for other communities in the eastern Arctic to create much-needed jobs. He also emphasized the need for better transportation infrastructure and better adult education to improve economic opportunities.

Willie Adams, an Inuk from Rankin Inlet who was my seatmate and later a fellow senator, had a hard time speaking English, but was able to convey his thoughts about his constituency. He said that fifteen houses had been built in Rankin Inlet the previous summer, but they were all built in two months, which didn't offer much by way of local employment and which meant that sections weren't the best quality. Tom Butters pointed out the economic potential of oil and gas in the Inuvik area (a topic that never goes away) and the value of reindeer herding (which has now largely disappeared).

Having heard the tone and tenor of other council members, I stated that the next four years would be the most important ever for the government and peoples of the North. We faced the challenge of getting Native people from the land into communities and the technological age and having economic development benefit the people. "Unemployment, lack of training, the anguish in adapting to a different society, frustration, all these invariably come up when Native people are discussed." With unemployment in the communities from 30 to 70 percent, economic development had to be dealt with by people and government jointly. "For too long Indian people have been consumers; they need to become managers and proprietors of businesses."

IT WOULD HAVE been impossible for me to do my job if I spent too much time in the big city, so I made a point of getting back to Fort Simpson at every opportunity. From there I would travel out to the smaller communities or to camps on rivers and lakes to meet the people who kept me focused on my mission to change government. One of those people was Joa Boots.

Joa lived at Willow River with his two brothers. I had met him a few times over the years and he was always happy and smiling. He was a "gentleman trapper," always neat in a white shirt with armbands to hold his sleeves in the right position. In the early 1970s, Johnny Tonka and I made a trip down the river to the Hire North camp to deliver groceries and return empty gas barrels. We stopped at Joa's house. What a surprise it was. Three brothers living together, Joa, Garcia and Victor, with everything so neat and orderly that you would swear there was a woman in the back somewhere. (Some years later Joa married Rosie Betsedia, Baptiste's daughter, but at this time it was just the three brothers.)

Before long, tea was served and a big pot of boiled beaver meat was placed before us on the table. Fine china dishes, normally not seen in town and never in the bush, were taken from a cupboard. When we finished, Joa served boiled eggs and oranges, amazing considering that the ice had just broken up and fresh goods were a rarity. That was the first time I had seen Joa at his home, and the impression stayed with me of a first-class guy.

The next time I visited Joa was with Commissioner Stu Hodgson. We had travelled to Wrigley by Twin Otter on floats for a community visit. When we were finished, I suggested we stop at Willow River to see the Boots brothers. We landed the Twin Otter at the shore and, to our amazement, the trail up the riverbank was covered with grass cuttings to make a neat pathway up to their house. The brothers came to the plane to welcome everyone, and when we entered the house they served tea and bannock. Stu was impressed with how nice the bush camp was and how they lived.

After Ted Trindell died I became even more attached to Joa. I was raised by my grandmother so I was comfortable with an elderly person, and never having a father, I guess I was drawn to a male figure.

That was the case with Ted and then Joa. He epitomized the ideal Dene. He lived out in the bush, didn't drink, spoke only Slavey and was very spiritual. He grew up in the era when people wore woven rabbit skin for clothing and travelled upriver by pulling canoes. He knew much of our history because he had lived it.

Joa's family were nomadic and travelled wherever there was game, from Tulita to Wrigley to Willow River, building cabins wherever they went. During his lifetime, he lived in sixteen houses spread throughout the Tulita and Wrigley area.

Spiritually, Joa had a unique blend of Dene and Christian philosophy. Feeding the fire, thinking about and praying for past relatives was a common ritual. Toward the end of his life he had a "teacher," who appeared to him every night in dreams and visions showing him amazing things—some biblical, others like the evils of polluting the earth and the destructiveness of alcohol.

AS THE SESSION progressed and the government proposed ordinances (as bills and acts were then called) and budgets, some of the criticisms became more pointed. Lyle Trimble began by saying that except for the laundry business in Inuvik, every business project started by the federal government and taken over by the territorial one had failed. He pointed to the sawmill in the Delta, started in Aklavik, then moved to Arctic Red River before it failed and was sold to southern interests. As well, the fishing and tanning projects collapsed despite large infusions of federal money. Lyle was adamant that government could not succeed because it did not follow private business principles. Small cottage businesses, such as the manufacture of northern equipment such as sleds, snowshoes and boats, could succeed if supported by government. The provision of firewood in most communities was an opportunity that "stared the Department of Industry in the face."

Weldy Phipps expressed concern about the lack of hiring of Inuit people by federal departments and agencies operating in the Arctic. Survey crews came through Resolute Bay with every man in the crew flown in from the south even though the only person who needed special training was the instrument man. The rest, like the rod man and people driving stakes into the tundra, could have been local Inuit workers. Another matter that required change, he added, were the bigoted attitudes of the white supervisors hired by the Ministry of Transport. Weldy said that from his experience, the Inuit labour force, though they had just come from a hunting tradition on the land, were reliable and competent if given the opportunity and treated properly. There were too many cases where inexperienced supervisors who had just arrived in the North treated the Inuit like dogs.

I raised issues on a number of economic matters, ranging from support to hunters and trappers working on the land, through the provision of radios, to the training and development of Native wildlife officers. More significantly, I criticized the entire focus of economic development that centred on giving grants to clean up communities or to create cottage businesses based on handicrafts. Instead, the government should be supporting people who wanted to get into house construction or viable ventures related to the oil and gas industry, such as seismic line clearing.

In Kakisa Lake, I said, I heard very wise words from the former chief, Philip Simba, who was concerned about the people's future way to make a living. Mr. Simba believed it was possible to develop tourism facilities along the lake. The people in his community were independent. His concern was that if the people were not helped to stay that way, they would become idle and dependent on welfare instead of vying for themselves.

Of course, it was impossible to talk about the economy without talking about the success—and failure—of the education system. This was a topic very close to my heart, given my experiences in residential school. Education officials had to change their concepts and attitudes toward the education of Native children. While I recognized that there had been progress, with 10,311 students in school, most of them Native, the Department of Education was making a gross mistake in not including Native parents in both the classrooms and student residences.

It was vital that the government acknowledge that education, mostly in residential schools, had often been a painful experience for parents. Moreover, many young children still attended residential schools far from their homes. Young children should not be torn from their families. Schools with grades up to nine should be set up in all communities; residential schools in the large centres should be restricted to senior grades. Parents, rather than churches, should operate the residential schools.

As to Native students attending school, I stated "there is little attempt to incorporate their cultures in the studies of the day. Their history, language, beliefs, whatever the parents have taught them are thought to be minor details and excluded as nuisance.... Great men arise in every society; great men have risen and do rise amongst Native people in this country. There is no reason why the education system, which purports to extol success and wisdom, does not recognize great men amongst the Native people and incorporate the stories of their lives and philosophies into the education system."

I did commend the teacher training program that had recently been started to produce young Native teachers, as well as the initiative to turn over education to the Dogrib people with a school and residence in Edzo where the language and culture would be part of the curriculum. Some people thought that the Indian language was outmoded and ineffectual. I denied this and, to show what I meant, I spoke in Slavey and said that at least one-quarter of the population in the North could understand me. Children who know their language and their culture have firmer backbones to cope with our modern society. (My instincts on this were proven right in later years, and there are now numerous success stories across Canada involving Aboriginal language use in schools.)

I elaborated my views considerably when the Department of Education came before us during the budget session. Bernie Gillie, the director, talked about the difficulty of creating education programs in Native languages for such a diverse population, which included Indian and Inuit people as well as non-Natives. They had to determine whether proposed programs were educationally sound, whether parents wanted them and whether they could be implemented. Implementation was difficult without Native teachers and local support, but progress was being made through the creation of local education authorities and training programs for Native teachers and classroom assistants, many of whom could be elders.

I made a lengthy response expressing my opinion on the matter of using Native languages and cultures in the classroom. "First of all, I am surprised that people who are supposed to be so well educated and top of their field should ask whether the incorporation of the Native language and culture into the school program is educationally sound. If you are aware of Indian society, their history, culture, and language, you would know that it has great value and it would be obvious that it should be part of the school curriculum. Every society has great people, leaders who have accomplished much, and where these peoples are alive, they should be approached and made teachers so their knowledge can be incorporated into the school program."

I had always felt that the education system was weakest at the grassroots level where it should be the strongest. It had never attempted to make Native parents part of the system, so when suddenly asked whether they should be involved, they would naturally be puzzled. "He has never been asked this question. He is not going to give a definite yes or no because this whole issue has never been asked of him and in the past fifty or hundred years he was made to believe that his culture, his language is really not important."

Turning to the subject of residential schools, I bemoaned the fact that hundreds of young children had to leave their homes and attend hostels. "I consider it most unfortunate that in this day and age, when you think the education philosophy or system would have progressed, you are still going with this system. I note that in Russia, where you have a socialistic or communistic type of society, that the state takes the children away at ten or twelve years of age, whereas in Canada, you take them away at the age of six or seven.... These children are torn from their parents [and] there is always a big fight between the parents and the education people who come around to pick up the children.... I find it incredible in this day and age that this should still continue."

Gillie responded to this latter issue to say that the residential school system had changed from my time in school and there were only 3 six-year-olds, 27 seven-year-olds, 36 eight-year-olds and 48 nine-year-olds—"just" 114 out of the one thousand students in territorial residential schools. Though the figures showed that the number of young students in residential school had been reduced, I felt alarmed that there were still so many.

Housing was another matter that captured a lot of attention. It was viewed both as an instrument of economic development and as a social need. Tom Butters spoke at length about housing, how he had been involved twenty years earlier in building a prototype of the first Arctic experimental house. Though he recognized that housing had improved since then, there were still many people living in what he called "dark boxes with ice shining on the walls, with a stinking bucket in a dark hole just off the kitchen." He called on the government to set up a housing authority that would "make sense out of the numerous and sometimes conflicting home building programs." Lyle Trimble put it clearly that the answer to the housing problem was for government to assist the people to provide their own houses stating that "giving people houses for nothing or very little will destroy people's initiative and pride."

We dealt with many other issues that first year, participating in debates and making numerous motions. David Searle addressed the matter of cabin fever both humorously and as a real problem facing people in isolated communities. Lyle Trimble proposed a motion opposing the diversion of northern waters for southern use; even in those days people were seriously concerned about the environment.

AND THEN THERE was the great problem recognized by almost everyone: alcohol and its effect on Native people in the North.

Alcohol was introduced into the North by the federal and, later, territorial governments through the establishment of liquor stores in all the major towns. Its impact on Native people had been devastating. Members cited many instances of alcoholism amongst Dene, Inuit and Métis people. Whites, too, were affected, but they had had a longer history of exposure to alcohol and seemed able to handle it better. If there was alcoholism amongst white people, they were able to mask it. As well, many white people came north for jobs and were accustomed, educated and trained to fit into the wage economy. In contrast, Natives came from a traditional, less structured way of life on the land and were just moving into communities and the wage economy. This was a major change to their way of life, and the availability of alcohol compounded the difficulty in making the transition. Living in communities required a different suite of skills that caused a certain amount of anxiety and frustration. Men and women who were great hunters and trappers and homemakers suddenly were faced with community living that didn't recognize these skills and practices. In this milieu there was frustration, social disorientation and upheaval, and people turned to alcohol to assuage their despair over these perceived shortcomings.

Council members made numerous suggestions to the government on how to address these problems. Alcohol was subsidized and was priced the same throughout the North, pointed out Lyle Trimble, while food prices, especially fresh fruits and vegetables, were extremely high in more remote communities. "Fresh food in the communities should be subsidized instead of liquor." The government made a profit of $3 million per year on the sale of alcohol but had allocated just $65,000 for alcohol education and $10,000 for treatment in the budget.

Tom Butters moved to set up community-oriented, low-budget alcohol treatment centres to address the problem. Normally, Tom noted, sick people went to a hospital. But, "the person sick with alcohol addiction wanders the streets and makes a nuisance of himself. He terrorizes and frequently assaults his family, ceases to provide for himself and his family, damages his body through the use of cheap alcohol substitutes, or improper diet." Lyle Trimble added "the problems encountered in the territories, especially among Native people who are still in a transition stage and learning how to handle alcohol, are very real, and I feel that this council and this government has a very real responsibility in this regard because we are the ones who sell the alcohol to them, and we derive a certain amount of revenue from those sales."

Commissioner Hodgson responded that he was sympathetic, but he was concerned about where the resources to deal with alcoholism would come from.

Trimble returned to the matter later when the budget was discussed. "I will repeat that I do not feel that we are justified in subsidizing the shipping charges of liquor. If we are prepared to subsidize the great cost of shipping liquor, then certainly we should be prepared to subsidize the air freight on milk which the babies require, and also fresh vegetables and meat which are required."

To refute the idea that dealing with alcohol would be too expensive, he described the costs of not dealing with it. There were large numbers of unemployable people in the North due to alcoholism. As to the profits that the government derived from liquor sales, we should also show the number of deaths from alcohol across the ledger. In 1970, there were thirty-one alcohol-related deaths in the Northwest Territories. And it was not only older people who concerned him; youth were increasingly being taken over by drinking, often landing in jail. Instead of jail, they needed education to overcome their problems and learn how to fit into the labour force.

These debates transformed my thinking and continued to affect me both personally and professionally for years to come.

Chapter 7: Key Issues and Major Fights

TO SOME EXTENT, I came to the legislative council as a bit of an innocent. I had my degree in political science and I had worked a few short
jobs in both the public and private sector, but the reality of the rapidly
changing government in the North was a far cry from the system of
democratic and responsible government I had learned in school and
that most people in southern Canada took for granted.

Until 1951, government for the North was handled by Ottawa
through an appointed commissioner and council that met in Ottawa
once or twice a year. Elected members were added in to the council in
1951, although appointed members still formed the majority. After the
1954 election, some sessions of the council were held in the Northwest Territories, but the majority of meetings continued to be held in
Ottawa, where the government administration was located.

In 1959, John Goodall, the postmaster from my hometown, was
elected in a by-election to the council. He used to say, "Give the Natives a pot of brew and they're happy as could be." That was his attitude and approach. Of course, treaty Indians didn't have the vote in
those days. Goodall used his position to ensure that his sons got contracts and to have lands lived on by Métis or Dene families transferred
to his name. Philip and Henry Lafferty believed that they owned the
land on which their houses were situated, only to learn years later
that Goodall was the legal title holder. My grandfather George Sibbeston, whom Goodall claimed to be his best friend, lived next door
to Goodall. Through the years the strip of land with their houses and
gardens got narrower and Goodall's land got bigger. Every spring the
causeway at the south end of the island would be torn out by river

ice, and each summer the Goodalls would get the contract to build a new causeway. This was not a role model for a young man interested in serving his community. Maybe that's why I originally planned to become a teacher!

By the mid-1960s, council sessions were being held in both Ottawa and throughout the territories, and in 1966, based on the recommendations of the Carrothers Commission, three seats were added to represent the eastern Arctic. At the council meeting held in Resolute Bay in October of that year, after a by-election, elected members held the majority for the first time.

In 1967, Commissioner Stu Hodgson moved the government and its administration to Yellowknife, landing with a plane loaded with files and staff from Ottawa. From that time on, all meetings of the council, which became the legislative assembly in 1975, were held in communities in the Northwest Territories. One of the more interesting things that the commissioner brought north was a collection of paintings of northern scenes by the renowned Canadian painter, A.Y. Jackson. Jackson had been seeking funds from the government to go north in the late 1940s and was finally given a few hundred dollars out of Northwest Territories liquor revenues in exchange for these paintings. The story goes that they were on the walls of various bureaucrats at Indian Affairs in Ottawa, and Hodgson, arguing that they were the property of the GNWT, went around personally to take them down and send them north. For years, they hung in the commissioner's office, but now they are on display in the caucus room in the legislative assembly in Yellowknife. That was the kind of man Commissioner Hodgson was: forceful, charismatic and determined to run the government as he saw fit.

Learning how to deal with the commissioner was the most important lesson I learned in my first term, one that served me well in dealing with strong bureaucrats in later years. One of my first run-ins with Hodgson was over economic development in the community of Wrigley.

Wrigley, north of Fort Simpson, was a community of a hundred people, mostly hunters and trappers. There was no highway connection, only a winter road for a few months each year. Some seismic work went on in winter months and, in the summer, crews were hired to deal with forest fires. Beyond that, there was little economic activity. Though trapping was still a means of earning a living for the older men, the young people were looking for jobs that provided a better and more stable income.

The oil and gas industry was growing, with seismic work every winter and the possibility of production in a few years. Oil had been found in Norman Wells in 1922, and the short-lived Canol pipeline had shipped it west to Whitehorse during the Second World War. I believed that with training and tools, jobs and even contracts might be obtained by people in the community.

With this in mind, I arranged for the commissioner and Economic Development officials to fly into the community. The meeting in the community hall was well attended, with tables set up at the front for the chief and band leaders on one side and the commissioner and government officials on the other. I sat in the middle between the two groups. The discussion focused on the potential of oil and gas and how the government could help local people get more of the work that was then being done by contractors coming in from the south. I encouraged the direction the discussion was going. Chief Edward Hardisty was silent but appeared supportive.

Then when Chief Hardisty finally spoke up, he said the community wanted a sawmill. I was astonished. I knew, from my own meetings in the community, that a sawmill wasn't the answer or what the people wanted; before the chief spoke, no one had even mentioned it. But Stu jumped on the idea, saying that if that's what they wanted, he would get them one. Emotions ran high as I challenged Stu Hodgson and the government officials to respond to the real issue of training, jobs and business opportunities and not look for a quick fix. The meeting ended with no decision having been made.

I must have offended Stu as he didn't speak to me and I was relegated to the back of the plane on the way back to Yellowknife. A few days later I ran into Val Wake, a CBC reporter who was with us in Wrigley to report on the meeting. He asked, "Aren't you afraid of Stu Hodgson?"

No," I said. "Not really."

Val shook his head. "He's the strongest man in the North."

It never dawned on me as a young politician, confident in myself, knowing people and the situation they faced, that I should be afraid to speak up truthfully and aggressively for what I believed in. Nonetheless, I did begin to realize how difficult it would be to really influence government without a few more tools in my kit.

A few weeks later, Chief Hardisty met with Stu Hodgson in Yellowknife. The sawmill was delivered to Wrigley later that summer and was set up a few miles up the river from the community. I visited the site a few times, each time witnessing Chief Hardisty himself struggling to make the sawmill work. I don't know if it ever produced any amount of lumber; after a few years it was moved to the edge of the riverbank in the community, where it still sits, rusting away.

Another time we travelled to Trout Lake, a community of about sixty people, to deal with housing issues. The people there were very self-sufficient and most had their own homes made of logs. However, some of the houses were getting old, and during the course of the meeting Stu agreed to provide materials for five new ones. There was not even a winter road, but a few weeks later a DC3 landed on the ice in front of the community to deliver the supplies. I admit I was pretty impressed; we weren't used to that kind of action out of the government. Hodgson made it a practice to visit every community each year and, in the course of community meetings, which went on for hours, he would invariably agree to change the capital plan to meet some local priority. It must have annoyed the civil servants who travelled with him to see all their hard work undone at the drop of a hat, but that's the way it was in those days: Hodgson was The Man. He made all the decisions. I have to give Stu credit for always keeping his word and for bringing government to life by making things happen in a quick and effective way. Although my role as a territorial council member was minimal, I knew intuitively that someday I and others from the North would be the ones dealing with issues and making government decisions.

IN 1972, I became a consultant to Northwest Project Gas Pipeline. This was one of the consortiums that proposed to build a gas pipeline down the Mackenzie Valley. I was cautious, as I knew the pipeline was controversial and opposed by many of the people down the valley. Despite this, I felt I could serve a useful purpose in educating people. The two consortia, the other being Foothills Pipelines, had a test site at San Sault Rapids, fifty miles or so north of Norman Wells. My job was to take community leaders to the test site to see for themselves what a gas pipeline might look like. Of course, the pipe was buried in the ground, but the pressure pumps and control panels were situated in facilities above ground. Tests were done with gas at various temperatures and pressures to simulate the operation of a natural gas pipeline.

I visited all the communities along the pipeline route beginning in Old Crow, Yukon, and working my way south from Inuvik to Fort Simpson. I provided information to the communities and arranged to fly the leaders and interested persons by Twin Otter to the test site. The tour included a thorough examination of the test facility and ended with a big meal put on by the camp cooks. The group from Old Crow consisted of the chief, some councillors and the well-known newspaper columnist Edith Josie. The tour went well, but as the plane was returning to Old Crow we ran into turbulence and people started getting sick. The pilots noticed people moving around in the back looking for containers and dropped the plane about a hundred feet, causing people to sprawl all over. Soon a number of them were throwing up. By the time we landed, the plane was a mess. Everybody was glad to get off and headed for their homes, leaving the pilots to clean up. I thought it served them right for purposely dropping the plane in midflight.

The consortium wanted an elders group from the communities to give it advice, so I arranged a number of meetings with gas company officials in Calgary and had Ted Trindell and Tadit Francis (the chief of Fort McPherson) and a few others as part of the group.

My work with the consortium often took me to Calgary, and I occasionally flew with the executives in their private jets to Houston, Texas, and Tulsa, Oklahoma. By the end of my two years with them I had become somewhat spoiled, staying in nice hotels and dining in the best restaurants. Meanwhile, Karen was living with the children in a small shack, and would chide me when I said something about the wieners and beans or the meatballs that were the common dishes at our home.

AFTER A COUPLE of years on the territorial council I had realized that the government was essentially the commissioner and his cohorts: the deputy commissioner and several assistant commissioners. The council, as we were often told, was merely advisory. But change was coming, and I needed more education if I was to be effective when elected members had real power. In 1973, while I continued to work hard to fulfill my duties as an elected representative, I stopped working for the consortium so that I could start studying for my law degree. I travelled back and forth between Edmonton and the North for the remainder of my term.

AS MORE AND more responsibility was devolved from Ottawa to the territorial government, many issues demanded attention. One of the first things we dealt with when the session opened in June 1973 was the announcement—delivered by telex—that all the remaining Indian and Northern Affairs responsibilities under the Northern Rental Housing Program would be transferred to the territorial government. We were to deal with thirteen bills that session, so the commissioner revived the legislative committee, which had been inactive for some months, and named me as chair.

The seventh legislative council, which lasted from 1970 to 1975, was a critical one for the development of government in the North. It was the last that had appointed members and the first where the opinions of elected members had significant impact on the actions of the government. We were laying the foundations for the structure of government while developing the physical infrastructure of communities and the programs and services for people.

The members of the council were a diverse lot. David Searle was a lawyer from Yellowknife, well-educated and methodical in his approach. Tom Butters, a journalist and newspaper owner from Inuvik, was steady and well-informed. Lyle Trimble operated an air charter company and was perhaps the fieriest of them all.

I would call the next category of councillors—Pearson, Phipps and myself—the second line as in hockey: not prolific, but scoring the occasional goal, adding important points and contributing ideas and views of our constituents. The others—Pedersen, Rabesca and Adams—were strong defenders of their constituencies. The appointed members, although placed there to give us guidance, often had very little to say.

It is interesting, from the perspective of forty years, how some issues that became critical were first raised in small ways during that seventh council, while other matters that seemed of vast importance wound up being of little consequence a few years down the road.

A good example of the latter was muskox ranching. We had several blazing and occasionally hilarious debates on the matter as we tried to determine how such an enterprise might be created and who should do it. Although no muskox ranch ever emerged in the Northwest Territories, the discussion does reveal some of the thinking around economic development that was prevalent at the time.

Qiviut (also qivik, or muskox wool) was a very valuable product. Previously the government had spent $5,000 on a project for people in Arctic communities to gather it on the tundra. This had not proven successful, and the latest proposal was for the government to spend funds either to set up a muskox ranch themselves or to find someone who, with government assistance, would take on the job.

In some respects, the debate over muskox ranching pointed to some of the difficulties of managing a territory as large and diverse as the Northwest Territories. The muskox came from the High Arctic, but creating a ranch there was uneconomical as it would be too expensive to provide feed. The Delta had similar issues and neither area had access to veterinary services, always a concern when domesticating and enclosing wild animals. Instead, the proposal was to move a small herd south under the management of a local farmer. Two communities were in competition for the ranch: Fort Smith, where a man named Plamandon had expressed an interest, and Fort Providence, where a man named Hendry would be the farmer. I supported the Fort Providence proposal, mostly because the local chief was interested in undertaking it as a joint venture with Mr. Hendry and it was a good opportunity for Aboriginal people to get business experience.

Of course, raising the muskox was only half of the equation. What would be done with the wool was the real issue. Some argued it should be returned to the High Arctic islands where the muskox originated, for use by local craftspeople. Bryan Pearson, on the other hand, wanted a small cottage knitting industry in Frobisher Bay (Iqaluit).

For others, cost was the real factor. David Searle from Yellowknife wanted nothing to do with the project at all, suggesting at one time that Fort Smith council member, Paul Kaeser, put up his own money if he was so keen on the project. That debate grew so heated that the commissioner had to intervene to end the discussion. The issue of government versus private expenditures came up again when Lyle Trimble questioned, with respect to the knitting shop, why we would approve "the expenditure of a hundred thousand dollars for a con-sultants' fee in order to provide seventy-five thousand dollars worth of labour for the people of the territories?" Bryan Pearson's response was, in effect, that you have to spend money to make money and he was tired of listening to debates over trivial amounts of money. We needed to take chances, as anyone going into any kind of business did.

At one point, we even had a discussion on the psychology of muskox and whether they could stand being taken to a southern cli-mate or being fenced! According to Louis-Edmond Hamelin, several had "committed suicide" when taken to a ranch in Fort Chimo, Que-bec. Bryan Pearson got in the funniest line of the whole debate, dur-ing the discussion of who would get to knit the qiviut into sweaters: "How about getting the muskox to knit? They could all stay home." The council voted seven to five in favour of the Fort Providence pro-posal, but nothing ever came of it.

Our concern for the economy wasn't confined to muskox ranch-ing, of course. While there were areas of the North with thriving econ-omies, notably Yellowknife with its two gold mines and government jobs, most places—even more so than today—struggled or experi-enced the difficulties of the boom-and-bust resource economy. Oil and gas exploration provided some seasonal work in the Delta and there was talk of building a gas pipeline down the Mackenzie Valley.

Justice Tom Berger would soon undertake his inquiry that would eventually make recommendations shaping northern political, social and economic development for years to come.

The territorial government had no real control over non-renewable resource development—those powers remain with the federal government to this day, though devolution will eventually be achieved—other than to tax the wages of those who worked in the mines (provided they were permanent residents of the Northwest Territories), but we were interested and engaged in other aspects of the economy, including tourism, hunting and trapping and other forms of renewable resource development. In particular, we focused on how government itself could create jobs and business opportunities for people who had been born and raised in the North, both Aboriginal people but also the growing number of second- and third-generation non-Natives in communities like Fort Smith, Hay River and Yellowknife. The best government jobs still seemed to go to recent arrivals and, in fact, the territorial government actively recruited for many positions in southern Canada.

I was very impressed by Dr. Ken Pugh from Alberta, who had undertaken a review of labour standards in the Northwest Territories. Hugh Campbell declared that there was a real problem in the North with contractors hiring local people who would stop showing up after a few days or after the first paycheque. In response, Dr. Pugh said it was essential to remember that Native people were making a transition from a hunting and trapping lifestyle to the wage economy. A certain amount of patience was necessary to succeed. He illustrated this by telling of the way his department, when he was the Deputy Minister of Labour in Alberta, trained Native people to work on the oil sands project. "I remember one of the prime contractors was mad at me because I was insisting that if somebody did not turn up after a weekend that they give him another chance. 'Look, this is ridiculous,' he said. 'If one of our old employees did not turn up after a long weekend and had been on a drunk, he would be fired, but you want us to forgive and forgive and forgive.' When somebody asks the Lord how many times you forgive a person, I replied, the Lord says seventy times seven, so keep on forgiving them. They do learn. They do appreciate the fact that the time-clock world is the white man's world, but the trouble is that we are just sometimes a little too hasty to think that we can change them overnight." Persistence paid off; 50 percent of one of the maintenance crews were Native people that his department had trained.

Pugh also disagreed with the idea put forward by Bryan Pearson that the standards of work should be lowered to allow Native people to get jobs. It wasn't the standards of work that needed lowering, he said, but the entry requirements into the workforce. He had seen the most perfect pressure welding of pipe by an Indian who had a grade two education. "The Indian could not write an examination, but after eight weeks of practical training he was the best welder we ever had."

Both of these ideas were influential on my thinking for years to come. The problem for Native people wasn't that they couldn't do the work; they could. The problem was they couldn't get the jobs and, until they got used to the wage economy, they couldn't keep them. Removing false barriers to jobs—especially government jobs—became a major goal for the rest of my political career. At the same time, I came to recognize that Aboriginal people had to make a transition from traditional to modern life. The government could help them do that but, in the end, it was something people had to learn to do for themselves—by being sober, working hard and taking control of their lives.

Bryan Pearson went on to suggest that every government job in every community now held by non-Natives from the south should eventually be held by northerners. The way to get there, he suggested, was to set up training positions and apprenticeships, not just in the trades but for office workers and managers, too. It was an idea I strongly supported.

On a related matter, I proposed a motion that the government begin contracting out highway maintenance work to local, and especially Aboriginal-owned, companies, starting with the section of highway between Hay River and Enterprise. It would not only be good for the local economy but it might also improve the conditions of the highway, which were notoriously dangerous. The commissioner was sympathetic but noted that even the highways were owned by the federal government; it was they who contracted the maintenance to the territorial government. Nonetheless, the motion passed without opposition, and when the highways were devolved to the GNWT, contracting out maintenance became standard practice and an important way to help develop local businesses.

Tourism was becoming more important in the North as roads started to be built and access to wilderness areas was improved by an expanding fleet of floatplanes. The government proposed creating small roadside and community parks for use by tourists and northerners for picnics, camping and other recreational areas. Though the proposed areas were small compared to the large national parks that would be created in later years, the issues we debated were the same as those we debate today when northern parks are established. How would communities be consulted, and how would they benefit? Would Aboriginal rights to hunt, trap, fish and otherwise use the land and waters in traditional ways be fully protected? How would we ensure that parks would not impede later development of mineral and other resources should they be discovered? The territorial council at the time approved the idea of creating parks as long as these matters were addressed. They also insisted that the final decision on creating parks be made by the commissioner-in-council and not simply by administrative fiat—in other words, as a political rather than a bureaucratic decision.

The creation of northern parks was an issue that continued to concern and sometimes trouble me over the years. While I have supported the reasonable development of parks and other protected areas, I've always remained cognizant of the need to balance environmental protection with resource development so that northerners can benefit from the mineral wealth with which we were blessed.

Another issue that concerned me was the decline of the freshwater fishing industry on Great Slave Lake, which the fishermen blamed on the imposition of the Fresh Water Marketing Corporation. The number of fishing operations both winter and summer had dropped by at least half since the corporation came on the scene in 1968. Over a five-year period, the price paid for fish had risen only from twenty-eight to twenty-nine cents a pound, despite high inflation at that time.

Through a motion in the assembly, I called on the commissioner to intervene and meet with the fishermen to assist them in their dealings with the corporation. The motion passed and the meeting took place, but the industry continued to suffer setbacks despite my ongoing efforts on behalf of my constituents. A small group of commercial fishers still operate out of Hay River to this day and in 2010 finally voted to leave the corporation and market fish on their own.

The elephant in the room remained the Mackenzie Valley gas pipeline, which had been proposed following the discovery of large gas reserves in the Delta. Although there was some support for the project among businesses and the non-Native community, the Indian Brotherhood was opposed to any development prior to the settlement of land claims. The Berger Commission (Mackenzie Valley Pipeline Inquiry) had been established in March 1974 to investigate the impacts of the proposed pipeline, but in the view of some, like Inuvik member Tom Butters, the project was already dead because of rising construction costs, resource battles between Canada and Alberta and the opposition of the Dene, who had threatened court action or more if the project went ahead without their approval. Others, like David Searle, wanted the government to throw their support behind the pipeline. It was clear where the commissioner's sympathies lay—he had spoken of the need for real and substantial economic development if the North was to advance. But he also knew that without a resolution of land claims, such development was unlikely to proceed. I opposed the pipeline at the time, though not fiercely, as I thought Aboriginal communities were not in a position to participate and benefit. Like many Native people in the North, my views have shifted, but although approval for constructing a pipeline has been given, the prospect of one actually being built seems as distant as ever.

ONE OF THE most critical issues—both then and now—that government faced was alcohol and its effects on people and communities in the North. The territorial council discussed the matter many times and heard expert witnesses and reports throughout its life. Beyond the direct discussions of alcohol pricing, distribution and treatment of abuse, the topic of alcohol permeated many of our other discussions: corrections and justice, health and even economic development.

The government commissioned Bill Wacko to prepare a comprehensive report on the problems of alcohol and drugs in the North and provide recommendations on possible solutions. He appeared before council on the last day of the session with his report, which contained seventeen recommendations. By way of introduction he stated that there was a trend in America toward liberalization of alcohol laws. Unfortunately, the greater the quantities drunk per person, the greater the number of deaths from cirrhosis of the liver and the greater the number of other resultant problems.

His first recommendation was for government regulations and programs "aimed at reducing the pattern of drinking which leads to drunkenness." Some measures that might reduce abuse included introducing weak beer into the liquor system, making food and recreation available in licensed premises and placing warnings on liquor containers. Higher pricing of alcohol was another method of reducing consumption.

I certainly supported the idea of weak beer, as lower alcohol brews would be similar to the home brew that people had grown up with. It had always amazed me that when the liquor store arrived in Fort Simpson in the 1960s, overproof rum and other strong liquors were made available without any thought about what they could do to people who were not used to them.

Equally important were the suggestions that controls be placed on the importation and sale of alcohol in smaller communities. This idea was supported by many members—some even calling for complete prohibition across the Northwest Territories—and by community leaders and chiefs from one end of the North to the other. While the government was not supportive of complete prohibition, both because of the impact on revenues and because of the difficulty enforcing it, the commissioner and deputy commissioner were agreeable to the idea of local liquor restrictions put in place through a community plebiscite. In fact, when the chiefs from the Dogrib (Tli'cho) communities asked that the decision on restrictions be made in the traditional rather than the southern way, that is, directly by leaders and elders, the commissioner agreed to that approach.

The Dogrib chiefs also asked that bars in Yellowknife not serve residents of their communities. The commissioner felt that this could not be imposed on private establishments but he would request that they do so voluntarily. (When later asked about the success of this measure, he reported that some establishments refused to try those restrictions, and those who tried found that patrons who were questioned would respond they were not Dogrib. What a baffling, powerful force alcohol can exert over people, even to the extent of denying their identity!)

The session concluded before we could discuss all of the recommendations in the Wacko report, but we nevertheless felt that it marked a significant event—the first real effort to grapple with the issue of alcohol abuse—and the report reverberated through our deliberations for several years.

Although many of our efforts were aimed at reducing alcohol consumption, we also were faced with the fact that many people were already addicted and were suffering great harm because of it. Alcohol was filling our jails and our hospitals and creating great social problems in communities, ranging from public drunkenness to domestic abuse to premature death. There had been numerous incidents of people dying from freezing to death in snowbanks because they were too drunk to get home or dying from suicide or accident while incarcerated for drunkenness. Sadly, incidents like these persist to this day.

A number of options were discussed. One that we were certain wasn't working was the existing practice of throwing people in the drunk tank to sober up. Bryan Pearson described it well in one of our debates as "a concrete room with scaffolds in the middle and a sloping floor…. [They] shut him in there, remove his shoelaces, belt and suspenders…until he sobers up; then release him the following morning after he has hosed down his mess…his vomit and all the rest of it… and he staggers out of there into the bright, blazing sunlight."

Pearson made a motion calling on the government to set up detox centres where there would be expertise on how to care for intoxicated people securely, providing immediate medical assistance if required and then treatment and counselling to treat the bigger problem. I spoke strongly in favour of the motion and gave the example of a well-run facility in Alberta called Henwood where people could go to dry out. Even more successful was a centre in Saskatchewan that was run by Aboriginal people. "Since alcohol is such a problem with Native people, it has got to be Native people who work in this area and it is only they who will be successful." For the Northwest Territories, I even had a location in mind: the old convent in Fort Providence, which was isolated from the bigger communities of the North and could provide opportunities for people to work in the gardens or even practise traditional skills. It seems ironic now that I would suggest an old residential school for a detox centre given how much residential schools contributed to the social ills related to drinking.

Tom Butters pointed out Eugene Yew in the gallery; he had started an awareness program on behalf of the Métis, "the first positive thing that has been done by any organization in these territories, including this government." Ultimately, the motion passed, and the government began to make greater use of detoxification centres and other treatment facilities. However, as David Searle predicted in the debate, it did not mean the end of the drunk tank.

On another occasion, we discussed developing a court workers program similar to that in Alberta. Since so many of the crimes committed in the North—from break-and-enters to domestic assault—were driven by addiction or fuelled by drink, it seemed a good idea to divert people into alcohol counselling or treatment as part of a system to help people understand the charges against them, the way the court operated and what options they had. I had met Chester Cunningham, who ran the Native Counselling Services in Alberta with a staff of twenty and a budget of over $200,000, and had seen how effective it was. Hoping for a similar program up North, I had started discussions with the Indian Brotherhood and Métis Association in the Northwest Territories and had even gained a commitment from the federal government to pay half the costs. Again, I thought it would be more effective if the program was run by Native organizations, operating outside government. As always when money was involved,

Deputy Commissioner Parker was hesitant to commit, but he did go so far as to say, "If the program that the administration favours in general is within our priorities, I think it would occupy a fairly important position so we would make our best efforts towards funding it." Eventually, of course, it became obvious that programs like these were essential if the court system was to deliver justice and not merely punishment.

Looking back on those debates, thinking about my own struggles with alcohol and thinking of all the people I knew who had even greater problems, it seems that so little came of all our talk. But still, it was a start and things did improve; the Northwest Territories would be a far worse place today if we hadn't taken those little steps then.

ANOTHER TOPIC THAT would resonate down the years was the structure of the territorial government and its relationship to regions and communities. Not surprisingly in a territory that covered one-third of Canada, the relationship of the Yellowknife-centred government to the far-flung communities of the North was a subject for great debate. During the life of the council, we discussed the role of community governments and their relationship to band councils, the function of hunters and trappers associations in economic development and environmental policy, and the organizational structure of the government and civil service.

One major debate that started out innocently enough concerned the Fort Smith Region. It began when I asked the commissioner in the 1974 winter session when he planned on getting rid of the Region. His response: "Not in the foreseeable future."

Fort Smith had been the administrative centre for all of the Northwest Territories until 1967, when the capital was established in Yellowknife. Fort Smith was left as a regional centre to administer the area along the Arctic coast and the Mackenzie Valley north of Yellowknife up to Inuvik. Eventually Inuvik became a regional centre to look after the Delta communities and the area around Great Bear Lake. The remaining area along the Arctic coast and the area south of Fort Norman remained part of the Fort Smith Region. From our vantage point in Fort Simpson, considering that all the airline and communication routes ran through Yellowknife, it seemed impractical and inefficient to have to deal with Fort Smith. Why not just deal with officials in Yellowknife who have the final authority to make decisions?

Others supported my view. Lena Pedersen, who came from Coppermine and represented the Central Arctic communities, saw Fort Smith as remote and inaccessible. David Searle pointed to the absurdity of the area office in Yellowknife reporting to Fort Smith even though the headquarters officials were right next door; envelopes travelled from the area office to Fort Smith, back to headquarters in Yellowknife for final decisions and then all the way back to Fort Smith for dispatch to the area office again. Bryan Pearson noted the large number of civil servants for such a small population—at the time 3,089 to govern 35,000. John Parker was quick to point out this included six hundred teachers and a number of seasonal workers, but Lyle Trimble retorted that the government was top-heavy and that we should do away with all of the regional offices, which were sucking up money and staff time. Commissioner Hodgson acknowledged that some of the members' views had merit and said he would hire Ewan Cotterill to look at these issues, including the number of civil servants required and the proper administrative structure.

I made the suggestion that Cotterill also consider the difference between the North and southern provinces. Here, as Native people emerged from living off the land, they needed help to adapt and make their living in western society. This required different approaches and skills by people working for the government. In the south, the people were better educated and the role and function of government was different. In the North we needed civil servants who could wield axes. "I notice that government has all sorts of expert people, people with Bachelor of Commerce, Bachelor of Science. I have always said the people that the government hires are too sophisticated, too advanced for our situation in the North. What good is a man with a Bachelor of Commerce to a guy in Wrigley or Trout Lake who is concerned with very fundamental sorts of problems?"

I then moved that the government begin a two-year phasing-out of the Fort Smith regional office and in its stead emphasize an area administration concept in such places as Hay River, Cambridge Bay,

Norman Wells, Fort Smith and Fort Simpson. Lyle Trimble immediately moved to amend the motion to include phasing out all regions in the North.

The debate that followed was lively and enlightening. Hugh Campbell, an appointed member, immediately asked if the motion was even legal, as the administration of the Northwest Territories was within the purview of the commissioner, not the council. Hodgson concurred, saying that his powers were prescribed by a minister of the government of Canada: "You know, if you want to play football, your first step is to get the ball."

I conceded that Hodgson had the legal authority to rule the North, but he also had a moral responsibility to take our advice as elected representatives; otherwise, "you will kill what little feeling of democracy there is in the North."

John Parker was quick to interject that "the record would indicate that there are a very, very substantial number of instances where the wish of this Council has been followed." It was the lack of funds and, indeed, power that prevented them from doing more: The chairman, Hugh Campbell, expressed his agreement with this sentiment and suggested we break for coffee, perhaps to give time for tempers to cool.

When debate resumed, David Searle added his support for the motion but expressed doubt that it could succeed. Tom Butters was concerned about the breadth of Trimble's amendment, and I agreed that I was mostly focused on the Fort Smith region. John Parker added that the more far-flung areas needed strong administrative centres close to home. Frobisher Bay, for example, should remain a regional centre, but perhaps some changes to other regions could be made over time as there were sufficient resources. Hodgson raised the debate to a higher level when he said, "I think one of these days that you fellows are going to have to make up your minds what you want to grow into being. Do you want to grow into being the government or do you want to grow into being the legislature, because there is not a legislature in the land that has this type of authority that you are advocating with your motion here today." It was a good question.

Eventually, Trimble's amendment failed six votes to five but my motion passed seven to five. Emboldened, I went on to set out the conditions under which the executive's budget should pass:

- The government was to do a study to look at the concept of area offices within the next two to three months.
- The government was to take into consideration the state of the Native people for whom they are setting up the administration.
- The government would state its intention to carry out these instructions.

John Parker sought clarification that the motion applied only to the Fort Smith region, but in essence he agreed to the conditions and would prepare a report to be completed by June 1.

A couple of other members expressed reservations about how long it might take for the changes I sought, as they could take years. I replied that it would take more than mere years to make the changes I really wanted. The type of changes that I envisaged would likely never come about. What I had in mind were major societal changes such as having half of the CBC programming in Native languages and substantial numbers of Native people working at the highest levels of government. These changes would never come about unless we had a revolution.

"Do not count on revolution to bring about what you advocate," said the commissioner, "because I have seen a few of them and I will tell you, they turn out much different than you think. After revolutions take place, guys like you and I are the first that are strung up because any revolution does not want ideas. That is not why they take place."

With that, the debate ended. What had started as a simple question turned into a soul-searching debate on democracy and an attempt to wield what little power we had to influence the budget of the government.

THERE WERE STILL many people in the North who could not speak English or who spoke it poorly. I had always considered myself fortunate that I had retained my own language while still being able to communicate in English. I had even retained a little French from my early days in residential school. I knew instinctively there would be benefits to teaching Dene languages in schools; at the very least, I felt it was essential that the government be able to provide basic services to people in their own tongue. Lena Pedersen and I both pressed the government to provide full-time interpreter services in hospitals, and I was constantly pushing for improved Slavey language instruction in schools similar to the Inuktitut offered to Inuit students in the eastern Arctic. It was a controversial subject, and I recall one parent in Fort Simpson saying, "If my child so much as learns a Slavey word, I will wash his mouth out with soap."

I was particularly annoyed with the CBC, who refused to program any Dene language programs. One time when the Northern Services director of the CBC appeared before us in Yellowknife, I challenged him to answer me in Slavey when I spoke to him in French. Only a few years later I was an on-air participant in the first ever Dene-language radio program in the Northwest Territories, a weekly program on CBC that ran for a couple of years.

THE JUSTICE SYSTEM was another area that was expanding rapidly in the North. The court assistants program was being developed and we approved the construction of a new correctional centre in Frobisher Bay, which sparked a considerable discussion of what was causing the increase in crime in the North. Not surprisingly, alcohol seemed to be the general consensus.

There was an incident just before one of our sessions that sparked considerable debate: a riot at the Yellowknife Correctional Centre on May 4, 1973. The warden of the jail, Clair Wilkins, appeared be-fore council and tried to put the riot incident in context describing what he called an inmate culture, which consisted of the dominance of the strong over the weak. He stated that the riot was an outlet for suppressed energy and "the more blood, the more there is a release from tension." Because of the parent–child relationship within the jail, small rebellions were not unusual and were usually put down by the staff.

Shortly after midnight on May 4, the three guards on duty in central control heard noise in the dormitory area. Two went to check and were attacked. The one remaining guard heard the commotion and left the station to see what was going on. He, too, was overwhelmed, after which the prisoners took control and the guards were let out of the building. Reinforcements, including the RCMP, arrived and negotiations commenced. During the process of airing complaints, tempers flared and the inmates threatened to burn down the building. A local journalist remarked that if they did, they would not likely get their gymnasium that was due to be built. That had a calming effect, and the men soon returned to their cells.

Wilkins praised the staff as being devoted. He said that they were in their jobs not for their salaries but with a "sincere desire to help their fellow man to become law-abiding citizens." Council members were skeptical. David Searle reported many calls from the staff who complained that morale at the jail was so bad that staff might simply leave the jail unmanned. He called for an independent review of the system. Under questioning from Trimble and Pearson, Wilkins admitted that not enough staff were present on the night of the riot to deal with the situation and mistakes had been made by those who were there. Lena Pedersen's questions revealed that the riot had been led by a single white inmate, and she speculated that the Natives had joined in only because they were scared. She also decried the lack of religious support in the institution, something that was particularly important to Native people. Pearson added that inmates needed something useful to occupy their times, such as vocational programs to provide them with employable skills on their release.

I said that in my experience, "those in jail are mild characters and are good people when they are not drinking." The majority were Native—which remains true in the North to this day—but there were few Aboriginal people working at the correctional centre. Wilkens claimed that their attempts to hire Native people were unceasing and that those he had on staff were gems. I was less than convinced and argued that the situation wouldn't change until someone was in charge who was passionate about including Native staff. To bolster my statement I moved that the corrections services undertake a special program to recruit, train and hire Native people. I added that if nothing was done within one year, somebody would have to go, meaning that they should be fired. The motion carried easily.

John Parker listed some of the changes that would be made to improve the correctional centres, including hiring more Native staff, making greater use of electronic surveillance and examining ways to let people serve their sentences in their home communities. A review of staffing procedures and policies was also promised. The commissioner expressed satisfaction at the way the council had handled the debate and declared that the government would "marry the good things of the past and the experiences of our programs that have proven to be sound" with new initiatives, increasingly focused on rehabilitation.

THIS DEBATE, LIKE many others in the territorial council, reflected a growing awareness that the territorial government had to adapt. Of course, it was evolving rapidly already. Federal programs were being devolved to territorial control and new relationships—if rocky and usually adversarial—were being established with Native organizations. The days of appointed members were coming to an end. In fact, one of the last acts of the territorial council was to pass legislation renaming the body as the legislative assembly in preparation for the 1975 election, when all members would be elected by the people. The commissioner would remain as head of government and oversee the work of the assembly, but elected members would play a more prominent role in decision-making, including having an elected leader in the assembly and seats on the executive council (cabinet) with ministerial authority over some departments.

It was no longer sufficient to be a government *of* the people of the North; it had to become a government *for* and *by* the people as well. Aboriginal people made up over half of the population of the Northwest Territories, and their needs had to be recognized in programs, whether through language instruction in schools, more Native people working for the government or the inclusion of Aboriginal practices and traditions in the operations and institutions of government. This view increasingly began to dominate my thoughts and became a central theme in my future political fights.

But first, I had to arm myself for that fight. I had to establish myself in the law in order to make real changes in the North.

Chapter 8: A Legal Interlude

HALFWAY THROUGH MY four-year term I realized the government was not yet ready for elected people to play more significant roles. I had been interested in studying law for some time and now decided to do so. In essence, I decided that I was wasting my time being a council member and should go back to university to become a lawyer. It wasn't just because the law would provide me with a good career; more importantly, it would better prepare me to someday play a greater role as an elected member in government. I was impressed by the political abilities of lawyers like David Searle. They had a distinct advantage over others in dealing with legislation. I had already studied political science and gained a Bachelor of Arts degree; I had come in contact with constitutional law issues there and was keen and interested in advancing my knowledge in this realm.

I applied to the Native Law Centre in Saskatoon and the University of Alberta. I was rejected by the former but accepted at the University of Alberta. Ironically, I had flunked twice from its Department of Education; now I was going to enroll in one of the leading professional faculties. For our family, it meant we were on the move again. Karen was not too happy being uprooted, but one fall day in 1973 we packed all our stuff in the back of a pickup truck and I headed for Edmonton. I had our two older sons, Glen and Randy, along with my cousin Arnold Hope with me in the pickup. Karen and our newest baby, Murray, caught a ride with Bill Granley in his private plane. Arnold reminds me often about the thirteen flat tires we had on that trip, as I couldn't afford new tires. Nonetheless, we made it to the city and settled in for the year at Michener Park university housing.

Despite now having three sons I loved and five years of marriage under my belt, I found that I was often uncertain in my role as a father and husband. I hadn't grown up in a household with a father myself, and my ten years in residential school had given me no understanding of normal family life. I wanted to be a good father but I didn't know how.

Even though I was now a law student, I was also still a territorial council member and flew back and forth to Yellowknife to attend sessions, leaving Karen to handle most of the childrearing. In the summer I returned to Fort Simpson to do constituency work, but come fall of 1974 I was back in law school. When my term as council member ended I didn't run for re-election (despite what it says on the internet), as I wanted to practise law when I got my degree. That degree came in May 1975, and I went to Yellowknife to begin my year of articling.

I had expected to work with David Searle's firm, but he wanted me to start right away in June, and I was set on building a house that summer. So I told David that I would look for another job down the street. I eventually got a job with Dietrich Brand's firm and was able to work on the house before beginning my articling in September. It made sense to have a house for my growing family, which now included three boys and a girl, Janice.

My uncle Charlie Hansen and Karen's father, Art, came up from Edmonton to help with construction. I also got a couple of workers from the jail on work release. They proved to be excellent workers: industrious and always on time. Interestingly, the biggest problem wasn't building the house but getting a mortgage. I went to all the banks in Yellowknife but none would give me a loan. They said I was a student, was just starting a job and had no background in building houses. I finally went to the local credit union and they agreed to loan me the money. If they hadn't, I planned to ask Bishop Piche for a personal loan. Nothing was going to stop me from building a house and nothing did. By the end of August I had the house finished and Karen and our children were able to move in. I thought to invite the bank managers for tea when all the construction was done to show them my work.

When I started articling with Brand and Co. I was given a small windowless room in which to work, and at first I had a hard time staying awake as I felt a shortage of fresh air after working outside all summer. Brand's law firm had distinguished lawyers such as John Bayly, Peter Ayotte and Don Cooper, who later became a judge. Articling involves working under an experienced lawyer in a law office for one year learning the practical aspects of law. Law school teaches you the theory and the principles of law through three years of reading thousands of cases, everything from criminal to constitutional law. In a law office, you learn to prepare documents involved in starting actions in court, drawing up mortgages, setting up corporations and preparing wills. Appearances in court before a judge teach the timelines and rules of court on a very practical basis.

I was the first Aboriginal lawyer born and raised in the Northwest Territories, and quite a fuss was made of it with articles in the local papers and a mention on CBC. I was asked to speak to the graduating class at Sir John Franklin High School in 1976, and I called on the students to "care enough to ask what can be done to get everybody... to the same level." I told them that their experience at Sir John Franklin, with white and Native students studying together, gave them an opportunity to learn each other's culture and to discover how to work together for the good of the North. After a full year of articling, I was admitted to the Alberta and NWT Bar Association. The press covered the event, which was attended by the assistant commissioner, John Parker, as well as several judges and territorial councillors. I was able to thank my wife, mother and especially my grandmother Ehmbee for all that they had done to get me to that point.

About this time I started a half-hour program with Joe Lemouel in Slavey five nights a week for the CBC. This was the very first time that Slavey was used on CBC Radio in a nightly program; I felt especially gratified given all my fights with the CBC in earlier years. The program only ran for a couple of years, but it was a start.

I set up my own law office in Yellowknife, renting space in the unused wing of a doctors' clinic and hiring a secretary, Monica Gates. I did general law, whatever was asked of me from clients coming into my office. Occasionally people came into our area of the building and began unbuttoning their shirts or blouses to show me their ailments. I or Monica would politely usher them back to where the doctors had their offices.

In 1978 we moved home to Fort Simpson in preparation for my entry back into politics. I continued providing law services out of our home, making enough money to live on by representing clients, often on legal aid, before the criminal circuit court that came into our area every month. Judge Robert Halifax was the territorial court judge who most often came to Fort Simpson and the surrounding area. He was young, brash and considered by many lawyers to be a difficult judge with whom to work. He caused more than one female lawyer to come out of his court in tears because of his harsh approach. Personally, I didn't feel intimidated by him, but I was never comfortable in his court. I certainly never dared to wear a moosehide vest or coat in front of him, though I did with other judges, lest I be reprimanded and told to put on a suit and tie.

I enjoyed representing people and felt that I was providing a meaningful service. I was from the area, spoke the language and understood the people, their lives and the situations they got themselves into. I simply tried to present their cases in a clear and truthful way to the court. During this period, some in the legal profession were trying to understand Aboriginal peoples and experimented with such approaches as sentence circles that involved the community. Judge Halifax didn't try any of these measures. He seemed set on staying with the status quo.

At one trial in Fort Liard, I represented an individual who had been among those arrested by the police at a house party where a brawl had broken out. The RCMP were pretty indiscriminate about whom they threw in jail. I thought I had precedents and evidence to support my contention that my client was innocent, simply swept up with the crowd. Nonetheless, Judge Halifax found my client guilty. I've always felt that he made a mistake. Had it been in a larger community where the RCMP were less prominent, or before a different judge, I think my client would have been acquitted. The judge seemed to be intent on protecting the image and status of the RCMP in the community.

Toward the end of my time as a practising lawyer, when I knew that I would be leaving the profession to go back into politics, I wrote a letter of complaint about Judge Halifax to the judicial authorities. I felt he was biased because of his friendship with the RCMP; a judge should be independent. The court party had arrived in Fort Liard and was met in a very congenial manner by the RCMP officers in their truck. When the court session was finished, Judge Halifax went off fishing with them. I never did know what became of my complaint, but because I didn't have to appear before him, I wasn't too concerned. Suffice that I had made the point.

Fortunately, not all judges were like Judge Halifax. I recall Judge Jim Slaven who held court in Wrigley where we were dealing with an accused who didn't speak or understand English. I tried to get an interpreter for the accused, and when this became onerous and frustrating I asked the judge if I could conduct the trial in Slavey and have someone interpret for him. I think we made history in this being the first occasion when court was held in the Dene language.

Judge Calvin Tallis of the Supreme Court was a joy to work before as he was always considerate and appreciative of your efforts. During a case in Hay River a number of defendants were involved in an altercation and were being tried before a jury. I represented one of them and, though he was found guilty, Judge Tallis thanked all the counsel for their good work and noted that it may have been the first time that a Supreme Court trial was handled by an Aboriginal crown prosecutor and an Aboriginal defence lawyer and clerk. I was gratified to know that someone in the judicial system appreciated what we were doing.

That said, I think I could have done more to educate the travelling judges who came into the small communities. When an incident occurred, there was usually some social reason behind it. Liquor was often involved, but there were also underlying community forces such as Indian medicine or family relationships and conflicts. All of these factors were unknown to a judge coming into town for the trial; the basic events were related by the RCMP and the person was sent off to jail. So much was missed that could have shed more light on the accused and his situation and provided fairer justice. I often made an effort to provide some of the context but was seldom encouraged in my efforts and was constrained by the rigidity of the legal system in doing more.

OF COURSE, TIME didn't stand still while I was establishing myself as a lawyer and preparing for my return to politics. The second half of the 1970s was a tumultuous time in the Northwest Territories. A proposal to build a pipeline to carry natural gas down the Mackenzie Valley was strongly opposed by Aboriginal people who wanted their land claims settled in advance of any development.

The Berger Commission, headed by Judge Thomas Berger of British Columbia, had been established in March of 1974 to investigate the social, environmental and economic impact of the proposed pipeline. Hearings were held in every community along the valley, in Yellowknife and in cities across Canada to hear the views, opinions and evidence of experts and regular citizens. Some of the testimony was dramatic, as when Frank T'selie of Fort Good Hope declared that he was "willing to lay down" his life to stop the pipeline. Robert Blair, one of the proponents, shocked some in the oil community when he agreed that "it's quite possible the critical factor that may require more time than anything else is good progress toward settlement of land claims."

In the end, that is what Judge Berger said in his 1977 report, "Northern Frontier, Northern Homeland," in which he called for a ten-year delay in the construction of a Mackenzie Valley pipeline, giving time for land claims to be settled. Ten years later, only one claim had been settled—the Inuvialuit—and in 1984 an oil pipeline was approved and built from Norman Wells to Alberta. Nonetheless, the Berger Commission and report gave a real voice to Aboriginal people and helped change the face of politics and society in the North.

The legislative council elected in 1975 (and renamed the legislative assembly in 1976) was the first that was entirely elected and the first that had a majority of Aboriginal members. The most prominent of these was James Wah-Shee, President of the Indian Brotherhood and, after the 1979 election, a prominent cabinet minister in the territorial government. Also elected for the first time were Ludy Pudluk, who served briefly in cabinet when I was government leader, and from Yellowknife, Dave Nickerson, who would later be the member of parliament for the district. Bill Lafferty was elected to replace me in my old riding.

The election of Wah-Shee was particularly interesting, as the official position of the Indian Brotherhood was one of distrust of the government. As the Brotherhood grew into the Dene Nation this opposition hardened, most often expressed by the phrase "This is not our government." Wah-Shee entered the assembly through acclamation from the Dogrib area north of Yellowknife and immediately disqualified himself from running for one of the two new elected positions on the executive committee (as cabinet was then called) because they "will be working directly for the government." By 1979, sufficient progress had been made for Wah-Shee and others to enter into cabinet on a trial basis.

The creation of the Dene Nation from the Indian Brotherhood and the proclamation of the Dene Declaration were considered radical at the time. The Minister of Indian Affairs likened it to separatism, and the Dene's determination to stop the pipeline by any means was referred to more than once as a terrorist threat. In reality, it was simply an assertion that Aboriginal people had occupied the land long before the Europeans arrived and still retained rights to that land, as well as the right of self-government. All of these ideas have gradually been recognized both by the courts and, in 1982, by the inclusion of Aboriginal rights, including the right to self-government (affirmed by federal policy in 1995), in the new constitution. Still, at the time it was heady stuff and a clear challenge to the status quo.

The idea of division of the territories—a long-held dream of the Inuit—got a boost at that time, too, with the creation of a second federal electoral district, so there was one for the eastern Arctic and one for the west. Approved in 1975, this split came into effect in the election of 1979.

I RE-ENTERED POLITICS with the 1979 territorial election campaign. Before I ran for that election, I was approached by both Liberal and NDP officials to be their candidate in the federal election that would take place in May 1979. I was flattered by the offers, but I turned them both down because I felt that during the next few years, political action would be in the North. Ottawa was so far away and removed from the daily lives of my people that I didn't see what I could do from that level. All the issues I was concerned about and could affect—housing, alcoholism, education, Dene languages and Aboriginal business—were in the North, and the legislative assembly was the forum in which they could be addressed.

The territorial election was held October 1, 1979. I ran on a campaign that I would not become part of the government per se, but that I would instead challenge its legitimacy. Bill Lafferty, who had replaced me as MLA in 1975, was my chief opponent, but the race wasn't even close. By the time the ballots were counted I had gained 71 percent of the vote and was going back to Yellowknife as an MLA. The number of seats had been increased from fifteen to nineteen, and thirteen of us were Aboriginal members. The newly named executive council had a majority of elected members and greater responsibility for running departments. For the first time there was an elected government leader, George Braden. True to my campaign promise, I didn't seek a position in cabinet.

I arrived in Yellowknife to meet all those who were elected from across the North. James Wah-Shee and Arnold McCallum, both first elected in 1975, were prominent in cabinet as was old hand Tom Butters. Meanwhile a raft of new members had come on the scene—Dennis Patterson, Tagak Curley, Richard Nerysoo and Nellie Cournoyea among them—who would all come to play dominant roles in territorial politics for the next decade or more.

Chapter 9: A More Determined Opposition

THE LEGISLATIVE ASSEMBLY had changed since I last took my seat, and not only in name. There were no longer any appointed members. The leader was elected, as was the Speaker, and MLAs now held a majority of seats on the executive council, though the new commissioner, John Parker, continued to chair it. Ministers appeared with officials and took the lead in answering questions about their departments.

However, it was still a long way from a body that truly represented the people of the North, especially the Aboriginal people. Interpretation was provided for Inuit members, primarily because many of the eastern MLAs only spoke Inuktitut, but Dene languages had no formal recognition. Stu Hodgson had worked very hard to instill the trappings and rituals of a Westminster-style legislature, with black robes, military processions and a mace. Although the assembly travelled to different regions of the North, it may as well have taken place in Ottawa for all that it reflected Northern culture.

I took my re-election to the legislative assembly seriously, as I had when I first ran for territorial council in 1970. Then, I had thought I was ready. I was married and had a fresh university degree. I knew about the disparities between Native people and whites. I was familiar with both cultures and believed all things were possible. I knew the hearts and minds of the people, and could speak their language as well as anyone. I had been taught to be kind and fair by my mother and grandmother. I thought I could go to Yellowknife and make the system work for us.

My first term had been a great eye-opener.

Now I was a lawyer. I had established my own practice. I had built a house for my family. I visited communities frequently and was up to date on the issues. No one in government could question my facts and my views. And I had a clear mandate from 71 percent of the voters. I was confident and felt fully prepared to represent the people from my area.

I had campaigned on the basis that my candidacy did not represent support for the government or the direction it was going. I was determined to go to Yellowknife and speak strongly for my constituency of Mackenzie–Liard and to represent Dene and Métis interests in the assembly. Naturally, I had rejected the idea of sitting on the executive but I also decided not to participate in any of the standing or special committees of the legislature. To my mind, these were instituting the European model of Government versus Opposition rather than the pure consensus style favoured by Aboriginal people.

The first session of the ninth assembly began on November 13, 1979. All the MLAs had already been in town for a few days, meeting in caucus to elect the Speaker and cabinet and getting to know each other. There were many new faces and we had much to talk about. The formal opening occurred in the usual way with the mace being brought in and the commissioner's address, the equivalent of the speech from the throne. Members had a right to make a reply to the speech, whether to speak about issues affecting their constituency or about matters they intended to raise during the session. I was first on my feet to make a response.

I started by highlighting the construction of the Liard Highway through the Hire North project, which had a training component for local residents. This, I thought, was a step in the right direction, but it was only a beginning. On the other hand, I expressed my opposition to the Norman Wells oil pipeline proposal that had come forward so soon after Berger's call for a ten-year moratorium.

Then I moved on to the major issue, one I would come back to time and again over the coming years: the problems caused by alcohol. Drinking had had devastating effects in the years since alcohol had become readily available, and the problem seemed to be getting worse instead of better. The government was selling and making money from alcohol but was doing little to address its consequences.

Liquor was literally killing people. Since 1968 when the liquor store opened in Fort Simpson, thirty people had died in our area from alcohol-related causes. In 1979 five people in Nahanni Butte, a community of less than one hundred people, died from the use of alcohol. I was determined to do something about this serious problem.

Father Posset, the local Catholic priest in Simpson, had said he was tired of burying people who had died from alcohol. In an attempt to inform people, he printed a six-page pamphlet showing graphically both the death toll and the amounts of money spent each year on alcohol. He was caught one night by the RCMP attempting to spray-paint "Booze Kills" on the outside of the liquor store. He had completed only B-O-O when he was caught, and thereafter he was called Father Boo by some people who were critical of him.

Native people had historically drunk homemade brew, which could be consumed in large quantities before you felt the effects. Hard liquor, ranging from vodka to overproof rum, was another matter. Consumption in Fort Simpson had dramatically increased; in small outlying communities residents flew in planeloads of liquor, leading to binges, family disruption, chaos and occasionally deaths.

Many meetings were held in the community hall in Simpson to debate the liquor issue. Some residents were strongly in favour of controls; others felt it was their Canadian right to drink as much and as freely as they liked. Many leaders favoured some kind of control on the purchase of liquor from the liquor store. Public opinion ebbed and flowed. When someone died, everybody agreed that liquor was the cause and that it should be banned or strongly restricted—but that feeling would fade.

Those of us like myself, Chief Jim Antoine and Mayor Orest Watsyk who were determined to limit the free flow of alcohol in our community would consciously plan to hold meetings about alcohol early in the week, when people would still be reeling from the weekend of drinking. After many community meetings, the final one of which was attended by Commissioner John Parker and officials from the Liquor Board, it was agreed to impose a restriction on the purchase of liquor.

A weekly allowance was set at 710 ml of hard liquor (two mickeys), one dozen beers and two litres of wine. This restriction was seen as a huge success—the first time that a community had a say in how much liquor should be made available. It made us believe that with concerted effort, you could change something as entrenched as the liquor laws. I recall visiting one elderly couple, Celine and Joseph Lafferty, whose son had a drinking problem, after the decision was made. Tears streamed down their faces as we talked about the hope that this measure might bring to their son.

I then talked about other territorial changes. The last few years had been traumatic for the people in the North. Thomas Berger's 1977 report, which called for the delay of further large-scale development until after land claims were settled, had been widely applauded, but it seemed that governments were already ignoring his recommendations. The birth and subsequent growth of Native organizations had been dramatic but had also led to conflict as various groups staked out their positions. The Dene and Métis had disagreed on approaches to Aboriginal claim negotiations. As well, a rift had developed between the past legislative assembly and all Native organizations regarding constitutional development.

While the Dene were advocating major changes to government with the Denendeh proposal, the eighth legislative assembly had adopted a position paper on constitutional development that would entrench the Westminster system. On every major issue during the past four years, the previous assembly had been directly opposed to the views of Native peoples in the North.

My support for the Dene Nation was unequivocal. My mission was to represent the Dene and bring about change. This government, I declared, was not the government of the Dene, Métis or Inuit people. We needed to change the face of government and make it truly northern and reflective of Aboriginal people. First, we should set up a Committee on Unity to meet with the Dene Nation and Inuit Tapirisat and resolve issues that had set peoples apart. It was also essential to make symbolic changes to demonstrate that this was the government of all the people. The establishment of a commission to change names of buildings, schools and geographic locales would be a good start. We needed to stop naming places after royalty, European explorers and southern politicians and start using Aboriginal terms or names. It was also critical to review the formality and practices of the assembly.

On a practical basis, the public service had to begin to reflect the people it served. As a start, the government could set up a wildlife officers' training program that recognized the traditional skills of Native people. The Native Employment Office needed an overhaul to make it more effective and visible. In particular, a plan to attract competent Native people into the top levels of government was vital to our future success.

It came as a pleasant surprise that some MLAs who had been part of the eighth assembly recognized that significant divisions existed in the North and that change had to come. Both Tom Butters and Arnold McCallum spoke to the issue. Butters was particularly eloquent when he said, "One of the shortcomings of the previous assembly was that it was a matter of 'other voices, other rooms' but, this time, sitting in this assembly chamber are recognized, dedicated, capable individuals who have served or are serving Native organizations. They are here. The debate will be joined here."

Other MLAs gave their inaugural speeches. Dennis Patterson from Frobisher Bay spoke at length about the creation of a separate Inuit territory of Nunavut. In the view of Nellie Cournoyea, the previous legislative assembly had been isolated and unresponsive to people, and in many instances opposed to what the people wanted; its biggest failure was in the area of land claims and constitutional development. That assembly criticized and ridiculed the land claim agreement-in-principle that the Committee for Original Peoples Entitlement (COPE) had signed with the federal government in 1978, yet had never approached COPE for clarification or an explanation. She went on to say that we should rescind the past assembly's constitutional paper and establish a new forum to deal with constitutional matters.

ACCORDINGLY, ON NOVEMBER 15, 1979, James Wah-Shee, former President of the Indian Brotherhood and now a cabinet minister, presented a motion that "this assembly not be bound by the content or substance outlined in the previous assembly's constitutional position." It was obvious, he said, that current members were not happy with the position paper, primarily because it was made without the involvement of Native organizations. I spoke first to the motion, calling certain provisions in the position paper absolute nonsense. It was nothing but a major grab for power proposing to entrench the present parliamentary system without consideration of the constitutional proposals of the Dene, Métis and other Native groups. Furthermore, many of the principles enunciated in the paper were contrary to the aspirations of Native people, particularly with regard to lands and the role that the GNWT would play in land claims negotiations.

The debate on the issue went on for a number of days. In the end, despite the opposition of members like McCallum and Stewart who were part of the previous assembly, the motion passed. Bob Mac-Quarrie called the setting aside of the constitutional paper historic. "It should never have been passed in the first place as it did not have the support of the majority of people in this territory."

Similarly, Richard Nerysoo, a young man from the Gwich'in area of the Mackenzie Delta who would later rise to prominence as the first Aboriginal government leader, moved to set aside the eighth assembly position on land claims because the principles were offensive and stood in the way of successful land claims negotiations by Native peoples. Those principles included that the powers of the GNWT were not to be eroded by land claims agreements, that Aboriginal groups were not to get any constitutional authority not yet delegated to the GNWT and that Native claims were not to prejudice local governments. A number of members, notably Nellie Cournoyea, spoke of how these general principles were interpreted by federal and GNWT negotiators to frustrate Native negotiators. The only member who spoke in favour of the principles was Arnold McCallum. When the motion was voted on, it too passed without difficulty.

Thus in just a few days the ninth legislative assembly undid the positions of the eighth assembly on the two important issues of constitutional development and land claims. The stage was now set for the new assembly to set its own course.

CLEARLY MUCH HAD changed. The infusion of new blood and the departure of Stu Hodgson as commissioner undoubtedly both played a role, as did the growing sophistication and prominence of Aboriginal organizations.

Commissioner Hodgson had worked for ten years setting up the territorial administration with its headquarters in Yellowknife. Regional administrations had been established across the North and municipal-style settlement councils, particularly in the Arctic communities, were promoted as the norm. Stu was protective of this work; he looked at the North as his kingdom. He visited all the communities each year, dispensing money as required, buying a tractor here and building houses or schools there. Politically, Stu was crafty and where he felt he could quell opposition by granting favours or giving gifts, he did so. At one point, he gave snowmobiles and new cars to chiefs in the communities.

He saw the development of the territorial council along Westminster parliamentary lines, with elected representatives as his crowning achievement. He introduced royal regalia and the mace and included military and police presence in territorial council openings and other formalities. He held an annual Commissioner's Ball with entertainment provided by southern orchestras and food by southern chefs. Only in the latter days of his reign, as it were, did a Speaker rather than the commissioner himself oversee the running of the council. A few elected members were added to the executive committee, though the commissioner and his assistants retained control.

Some members felt defensive of their positions and sneered at Native groups who were advocating other forms of government. No wonder there was no communication between them. A chasm had developed between whites and Natives that led to discord and frustration among northern peoples.

Many MLAs including me recognized the situation and wanted to do something about it. The new assembly was full of MLAs who were members or leaders of Native organizations and they were joined by progressives such as Bob MacQuarrie and George Braden in creating a process that would undo the misunderstanding and distrust that had developed. We wanted to unite people to formulate a government for all northerners.

Similarly, Aboriginal organizations had shown a willingness to work with the new assembly. A few days after the election, the Inuit Tapirisat and the Dene Nation had sent letters to all MLAs asking them for a meeting to discuss their political positions. As a first order of business they asked that we withdraw the previous assembly's constitutional position paper. They called on members to start work on a new approach that would recognize the aspirations of Native people. We had already achieved the former; now, we needed to figure out the latter.

In the following days, I proposed a motion to set up a committee on unity. Its purpose was "to determine the means by which political consensus might be generated amongst the peoples of the North." The members on the committee were to be Bob MacQuarrie, Robert Sayine, Peter Fraser, Tagak Curley and me. We would spend up to a year meeting with Native leaders, listening to their proposals and seeking a consensus on one form of government for the North.

All members spoke in favour of the motion, and when Don Stewart raised a point about the necessary funds, Tom Butters came to the rescue by suggesting that the Commissioner's Ball be scrapped for the year and the money used for the Committee. The motion passed unanimously and Commissioner Parker prorogued the assembly until January 31, 1980.

THE NEXT SESSION began where the previous one had left off. Commissioner Parker, in his opening address, affirmed the constitutional initiatives of the new assembly. The Inuit Tapirisat's policy paper entitled "Political Development in Nunavut" as well as other serious proposals of political and constitutional changes would be critical elements of the session's debates. Parker went on to recognize the ongoing land claims negotiations and urged northerners to deal with them in "a spirit of unity."

On March 11, 1980, Bob Overvold of the Dene Nation appeared before the assembly. He began by recognizing the new and positive relationship developing between the legislative assembly and the

Dene Nation. Despite this new relationship, the Dene Nation could not support the present system of territorial government and the legislative assembly because it entrenched values that were not Dene.

The Dene Nation's response to the Drury Commission—the federal government–initiated review of constitutional development in the North that had been issued only a few days before—was that it was already outdated. The commission's report argued that, with few people scattered across a large territory coupled with undeveloped resources and financial dependence on the federal government, the North faced real limitations on its political independence. Overvold said that the report had "no imagination, just old ideas" and must be dismissed out of hand.

On Aboriginal rights, the Dene Nation was seeking unity between the Dene and Métis. Overvold suggested that there should be one settlement in the Mackenzie Valley for both groups, and negotiations should be with the Dene Nation.

The initial Dene claim of ownership to 450,000 square miles in the Mackenzie Valley had evolved over time as expressed by the Dene Declaration in July 1975, the proposed Agreement in Principle (1976), the Metro Model (1977) and finally the proposal for a Dene government. A Dene form and style of government would be based on decentralized decision-making, not only decision-making by a few elected representatives. It would include recognition of the rights of all citizens and would be committed to one government for all people of the North based on sharing of power with the federal government. Negotiations had recently broken off and future progress was uncertain. Overvold asked the legislative assembly to support the Dene Nation in getting negotiations going again with the federal government.

In support of that request I moved that the legislative assembly urge the Minister of Indian and Northern Affairs to reinstate loans to the Dene Nation to prepare for negotiations and to make a commitment to begin negotiations within six months after funding was provided. The motion was carried unanimously.

Of course, supporting change and recognizing Dene approaches was easy to do in theory, but in practical terms it was a matter of two steps forward and one step back. I recall questioning the Minister of

Local Government, James Wah-Shee, on the situation in communities. Since the territorial government came into the North, they had established settlement councils in many of the Dene communities, often in competition and conflict with chiefs and band councils. Would that policy and approach change? The minister recognized the problem; he had met with the Dene Nation to find a solution. Meetings would be arranged throughout the summer between municipal councils and band councils to find solutions. In reality, these discussions went on for many years. In some places, such as Fort Good Hope, the two bodies did come together, merging into a charter community with its own constitution; in others, conflicts between bands and municipalities continue to this day.

ANOTHER MAJOR ISSUE I focused on during that session was the structure and operations of the government.

In January 1980, when I gave my response to the Commissioner's Speech, I took the opportunity to review the budgetary powers of the members. When I was a councillor in the 1970–74 era, we were told that we had no power to effect changes—we were only advisors. The commissioner held all power and did not need to abide by our recommendations. Ten years later, we had John Parker as commissioner, a partially elected executive committee (cabinet) and a more informed and active assembly.

Our power as assembly members rested in our ability to withhold consent to the budget, or parts of it, and not pass the ordinance authorizing money for the government. Elected executive members could be changed or dismissed if they did not abide by the assembly's instructions, made through motions or statements in the assembly. The Northwest Territories Act made the commissioner the chief executive officer, and though we could not fire him directly, we could exert pressure on the federal Minister of Indian Affairs to revoke his appointment.

I went over this. This political science lesson was not to show off my newfound expertise in the law. I wanted to bring my fellow MLAS around to the view that we, as elected representatives of the people, were the real authority now. Power is only real, however, if it is used.

By pointing out ways we could use our power, I hoped to bring about changes to the way the government operated both politically and on a day-to-day basis.

The commissioner was only the focal point for a broader issue. Civil servants handled things in the North the way they saw fit, often contrary to the ways elected representatives thought things should be done. I used the example of game wardens, who required university degrees but faced no requirements for knowledge of people, the land or common sense. I also stressed the necessity of the government becoming more reflective of the people they served. More Native people had to be brought into government, especially at the higher levels. The inability to accomplish this had been Commissioner Hodgson's greatest failure. He looked at bright young Aboriginal leaders as threats. The new government had to do better.

Later in that winter's budget session, I was able to point specifically to ways in which the government was on the wrong track when it came to staffing positions. We were reviewing the Department of Justice's budget. The government had been hiring an inordinate number of ex-military and RCMP personnel throughout its offices. Some of us were of the view that former Commissioner Hodgson liked hiring them because they followed orders without hesitation. This fitted the type of top-down administration that the commissioner ran in the North. Unfortunately, nothing seemed to have changed under John Parker.

I raised the question with Minister Butters. He admitted that many of these ex-military and RCMP were hired in the Safety Division as fire inspectors but said that no special efforts were in place to hire them. It was simply that former RCMP officers, who had spent many years in the North, particularly in small communities, were valuable because of their legal background and experience. The Department of Justice must be independent, I argued, and a high number of ex-RCMP and military personnel might make people, particularly Native people, uneasy.

Similarly, in my first speech in the fall of 1979, I had raised the issue of Native employment—specifically, the need for the government to hire more Native people and the lack of Native people in the higher levels of the public service. During the 1980 budget session I asked Bob Pilot, the deputy commissioner who was responsible for the Department of Personnel, about the Office of Native Employment. Neither of the two people employed in the office was Aboriginal. Wasn't it ironic? How could the office deal with resistance by departments to hire Native people when they had none themselves? Was there even a way to monitor departments' hiring practices?

In my view, the office would be more effective if it had greater resources (it had two people and a budget of $85,000) and reported to the executive. I proposed, first, that the government consider having the Office of Native Employment report directly to the executive committee and, second, that the office be expanded. I stressed that the employees working on Native employment must be able to speak a Native language. Don Stewart argued that my first motion set up a new department, and before we did that we should have policies and a paper to consider the issues. Nevertheless, the motions were voted on and passed.

A year later nothing had changed in the Office of Native Employment, although there was an affirmative action program whereby Native people had first preference for training programs. I suggested that there ought to be a policy covering actual Native hiring, not just a preference for training, and I continued to insist that the office should have more staff and report to the executive committee so it could have a higher profile both to the public and in the government hierarchy. In addition, more had to be done to move Native people into higher levels of government. Further, in any government apprentice or training program, the employee doing the training should hold his or her job only until a Native person was qualified.

Commissioner John Parker entered the debate as the person primarily responsible for personnel. With respect to the previous year's motion to shift the Office of Native Employment to the executive, he said that "from a functional standpoint, it simply did not make any sense to divide off a small office from the major personnel function." As for expanding the staff, he said that "we already have two people designated in the regions as persons working for the Office of Native Employment and there was money in the budget to hire two more persons." Employing more Native people, Parker said, was a priority of the government. Jim Blewett, the civil servant responsible for personnel, added that all fifty-five officers in his department saw Native employment as a major issue.

I was blunt in my response to Blewett. Quite simply, I didn't believe that all his employees were committed to northern hiring and I didn't believe that enough was being done. There were still systemic barriers in place, such as the requirement that applicants already know the government's financial reporting system, effectively barring external Native applicants. Again, I moved that the Office of Native Employment report to the executive committee and that more staff be hired, and again the motion carried.

Having had limited success on the broad issue of Native hires, I decided to take a more specific approach. I proposed the establishment of an on-the-job training program to train and hire local hunters as game officers. I was very specific about the type of program that I believed the government should set up. Experienced and mature people, perhaps with little formal training but with a wealth of experience and knowledge about the land, should train and work with an existing game warden to learn the administrative side of the job and after two years take over his position. The government's program required entry with a minimum of grade eleven or twelve followed by four years of college-based training on the job. I challenged the government to try a new approach and get experienced people who otherwise would never fit into the present government system. If their traditional knowledge of animals and the land were given recognition they would be effective in assisting people to make a better living on the land. The government was reluctant at the time, but traditional knowledge and land-based skills were eventually recognized as equal to formal education. The concept of equivalencies slowly seeped into their consciousness. Still, it would be years before formal qualifications stopped being barriers to competent Native people getting jobs in the public service.

EVEN IF TRADITIONAL knowledge or land-based skills were given proper recognition, education was still a critical issue. Just as I had

had to become a lawyer to be effective as a politician, young Native people would need a better education to succeed in the changing world. The Tli'cho people (or the Dogribs, as they were called then) had recognized early on the need to learn from both cultures. In 1969, Rae-Edzo was the first Indian band in all of Canada to take control of their local schools. Chief Jimmy Bruneau (whose name lives on as the name of the local high school) wanted people to learn both ways of life so that they could "be strong like two people."

Formal education had first come to the North in the 1880s when Catholic and Anglican missionaries established rudimentary schools designed to provide a basic education while Christianizing Native people. These developed into the residential school systems which were run by the churches under federal government auspices and funding. The territorial government began to take over this system in the early 1960s. By 1979 there were 12,766 students and 580 school staff working for the GNWT. The assembly had passed a new Education Act in 1977. A new curriculum with Northern components was introduced in all grades; teacher assistants and Native teachers were being trained. Cultural inclusion and Native languages were finally being used in the schools, particularly in Aboriginal communities where there was some support for teaching the language.

For post-secondary education, a significant student grant and loan program had been developed to send Northern students to southern universities. However, few Native people were benefiting from the program. In 1980, I had obtained a list of Northern students in southern schools; only 15 percent of those attending technical schools were Native and 7 percent of those attending university. Most of the so-called "Northern" students were the children of civil servants. I made the argument that civil servants who came north had good incomes, good government houses and benefits and, on top of this, took advantage of higher education grants. I said that the grants policy should be reviewed and that money currently going towards the grants should be channelled into improving the basic education of Native peoples in the North.

Later that year, a report was presented in response to these claims that utterly failed to address the matter. The Student Grants Program remained a generous benefit for well-off civil servants whose children were taking advantage of the program, while very few Native people attended universities and technical schools.

I spoke directly to Butters, the Minister of Education, and told him that he himself had four children taking advantage of the program while he was making at least $47,000 (a princely sum in those days) and John Parker "perhaps" had children attending university while he was making $60,000. Non-Natives made more money than Native people and non-Natives held the highest positions in government and industry; therefore, they should pay for their children's higher education. This position was supported by Dennis Patterson, who would later serve a number of years as Education Minister, and the assembly passed a motion sending the department back to the drawing board.

TRYING TO CHANGE the day-to-day operations of the government was only one tack I took in those early days of the assembly. I knew we needed to make changes at a more basic level. The power of symbolism should never be underestimated; Stu Hodgson had used it in full measure to try to establish southern approaches to government and the Westminster style of government. In February of 1980, I raised several issues designed to reverse that tide and use symbolism to the advantage of Native people.

My first target was the recently opened Prince of Wales Northern Heritage Centre in Yellowknife, which was the GNWT's museum and archives. It had been officially opened in April 1979 by Prince Charles himself. Nonetheless, I proposed that the name be changed to reflect more authentic Northern traditions. Commissioner Hodgson had not consulted the peoples of the North on the name or even the design of the museum, which created dissatisfaction throughout the North. Moreover, many geographic places and buildings were already named in honour of the royal family; I had compiled a list of fifty-seven royal places names, scattered across the North, which I distributed to all members. I had also drafted a letter to Queen Elizabeth calling on her to accept a change to the name of the centre. My motion simply asked that the executive committee be given the task of finding a more appropriate name. A substantial debate ensued.

Some of the MLAs were cautious, recognizing that Hodgson hadn't consulted the people, but concerned about the adverse publicity and possibly perceived insult in taking down a royal name. While not against renaming some geographic features, they were against renaming the museum itself, as it would dishonour the prince. Further, significant costs had been incurred in naming the centre after the Prince of Wales, including the fact that a director in the government had gone to the United States to purchase and transport a painting of the prince (which still hangs in the museum). A number of members did support the idea that names of original people should be considered in the future in naming buildings and geographic features.

Others had no difficulty in supporting the motion. Non-Native people had a bad habit of naming features after other non-Native people, and it was important to have northern names even if feelings were hurt. Mark Evaluarjuk said, "It's just a name," and Ludy Pudluk would not support the motion because it involved only one name; if all the geographic and building names were to be changed, he would support it.

When everyone had spoken, Commissioner Parker offered information about how the museum and name came into existence. Obtaining funding for the construction of the museum had been difficult; getting the royal family's consent to use the Prince of Wales's name and having the prince attend the opening had ensured that funds were made available. Further, the picture of the Prince of Wales, which had been painted especially for the opening, was brought from the home of the artist in the United States by vehicle. This was the least-cost approach and was undertaken with much difficulty through rain, snow and customs. He made it sound like quite an adventure.

I made one last pitch to win support. "Are we saying now that what is past is done and we cannot undo it absolutely?" I predicted that one day the museum's name would be changed through the land claims process. As it turns out, I was wrong. The Prince of Wales Northern Heritage Centre remains. However, many other names have been changed, including names of lakes, rivers, parks and communities across the North. Rae-Edzo became Behchoko and Frobisher Bay is now Iqaluit. Numerous buildings—built by the GNWT and Aboriginal governments, as well as business—bear the names of prominent northerners, both Aboriginal and non-Aboriginal.

Only five MLAS—Fraser, Noah, Curley, Cournoyea and Sayine—had supported my efforts, but the seed had been planted and change would come.

LANGUAGE HAS ALWAYS been important to me. I knew that my ability to speak my own language had been an invaluable resource, not only politically but in terms of my ability to see multiple sides of a situation and to come up with creative solutions to problems. During my time away from the assembly, I had helped bring the first Slavey language program to CBC Radio, but little more had been accomplished since. However, in 1981 I had Doug Ward, the Northern Services director of the CBC, come before the assembly to explain why this was so.

When Ward appeared, I made a number of points. In the Yellowknife broadcast area, Native people were one-third of the listening population, yet of the nineteen-hour broadcast day only two hours were in Dene languages. Although this represented some progress, it was a long way from satisfying the Dene. No original Dene news was broadcast, only a repeat of the English news translated to Dene languages. I suggested that a broadcaster providing daily Dene news with a Native viewpoint should be placed in Fort Simpson to serve the Mackenzie Valley. Given the failure of the CBC to provide Dene broadcasts of any kind in the Sahtu or other areas of the western Arctic, perhaps if Dene people wanted to hear more of their own language, they would have to do it themselves by setting up a Dene broadcasting system down the Mackenzie Valley. Ward was not able to respond positively to my concerns except to say that through the use of satellite technology, more Dene broadcasting might be possible in the future.

While getting Dene languages on the public airways was important in terms of serving the people effectively as well as a symbolically powerful statement that the Dene and Métis were part of the North, there was a more important venue for language use: the schools and other public places where people worked or received services. My first experience during the seventh assembly in trying to get Slavey into the classroom showed how difficult it would be in communities where there was a mixture of Dene and non-Native people.

During the 1980 budget session, I raised the matter of Aboriginal languages in schools on several occasions. I felt discouraged about the approach of the Department of Education. Dene classroom assistants provided some interpretation services for students, but teachers weren't able to provide a high level of instruction in Dene languages. Young Native people who did not know the language very well but had received teacher training were hired over linguistically skilled older people who, because of the insistence on formal qualifications, could not get teaching positions. Ted Trindell, for example, who was known as the Shakespeare of Slavey, could have brought the language to life in the classroom, but he did not fit into the system.

In communities like Fort Liard and Trout Lake, where children were fluent in their Dene language, parents looked to the school to teach them English so they could obtain jobs. They did not want Slavey in the classroom because they didn't understand the benefits of learning in one's own first language. This reluctance to have Slavey in the community—I had certainly seen the opposition in my hometown of Fort Simpson—came from loss of morale, which made people think there was no value in keeping their Dene language. Only English mattered because English would get you a job. Promises to do better were made, but progress has been painfully slow. Even as recently as 2011, I needed to present a paper to an education conference in my hometown showing the growing body of evidence that scientifically proves the value of retaining your first language. Educators across Canada finally seem to be taking heed.

In 1981 when the budget for territorial libraries was being presented, I tried to take things a step further. I wanted the minister, George Braden, to do something for people who didn't know how to read English. At the time, the entire library budget went to English products and services. "What about the Dene who do not read English?" I asked. Tapes or videos in Slavey had a place in libraries. "Buy everybody a tape recorder if you have to, so they can access these tapes and use them."

I had to make the government understand that services should be available to all citizens, even those who do not read and understand English. In the communities, people live and breathe the Dene language, not English. They didn't benefit from government-supplied services that other citizens took for granted. I challenged Braden to do something, not just with respect to libraries but to examine every aspect of government and see where else people who do not understand English were being denied services. "You cannot have this government continuously insisting, 'Well, you want to use our services, learn English.'" I went on that "A lot of my constituents do not really accept this government.... [T]hey just see it basically as a white government, a bunch of white people running it...because in many ways they are not able to take part in the government and they do not benefit from a lot of the programs." If the GNWT ever expected to be viewed as legitimate, it would have to take Dene concerns seriously. As a first step, they could begin to serve people in their own language.

LIKE EVERY MLA, I had to make sure my constituency's interests were served. Although government programs and services (and capital expenditures) were supposed to be equally apportioned, it was clear, as the old saying goes, that some regions were more equal than others. I was particularly aware of the differential treatment accorded the Inuit areas, perhaps as a holdover from the Hodgson days when he had a special interest in establishing government in the High Arctic. In the 1981 budget session I put it this way: "In our part of the North, in the Dene part...the government does not provide as much as it does up in the eastern Arctic. I have had teachers who have come from the eastern Arctic to my part of the North and they are just appalled.... As an example, the teacher that is teaching now in Nahanni Butte last fall, almost could not believe it, that there was just nothing to teach with."

Dennis Patterson from Baffin Island quipped "You got trees," but I continued, "Up in the eastern Arctic the teachers have good schools. They have good equipment, good supplies and there just seems to be no lack of money." I described how it seemed that there was no end to the equipment and supplies available for municipal services to Inuit communities in the eastern Arctic. For the next few years, I suggested, the government should concentrate on our part of the North. I asked Deputy Commissioner Bob Pilot, responsible for Department of Public Works, if my impressions and allegations were true, that the east had more than the west. Pilot avoided the question, saying that it was the Department of Local Government that bought the municipal equipment and the Department of Education that bought the school supplies.

A few days later I asked James Wah-Shee, Minister of Local Government, to review the situation of municipal equipment for communities in the Mackenzie Valley to see if they were indeed getting less than communities in the eastern Arctic. At the same time, I suggested he could review the department's generosity to his own constituency. The budget identified $350,000 for a four-bay parking garage for Lac la Martre; $100,000 for a settlement office and $200,000 for a community hall in Rae Lakes; and $64,000 for a community hall in Snare Lakes. In contrast, Fort Simpson was getting $50,000 while another community was getting "a small amount." I asked whether this extravaganza of buildings was happening because he was on the executive. Wah-Shee sidestepped the issue by saying that perhaps the communities in my riding had not made their requests for building and equipment yet. I left it at that, having given notice that I would be vigilant about such matters in future budgets.

ONE OF THE biggest issues facing the assembly in 1980–81 was the proposed construction of a pipeline to carry oil from Norman Wells to Alberta. Oil had been produced in the area since 1933 and had briefly been shipped to Alaska during the Second World War through the Canol pipeline. Now, Imperial Oil wanted to send it south, and the federal government was a willing partner. (In fact, it eventually assumed part ownership of the pipeline in lieu of royalties, which has proved very lucrative to federal coffers over the years.)

This was a much smaller pipeline than that proposed earlier to take natural gas out of the Beaufort–Delta: twelve inches rather than thirty-six and only half the length. Still, this proposal had come forward barely three years after Berger had called for a ten-year moratorium on major developments to give Aboriginal people a chance to settle their claims, and Native people considered the pipeline a serious affront to the gains they had made. In June 1980 I moved that the project be delayed for three or four years. This motion had come out of meetings between the executive and representatives of the Dene and Métis. I had worked closely with Government Leader Braden to craft wording that would be acceptable to the GNWT.

In the debate that followed, I insisted that people were not against development. Many Aboriginal businesses and workers were involved through Hire North in building the Liard Highway, which would occupy them for three or four years. But people were not ready for a pipeline project. I pointed to the recommendations of the Berger report and questioned why there was talk about pipelines when land claims had not been settled.

The land claims negotiations had just started. It would create chaos if a Norman Wells pipeline went ahead now. A Dene and Métis regional meeting had recently passed a motion that the rights of the Dene be settled through negotiations with the federal government before any kind of development occurred. My motion to delay the pipeline for three or four years was therefore a moderate position.

George Braden spoke in support of the motion, noting that discussions had been held with the Dene and Métis, and although there was still disagreement in some areas, a consensus had been reached on others. A joint position paper had been developed and adopted and discussions had been held with the minister only a few weeks before. The minister had agreed to take the matter to cabinet. We needed to take a stand. Before we supported the pipeline, the federal government had to make tough, but fair, decisions, including getting negotiations started with Native people on Aboriginal rights.

As well, the federal government had done nothing for years in the Mackenzie Valley; they had had no plans in place for economic development since 1970. Economic development had to be done with the benefit of northern people in mind. This meant having northern authority over resource management and a share of the revenues from development.

Braden also presented an analysis of the finances of the project. Since 1950, Imperial Oil (Esso) had made over $100 million in profits from Norman Wells. Federal revenues over the same period were $32 million. Under the current system, the GNWT could collect only indirect taxes—that is, income taxes from labour on pipeline construction, estimated to be a mere $1.2 million from a $375-million investment. Northern resources would be depleted and most of the revenues and benefits would flow south. Esso would not even do training, leaving it up to the GNWT to provide those services. Meanwhile, demand for labour would drive up prices, affecting all other projects in the North. The GNWT could easily go broke from increased demands on programs and services, while industry and the federal government reaped the benefits.

By calling for a delay, the GNWT was not being anti-development, as there were many projects going on. The executive was prepared to work with the federal government to get a good deal for northerners. The Norman Wells pipeline, delivering 25,000 barrels a day, was an important project for Canada but it also needed to be of significant benefit to the North. Braden asked all members to support my motion. In the recorded vote that followed, only Lynda Sorenson voted against, while Pete Fraser abstained.

Some months later, in the 1980 fall session held in Frobisher Bay, it appeared that little progress had been made on delaying the project. I thought it expedient to follow up with a motion to look at legal avenues available to the GNWT to stop the construction of the pipeline in the event that there was a decision by the federal government to proceed. The motion was sweeping in its intent and included the extent to which territorial legislation or regulations could be used, the extent to which federal regulatory bodies could be used and the powers of the legislative assembly to pass legislation or refuse to pass the budget to stop the pipeline. I submitted that we were not defenceless in our ability to thwart the pipeline: "[T]his possibility of challenging the federal government has only come about with the election of this assembly.... [T]o challenge the federal government is a sign of growing up. It is a sign of becoming more responsible." My motion passed.

In May 1981, after the National Energy Board had issued a certificate for the pipeline, the minister of the federal Department of Indian Affairs and Northern Development (DIAND), John Munro, came before the assembly in Hay River and I asked him two questions: first, whether the GNWT needed his permission to legally challenge the National Energy Board decision; and second, whether he would delay the start of the construction of the Norman Wells pipeline project at least until 1983. His answers were that he did not think his permission was necessary and he was considering delaying construction.

The following day I asked George Braden whether the executive committee would challenge the decision of the National Energy Board. He replied that they had not fully considered the matter. The federal government approved construction in August of 1981 but, in the end, the economy accomplished what the federal government refused to do; the global recession reduced oil prices and demand, and thus delayed the pipeline by several years.

DURING THE FALL of 1981, Canada was deeply immersed in constitutional issues as Prime Minister Pierre Trudeau worked toward repatriating the constitution. At a federal/provincial conference on the constitution, nine provinces (excluding Quebec) and the federal government had agreed to a constitutional accord. As discussions proceeded, it was clear that no provisions were being considered to protect Aboriginal rights, creating much alarm among all national Aboriginal leaders as well as our government. The executive committee had sent telexes to the prime minister asking for a meeting to clarify the situation.

At the legislative assembly, Commissioner Parker celebrated the accord, which included repatriation, an amending formula and a Charter of Rights. He had barely finished speaking before we waded into the constitutional issues that were most on our minds. Members were supportive of the proposed repatriation but condemned the exclusion of Aboriginal rights and the involvement of the provinces in the future of the North, including the extension of their boundaries north. Dennis Patterson went further by condemning the process it-self, which took place "without the Northwest Territories, without the Aboriginal peoples, without Quebec." Others, including Bob MacQuarrie and myself, expressed fear that the provisions of the ac-cord would thwart the aspirations of Aboriginal people in the North. I went on to say that the involvement of provinces, some of which had not historically recognized Aboriginal rights, would seriously limit Aboriginal rights in the constitution and across Canada.

We needed to take a stronger stance than simply sending telexes to the prime minister. MacQuarrie and Patterson both broached the idea of going en masse to Ottawa. Tagak Curley took up the cudgel, saying that the atmosphere in the legislative assembly was like we were mourning for someone who had died. He moved that we ad-journ for a week and go to Ottawa. Tom Butters spoke up and stated that the motion was premature, as the executive committee was doing as much as possible. I said that was nonsense, that the executive com-mittee did not have direction and that Tom was up to his old tricks to delay or put impediments in the way. Tom rose on a point of privilege, stating that my comment was uncalled for and asked me to withdraw. "Never!" I said, and the debate went on.

Eventually, Curley was persuaded to withdraw his motion so that he and I could meet with the executive and reach consensus on a plan of action. Curley's new motion was to establish a permanent constitution committee of all MLAs to co-ordinate an action plan. We suspended until the next day when two new motions were adopted. The first, moved by Tagak Curley, proposed that the MLAs meet with the prime minister in an effort to reinstate Aboriginal rights, delete provisions relating to the extension of provincial boundaries and re-store federal jurisdiction on the creation of provinces. I followed up with a motion to establish a special committee on the Constitution of Canada, to be chaired by Nellie Cournoyea and George Braden, empowered and funded to go to Ottawa and lobby on behalf of the Northwest Territories.

When we arrived we were forced to stay at a hotel across the river in Hull, as all the rooms in downtown Ottawa were booked. Still, that didn't stop us from meeting with Prime Minister Trudeau, Justice

Minister Jean Chrétien, Opposition leaders, members of parliament and senators. Over the next ten days we broke into small groups to meet with as many politicians as possible to express our concerns.

On November 27 we reconvened in Yellowknife. Nellie Cournoyea reported that the federal government, with the agreement of all of the provinces, had reinstated Aboriginal rights in Section 34 of the constitution by adding the words "The existing Aboriginal and treaty rights of the Aboriginal peoples of Canada are hereby recognized and affirmed."

George Braden reported that the constitutional provisions dealing with the extension of provincial boundaries and giving provinces a role in the creation of provinces were issues that many politicians in Ottawa were not aware of and which we were instrumental in bringing to their attention. These provisions were unchanged, but they had received commitments from Opposition leaders and assurances from Minister John Munro of Indian Affairs that they would be changed once the constitution was repatriated. In fact, such provisions were never removed, though any changes would require the consent of the federal government and seven provinces. However, given subsequent developments it is unlikely that these provisions will ever be utilized.

All members commended us for our success in Ottawa. Tom Butters admitted that he had had reservations when Curley first raised the idea of going to Ottawa, but acknowledged that we were successful beyond our wildest expectations; he saw our actions as being the art of the impossible. William Noah was certain that it had been instrumental in restoring Aboriginal rights. Others expressed the view that it demonstrated the strength of our consensus style of government. I hoped we would learn from this historic mission and be open to try new things and different approaches in dealing with problems unique to the North, notably the Dene Nation's Denendeh proposal as well as others that we would be considering in the weeks ahead.

During the first two years of my return to the assembly, I had used every means I knew to bring issues concerning Native people to the fore. I debated, made motions and asked questions, I used all the mechanisms of the legislature, of the press and of public opinion, to try to change attitudes of government ministers and officials.

I certainly had my share of successes, but I also experienced frustration. It sometimes seemed that the very process of opposition further entrenched the Westminster system. I could also see how easy it would be to become part of that system, used to the processes and forms of the legislature. It was a real danger for Aboriginal people—to start by opposing but then become co-opted by the perks and benefits of power. I could see it among some of my colleagues and was determined not to fall into that trap. I knew it was time to abandon some of the niceties of the assembly in order to force the government into real change. Beginning in late 1981 I began a concerted campaign to challenge and change the very appearance of government.

Chapter 10: Changing the Face of Government

SOMETIMES THE COURSE of events seems to move at a snail's pace. Issues are raised but not resolved; changes occur but only incrementally. At other times, change is rapid and dramatic; the stars align and nothing is ever really the same after. For many people in the North, the events of 1982 had that latter character. It was a turning point, and much of what you see today in terms of political structures and systems in the North had their origin in that fateful year. In retrospect, one can see all the small elements that led to this dramatic shift, but at the time there was a sense of hurtling into the future.

Canada changed in 1982 with the repatriation of the constitution and the introduction of the Charter of Rights and Freedoms. It was the last step in a process that had been going on for decades as Canadians threw off the last vestiges of their colonial past. Yet at the same time it seemed remarkably fresh and new, as if the whole country had been recreated. No one then could see all the results, but we all knew something had shifted in the way Canadians saw themselves and each other. It was a big year for Aboriginal people, as well, with the recognition of Aboriginal rights in Section 35 of the constitution. Section 35 laid the basis for tremendous advancements in the ability of Aboriginal people to regain control over their lands and governments, though much remains to be done.

In the Northwest Territories there was a similar acceleration of changes that had been in the works for decades. As early as 1963 there had been a proposal to divide the Northwest Territories into two separate territories. The legislation, introduced in the dying days of the Diefenbaker government, had been largely administrative in nature but nonetheless reflected both the reality of trying to govern such a large area and the aspirations of the Inuit people to be treated differently from people in the west. Despite being dismissed by the Carrothers report (from the Advisory Commission on the Development of Government in the Northwest Territories), division was an idea that would not die.

In 1976, the federal boundaries commission, consisting of Judge William Morrow as chairman and Nellie Cournoyea and Ross Payton as members, toured the Arctic to consider the boundary between the western and eastern Arctic areas for the purpose of the federal election. At the request of Judge Morrow, I was secretary to the commission and travelled with them. We spent the summer and fall travelling to most of the communities in the Arctic, and when all the travel was done, the commission drew a line that placed all the Inuit communities from the west to the east in one constituency. Nellie played a major role in convincing Judge Morrow of the importance of placing all of the Inuit communities together in the eastern constituency. I believe this line on the map was significant and was the prelude to the eventual establishment of an eastern territory.

The Inuit Tapirisat also raised the issue again in 1976 as part of their proposed land claim, and it was this desire for division—as well as the need to reconcile Dene and Métis interests—that led to the creation of the Unity Committee early in the life of the ninth assembly.

The Unity Committee met a number of times under my chairmanship and reported late in 1980 that there was "no consensus on a united territory." In other words, division of the territory was necessary and inevitable. The following year the assembly debated the issue and voted sixteen to one to support the concept of two territories. A plebiscite was proposed with the vote to be held on April 14, 1982— just two weeks after the repatriation of the constitution with much fanfare in Ottawa. The question was simple: do you think the Northwest Territories should be divided into two?

I had been fully engaged in the discussions of the Unity Committee and had come to believe that the issue of division had to be settled before we could really move forward to create the kind of territorial government satisfactory to the Dene and Métis people. Some saw it as a risk; without the Inuit, Aboriginal people would no longer form a majority of the population of the Northwest Territories, especially if the Inuvialuit chose to go into Nunavut rather than remain with the west. This was a real concern at the time, as they were drawn to the east by ties of language, culture and family and held to the west by natural transportation routes and economic links.

However, I believed that the Inuit were too focused on their desire for a separate territory to be reliable allies of the Dene in their struggle to attain their rights. I also felt it was just and sensible to divide the territory. You just have to travel from the west to eastern arctic communities to realize how distant the Inuit communities were. It was not really feasible to govern the far-flung communities of the Arctic from Yellowknife. Inuit interests, too, were different and unique. A vote for division, which would still take years to implement, could be a spur for other changes. So during the plebiscite, I actively campaigned for the yes side throughout my constituency, at a time when many western leaders were indifferent or even mildly hostile to the idea. I remember going into Tungsten, a small mining community situated remotely in the mountains in the southwestern corner of my constituency. Because they were so far removed from the rest of the communities in the Northwest Territories, the issue of division was not relevant to them, but I still was able to attract some of them to attend a public meeting where I outlined my reasons why they should vote yes in the plebiscite.

When the ballots from throughout the North were counted, the vote was quite close. Only 56.6 percent voted yes with 43.4 percent voting no. In the eastern areas, turnout was large and overwhelmingly in support of division. However in Yellowknife, the no side had a significant lead, though voter participation was relatively low. In my riding, we won a clear majority in support of division. Although it would take another seventeen years to achieve, division was on its way.

MEANWHILE, IN THE legislative assembly, I was continuing my fight to win greater rights for the Dene, both in practical ways and symbolically in terms of how Aboriginal cultures could and should be recognized in the Assembly's decor and manner of operation. I still recalled my culture shock when I experienced the opening ceremonies of my first council session in 1970. Often with the prime minister or the minister of Indian and Northern Affairs in attendance, the opening of the assembly back then had a military air. Men in uniforms wearing polished boots paraded in. Someone yelled "Order!" as a procession led by the commissioner and the sergeant-at-arms, carrying the mace, marched in. Sometimes bagpipes blared as men dressed in Scottish kilts strode in at the end of the procession. Nine years later when I became MLA again, the formality was the same and looked very like it was becoming entrenched as the way that our assembly functioned. I would grit my teeth wondering where the Dene, Métis, Inuit or Northern culture was represented. We were in the North, not somewhere in southern Ontario. I did not identify with any of these kinds of ceremonies. I had attended many Dene gatherings and had never encountered such peculiar practices. Solemn drumming and chanting marked Dene occasions, along with ceremonies like feeding the fire, which had spiritual meaning and significance in people's lives. I decided that the winter session in 1982 was my last real chance to make changes before the election the next year.

I had been raising the matter of Aboriginal languages since my earliest days in the territorial council. The government, as a matter of course, had been providing interpretation services for Inuit members for many years. It was a necessity since most spoke limited English; some spoke none at all. Dene politicians could speak fluent English and represent their constituents, but I felt there was a greater issue than simply being heard in English. The Dene language had to be spoken and heard in the legislative assembly. The Dene people were an important part of northern society and their representatives must represent them in their languages. I had pressed the government to provide Dene languages in schools, and there had been some baby steps made in that regard. I had started the first Dene language program on CBC and pressured them to expand their services in various Aboriginal languages. Progress had been made in many areas but in the assembly only two languages were recognized—English and Inuktitut. Promises had been made to provide Dene languages interpreters, but so far they had been empty words.

The 1982 budget once again failed to provide funds for Dene languages in the assembly. Obviously, I was talking myself blue in the
face without success. What else was there to do? The idea came to
me one day that if I spoke in Dene, no one would understand me and
something was bound to happen. I wasn't sure just what it would be,
but I was willing to bear the consequences.

I began my presentation in the usual way by admonishing the
government for its broken promises: "I was disappointed yesterday
when the budget was tabled … given the fact that we had made such
a fuss, we had made such an issue of the fact that Dene languages
ought to be a top priority of government." I continued in English for
a few more sentences, concluding with "Maybe by my insisting on
speaking the Dene language, it will force, somehow, in a small way,
this government to begin to be serious about the Dene languages.
If anybody does not like it, they can learn the language, or else get
an interpreter." At that point I switched to the Dene language. The
assembly ground to a halt. Everyone looked bewildered, moving
uneasily in their seats.

Finally Nellie Cournoyea, who was sympathetic and wanted to
resolve the situation, rose on a point of order: "Mr. Speaker, I would
request that this assembly provide an interpreter, so that we may
understand what the Honourable Member Mr. Sibbeston is saying."

Don Stewart, the Speaker, responded that the assembly was not
equipped to be able to meet that request at that moment, though he
allowed that there were probably procedures that could be taken to
do so in the future.

Nellie responded that in many communities there were no sophisticated translation systems, but someone would stand next to
the speaker to interpret after each statement phrase. The Speaker re-
iterated that the House only recognized two languages, and until it
recognized another, he could not himself rule that another language
was acceptable. Meanwhile, if I continued to speak, I was probably
breaking assembly rules by wasting time. He noted that I was "fully
aware that a request could be made to include the Slavey language
and having a ruling provided. However, as Speaker, I do not have that
authority."

He had given me a perfect opening. I rose and said that I wished to get a ruling from the Speaker on whether I could speak my Native language. "Is your ruling that it is not acceptable to speak Slavey or Dene language in this House at this time?" The Speaker claimed he had not made a ruling and asked how long I planned to continue. I smiled: "Maybe a few days, until we get an interpreter." The Speaker recessed the House for a caucus meeting.

The caucus lasted over an hour and the discussion was frank and thorough. The government once again promised they would do more for Dene languages. Finally, I agreed to come back into the assembly and speak English. I finished my reply and said I was looking forward to the government hiring interpreters and tripling the money it was currently spending on Dene languages. Further, I was aware that the Inuit received one million dollars for interpreters and felt that the Dene should expect nothing less; currently, not one cent of government funds went toward Dene interpreters. Beyond that, given that few people could read Slavey, the government had to find creative ways to communicate with the Dene people, even if they had to make cassettes of news and messages to distribute to people in the communities. For the next few days and weeks, until they set up a proper translation system, the Speaker provided me with an interpreter whenever I wanted to speak Dene in the assembly. I had won.

I had also been thinking for some time how to approach the issue of dress. The rules simply stated that we had to dress "in a manner appropriate to the dignity of the assembly." It was assumed that this meant suit and tie, though Native dress was permitted, allowing people to wear the traditional clothes they might have worn at important ceremonies. However, members seldom exercised this option and, on any given day, everyone in the assembly wore a suit and tie. I had raised the issue at every session going back to the early seventies, to the point where some MLAs were getting tired of it. Inuit representatives, whom one might think would have been supportive, were not. They seemed to believe this was the Canadian way, the white man's way, and they were content to follow "suit."

I decided that early in the session, when I made my reply to the commissioner's speech, would be a good time to make my move.

The day before, I had worn my suit without a tie. Late in the day, the Speaker had sent me a note asking if I had forgotten it. I sent a note back saying that I did not intend to wear a tie ever again in the assembly, though if he was willing to take his black cloak off, I might reconsider and put a tie on. His long black gown was the type of thing that Speakers in the south were wearing as part of their formal dress. The exchange of notes had set the stage for my move to demonstrate the difference between being *allowed* to wear Native dress and exerting the *right* to do so.

So the next afternoon, I entered the assembly wearing my best suit and tie, much, I am sure, to the Speaker's satisfaction. Eventually, my turn came to reply to the Commissioner's speech. I first made a number of points about constituency issues, but then moved on to the whole concept of the inclusion of Native people in government and how they did their jobs. There might be more Native people in government, but they had to comply with the government way of doing things. Governments by their nature were organized into systems with policies and set procedures. Native people who came from a different background and culture found it intimidating to do their jobs as prescribed. To an extent, the hidden message was "you are welcome to have a government job, to take part in mainstream society, as long as you give up everything that makes you Aboriginal." It was a softer version of the old Indian Affairs mandate for residential schools: to educate the Indian out of the child. But I was no longer a child, and now it was the white-based government that needed to be educated, that needed to put the Native back in.

I referred to the recent constitutional conference in Yellowknife, which was a serious beginning on creating a new government in the western part of the North for all peoples: Dene, Métis and whites. I reasoned it should lead to a better government, one significantly different from what we had now, more reflective of the people of the North: "As Native peoples, Dene people, it is important to be strong, in terms of your culture, your language, free expression of ideas and also in dress."

At that moment, I removed my suit jacket and vest and let them drop to the floor. To the rising murmurs of fellow members,

I loosened my tie and cast it aside. Then I reached under my desk and pulled out a beautiful moosehide jacket: smoke-tanned leather trimmed with fur and decorated with intricate beadwork. I quickly slipped it on. According to the rules, I was still dressed acceptably. (Of course, the rules said nothing about using the assembly hall as a changing room.) I had demonstrated the seriousness of the matter in as dramatic a fashion as I could.

I continued to speak: "I do it in a symbol of throwing off...I was going to say 'shackles,' but chains of colonialism, chains of cultural domination by non-Native people." I encouraged my Dene and Métis colleagues to do likewise and not feel that they had to wear three-piece suits and oxfords to work for the government or be on the executive. A few weeks later, Nellie appeared in the assembly with a bulky muskox coat, causing a stir and some laughter as such outerwear would have been hot indoors.

Both my filibuster in Slavey and my gesture of removing my suit in favour of a moosehide jacket received a lot of attention in the media, as was my intention. Southern papers talked of a northern MLA "stripping off his clothes" in the assembly, and *News/North* called it a strip-tease, making it all sound more risqué and dramatic than it really was. There was even an editorial cartoon in the northern paper showing me removing my tie while fellow MLAs yelled, "Take it off!" Despite the humour, I was quite satisfied; I had wanted public attention and I had gotten it. I knew that sometimes a little joke was a good way to loosen people up to make them listen to the serious issues I wanted to raise. Generally, in fact, the response of the media and, more importantly, my Native constituents was positive. It was a good opening salvo.

On February 17, I was ready for the next round, quite literally as it turned out. I made a motion, seconded by Nellie Cournoyea, for a committee "to review all the rules, decor, dress and practices of the legislative assembly with a view to making such rules, decor, legislative assembly staff and Speaker's dress and practices more appropriate to the custom and tradition of the people of the North, instead of continuing the British practices and styles thus far adopted." I added that the mace should also be reviewed, with the committee travelling throughout the North to consider a more appropriate symbol of authority. All of this information should be reported back to the assembly in the fall so that changes could be in place for the next assembly.

Before my opponents could raise it, I self-acknowledged that I was obsessed with this issue and asked, rhetorically, "Why not simply deal with the substance of budgets and legislation?"

Tagak Curley yelled, "Yes!" indicating his displeasure at the discussion.

I was obsessed, I said, because "I was human, had a conscience, emotion, have a big heart and ... a responsibility to my constituents."

Lynda Sorensen piped up that "You sure do not like mine. You have no heart as far as I am concerned."

I didn't like the heckling, but I persevered. I emphasized that the Dene Nation did not approve the formality of the assembly and made fun of it. They used a traditional approach of voting by a show of hands. I didn't appreciate this strange instrument called the mace, the bland black robes used by the Speaker and all his clerks, or the marching RCMP officers. At Fort Liard in my constituency, the people were in a battle with the RCMP because they had swooped in with a Twin Otter and seized all the band's office files. Every nationality had customs they were proud of and wanted to see represented in their governments. The Dene would like to see their culture represented in this assembly so that when they were present, they could identify with the proceedings and they could feel comfortable in this setting. I reminded everyone that we talked of big constitutional changes but had a hard time dealing with small things like the decor and dress in this House.

Changes had to be made. Firstly, we should have interpreter services so that Aboriginal MLAs could speak in their mother tongues. Secondly, the rules concerning dress were stifling. All members should be able and encouraged to dress according to their cultures and custom and not feel compelled to wear suits and ties. Thirdly, the Speaker or the Members Services Board should commission Dene art such as moose hair tufting. The assembly should get Dene art from the five regions of the North. For example, the North was famous for polar bear hides, and there should be a few draped in the House. "Maybe a polar bear hide can be used for the Speaker to sit on, or else he can have it to lay his weary feet on." This last elicited laughter but I continued: "For the Dene and Métis, we do not have polar bears, but we have beaver skins and we have black bears.... Of course we have moose, we have caribou hides.... From the Delta, Ms Cournoyea, we have muskrats, muskoxes."

Even the Speaker's chair was not spared from my remarks. It was a nice chair, even impressive, I told the assembly, but it was not from the North. "That in itself should be revolting to many of us, just the fact that it came from Ottawa." It had been presented to the assembly by officials in Ottawa, who wanted to ensure we were on our way to the British Westminster model of government. "We should have a northern-made chair, made with local wood and with various resources from northern industry embedded for decoration."

As to dress, I told the Speaker that his present wardrobe was pretty drab and unimaginative; he looked like a judge from England. He should have the fanciest formal wardrobe in the North. With all the Native sewers available, he could modify his black robes. "You could have some caribou, a little bit of moosehide, some furs, some beadwork. I daresay, you could be pretty dazzling!" Something similar could be done for the clerks, though perhaps not as fancy. I noted that the pages had already made a bit of a transition with the addition of northern vests, but even these could be improved.

I finished by speaking about the mace. In the British tradition it was a symbol of authority, but while "I do believe that it was made from materials from the North...I do not know when it was made. If it was made without public knowledge, without public consent or input, it was as if it was made in hiding, so I think we should publicize the mace and see if we can improve on it and give the people of the North a chance to have input into it." I asked, whimsically, if there was something in the mace that was special that people bowed to it and held it in such reverence.

When I sat down, George Braden immediately rose to congratulate me on my speech and say how much he enjoyed it. "I would just say that I think we really have to make a concerted effort for the next few years to pull together decorum and to bring together some of the artifacts, art and so forth, which I know all members will agree will look very nice in the new legislative assembly building that will one day be built here in Yellowknife as capital city."

Other reactions were mixed. Tagak Curley was "tired of fooling around with too many little things when we could be trying to improve the economy and employment opportunities for people." Mark Evaluarjuk didn't care what we wore and what artifacts we had in the House; he just wanted to represent the people who elected him by discussing the issues. He said that he would abstain from the vote because it did not affect him at all. Dennis Patterson too would abstain, saying that he was more interested in customs and practices of the forthcoming Nunavut Legislative Assembly. Bob MacQuarrie supported me in developing an assembly that in some better way reflected the society that it represented, though he took issue with the "dramatic moves" I had made.

I had the opportunity to close the debate. I said that I was disappointed with some members, particularly Native members, who dismissed Dene and Métis concerns and my very serious motion. I spoke about the racism toward the Native people in this part of the North, and how white people had imposed their system on us. In frustration, I declared "I am serious to the point of crying on this issue."

Tagak Curley, who was sitting two seats away from me, interrupted. "Cry! Cry tears!"

I turned on him. "You had better watch out or I will go and give you a punch." As I began speaking again he continued making rude remarks, and I lost my temper. I stalked over and hit him on the side of the head with my fist.

There was a collective gasp in the House. The Speaker reacted immediately: "Mr. Sibbeston, you will leave the House. You are expelled for the remainder of this day."

With my mind in a turmoil, I wasn't sure what he had said, so I went back and sat in my chair. He looked at me sternly: "What I said was you have no right to…touch any other person in this House. You are now being asked to leave the House for the rest of this sitting day."

I rose on a point of privilege but was not allowed to speak. I hesitated, muttering under my breath, "You're going to have to drag me out of here." But after a moment I decided not to create any further disruption. I left the assembly. I went out into the lobby area of the hotel where we were meeting and waited for members to come out, some of whom were sympathetic with me and understood my frustration. When Tagak eventually came out into the lobby, I walked over and apologized, and we made peace.

The next day, as the assembly started, I apologized for my conduct. I then closed the debate on my motion, again stating that it was a sincere attempt to make changes because the Dene and Métis were excluded from the decor and customs of the House. I reminded them I had the support of my constituents and the Dene Nation and Métis Association for the changes. While the Inuit in the east were secure in their future, with division we Aboriginal peoples in the west might well be in the minority. Our future was not as secure, and hence the need to make changes while we could. In the end the motion did pass, with only Evaluarjuk, Curley, Noah and Fraser voting against it.

Naturally, my actions garnered lots of media attention: positive for the results; not so much for the methods. I still have a framed copy of an ensuing editorial cartoon in my office. I have a fierce expression as I make a point in the assembly, while a nervous-looking Tagak Curley, wearing a hockey helmet, looks on.

The passage of this motion and the eventual report and recommendations were a highlight of my career as an Opposition member. I had fought for ten years to improve the treatment of Dene and Métis by the GNWT and to ensure their cultures were reflected in all aspects of government from the assembly right down to basic services in communities. Yet all I had really accomplished was to elicit further promises of change from the executive and from my fellow MLAs. The process of delivering that change continued to be slow, bureaucratic and often immensely frustrating. Sometimes, as in the case of punching Tagak Curley, I let my emotions get the better of me. It wasn't the first time and it wouldn't be the last.

A FEW WEEKS after my round with Tagak came another incident. The day started like any other. My family and I were living temporarily in an unused government house on School Draw Avenue in Yellowknife.

There wasn't much furniture there. As usual when Karen and our six children—Jerald and Laurie were our two youngest—joined me while the assembly was in session, we camped out with foamies and cardboard boxes in a vacant government house for a few weeks.

Around nine I went uptown for our usual caucus meeting before the assembly started in the afternoon. We were a few days into the budget, and the Department of Local Government's budget was up for debate in the Committee of the Whole. Minister James Wah-Shee was defending; Peter Fraser was the chair.

I began on a positive note, stating that the band councils in the communities of Fort Providence, Fort Liard and Wrigley were taking over municipal functions, and even the Village of Fort Simpson had improved in that a couple of Native people had been elected to the council. However, Nahanni Butte was experiencing problems as the community was in disarray due to alcoholism. The discussion turned critical as I noted that local government officials from the regional centre in Fort Smith did not visit the Deh Cho area and, while interest was growing in forming regional councils, there was no financial assistance to communities down the Mackenzie Valley to do so. The Baffin and Kitikmeot regions had funds provided to them for their regional councils but there were none in the west.

Wah-Shee responded sarcastically: "I had the impression the honourable member did not recognize this government. I do not really know why he wants to organize more councils."

Undeterred, and still trying to be diplomatic, I said that a lot of people shied away from settlement and village councils and turned instead to the band and the Dene Nation. But, I said, "there is some merit in becoming involved, not to necessarily endorse this government, but just as a matter of practicality." The Inuit had gained much by being open to government services, and I planned to do more in my area to get Native people involved in this government's programs "as a means to obtain services on a day-to-day basis."

Wah-Shee became testy. He was adamant that the communities had good relations with and recognized the territorial administration. I replied that in all my communities, it was the band councils, not the municipal councils, that represented the people. This indicated to me that a lot of people in my constituency did not support or understand the territorial government. When there was a Dene Nation general assembly, people flocked to it, but there was not a single Dene other than a man from the CBC at this assembly.

My remarks unleashed a brief flurry of responses. Wah-Shee, highly irritated, said that he would go to my community and challenge my allegation that the people did not support the government. Mark Evaluarjuk indicated that rather than adversely comparing the government's response to the Dene with that to the Inuit, I should tell my constituents that they should be working hard, not just trying to push the government. Nellie Cournoyea came to my defence. It was undermining my representation for the minister to say he would go to my communities to try to get a different opinion; my comments about my constituents' concerns should be respected.

Wah-Shee backed down. His experiences in travelling to communities differed from mine, and he disagreed with my view that no one acknowledged the territorial government, but he acknowledged that there was something to what I had said. "I think that evolution has to take place. I am well aware that many of the communities are not happy with the present set-up and they would like to see some changes." He apologized to me and promised not to raise the issue when he came to my region.

Still, I felt I needed to demonstrate the basis for saying that people did not support the government. Impassioned, I said that Native people were coming from the bush and settling in communities and they did not have the education and skills to obtain government jobs. Their lands and resources were being exploited while they received neither jobs nor benefits; southern people got the jobs and all the accompanying benefits of housing, vehicles and trips south. Meanwhile, the government had introduced alcohol into the North, selling it from liquor stores and licensing bars. Alcohol had had devastating effects on Northern people. Rather than providing alcohol, the government should outlaw it, just as they outlawed marijuana and other drugs that were bad for people.

Peter Fraser, as chair, interrupted me—"Could we get back to municipal affairs, please?"—but I continued my presentation. The leaders of the Dene people were aware of all of these issues, I said, and that was why they had negative feelings toward the government. To make matters worse, the bureaucracy and its red tape made it difficult for government to operate and get things done for people in communities.

Fraser interrupted again to say my time was up.

I pressed on. "Much to your dislike, I will continue, Mr. Fraser, because I am probably stating some truths that you do not perhaps like." I described how the band council and the Dene Nation were the organizations closest to people. These were the organizations who fought for land claims settlements, who challenged the resource companies that came into Dene areas. Native people were suspicious of government; it was these gut feelings that I represented and tried to express to the assembly.

When I was finished, Fraser immediately called out Municipal Affairs to get approval for this item in the budget. I protested the unreasonable haste. He disregarded me, going on to call three other items in quick succession. Equally quickly, members gave their approval by saying, "Agreed."

Frustrated, I spoke again: "I would like to think that these are important things, and I despise the fact that you are just trying to not have any further discussion on the things that I raised…. You seem to be more interested in passing the budget than even thinking…"

Fraser interrupted me. "I think everybody in this House has heard those statements before, two or three times. I do not want to listen to them again."

I asked that the ministers or their officials have the opportunity to respond to what I had said. "I have made some statements which I am sure the government either thinks are untrue or do not like." I looked directly at Fraser: "You have been rather insulting, Mr. Chairman."

It was as if I were invisible. There was just stony silence on the other side where the ministers sat. Emotionally drained, frustrated and upset, I picked up a coffee cup from my desk and threw it in the direction of the chairman. The cup came crashing down on the floor in front of him and broke into pieces. Everyone fell silent, aghast at what had happened. I was surprised myself. Then I stood and walked to the exit: "If that's all you care about the things I said, stick this council up your ass. I resign!" With that, I slammed the door and went out into the lobby, where I broke down in tears.

John Parker was the first to come out to ask how I was doing. He consoled me, saying that someone should have responded. He reminded me that we were making progress, and urged me just to have a rest and not resign. I agreed that I would go home and talk to my constituents.

I eventually walked home to Karen and my family and told her about the incident. She similarly comforted me, and my children all gathered around, hugging me and telling me, "Daddy, it'll be okay."

News of the incident travelled fast. Within an hour Pat Moore had called and invited me to go skiing. I spent the rest of the afternoon on the cross-country trails, far removed from the affairs of government. Falling down, standing up and trying to stay on the ski trail seemed a lot more important than staying within the ropes of the assembly.

The newspapers and CBC had a field day reporting the event. The news of an MLA throwing a cup at a colleague appeared in the *Edmonton Journal* and many of the southern newspapers. The Native press and *News/North* had headlines about the incident and the latter an editorial headlined "Temper."

I spent the next few days packing up and moving my family back to Fort Simpson, worried and unsure about the reception I would get from my constituents. I shouldn't have worried. In the stores, in church and on the streets, people greeted me like a hero. They found it amusing that I had thrown a cup in assembly. I soon realized that what had seemed like a serious incident in Yellowknife was not seen that way at all by the people. Some said, "It's about time someone shook things up in Yellowknife" while others said, "You should have thrown more cups." The chief, Jim Antoine, commented on CBC Radio that it was Peter Fraser's fault and he should be the one who resigned.

In the ensuing weeks I visited every community and explained exactly what had happened, always ending by asking, "Should I resign?" The answer was always a unanimous "No," and they urged me to get back in there and keep fighting for them. I had lived up to my commitment to get the feelings of my constituents on record. Their reactions reinvigorated me. I felt ready to do battle again.

IN RETROSPECT, MY political passion to see that right was done for Native people was no doubt linked to the traumatic repression of my years at residential school.

It would be wrong to give the impression that all I did that fateful year was raise hell in the assembly or spend my entire life fighting people. In fact, my experiences outside the assembly ropes were quite the opposite, the picture of cooperation and collaboration, often with the same people I fought with when the House was in session.

The Unity Committee Report in early 1981 had dealt with the division of the territories and what would happen in the west if division occurred. A Constitutional Committee was struck to explore with interested organizations a process to deal with constitutional development and, possibly, hold a conference to deal with the creation of a western constitution. I was appointed chairman of that committee, and Bob MacQuarrie, Peter Fraser, Donald Stewart and James Wah-Shee were full members. George Braden was an ex-officio member. Throughout the fall, I contacted Aboriginal organizations and the Association of Municipalities to gauge their interest. On December 3, 1981, I was able to report that a constitutional conference was to be held on January 19 to 21, 1982, in Yellowknife, and that the Dene Nation and Métis Association had agreed to attend.

The conference opened a day late because I attended the burial of my old friend Ted Trindell in Fort Simpson. When we finally met, it was the first time that all these Native and non-Native political leaders had gathered together in one room since the divisive years surrounding the Berger Report. After briefly setting the stage, I emphasized the importance of the matters we were about to discuss. With division looming, the peoples of the west had to decide on a process for the formation of a new government. Native organizations, like the Dene Nation and COPE, and the legislative assembly had advanced proposals or at least principles for what a new government would entail. Communities throughout the North would be affected, so representatives of all communities greater than five hundred people had been invited along with such organizations as the Chamber of Mines, the public service and teachers' associations. This conference was the opportunity for people to sit across the table from each other to explain and get reactions to their already published positions.

Georges Erasmus (later the National Chief of the Assembly of First Nations and co-chair of the Royal Commission on Aboriginal Peoples) began with the Dene Nation's proposal, "A Public Government for the Peoples of the North." The common interests of many northerners made their proposal a possible solution. The main features were a government in the tradition and style of the Dene, guaranteed representation, a ten-year residency voting requirement, a senate to protect Aboriginal rights, strong community governments with the active participation of people and limited powers to elected representatives. The large transient population of workers coming north to work on resource development projects and the likelihood of the Dene losing their majority were the reasons for many of the provisions.

Jim Bourque of the Métis Association supported the Dene Nation proposal and saw a role for the commissioner and the legislative assembly to bring about these changes. Sam Raddi of COPE, which proposed a regional government based in the Beaufort area, stated that his organization was only an observer because it did not know whether the communities in the Beaufort area would go with Nunavut or an "Indian" government in the west. James Wah-Shee, speaking as the territory's minister of Aboriginal Affairs and Constitutional Development, said that the executive committee supported division and outlined the contents of a discussion paper titled "Our Land and Our Future," as well as principles dealing with regional governments.

These four opening presentations were followed by shorter speeches from a range of delegates representing a variety of organizations. There were representatives of roughly ten municipalities or band governments, including Vince Steen (Tuktoyaktuk), Mike Ballantyne (Yellowknife), Frank T'selie (Fort Good Hope), Joachim Bonnetrouge (Fort Providence) and Ted Blondin (Rae Edzo). Most western MLAS were in attendance, as were Cliff Reid from the

Federation of Labour and Terry Daniels from the Chamber of Mines, among others.

On the second day we got down to the real debate. Cliff Reid started on a positive note, recognizing an aura of understanding that hadn't been there before. Georges Erasmus elaborated on the Dene proposal and responded to concerns about the ten-year residency requirement. Six months or even two years were not enough; a large industrial camp close to a community could overwhelm and out-vote permanent residents. A senate was needed to protect Aboriginal rights—how else could negotiated rights be protected in the future? The Dene were committed to a public government instead of an exclusively Aboriginal one. They looked to a constitutional negotiation process involving the federal, territorial and Native organizations, with input from municipalities when local governments were discussed.

Individual delegates had their own concerns about the Dene proposal and had an opportunity to express them. Mike Ballantyne, the mayor of Yellowknife and later a territorial minister, questioned the effectiveness of referendums as a way of involving citizens. The Dene Nation's intent to reconsider the location of the capital was problematic as it would cost approximately $500 million to establish a new capital. Ballantyne also opposed the lease-only approach to land tenure in communities to replace fee-simple land ownership. Vince Steen asked why the Inuvialuit communities should stay in the west; Erasmus identified the close proximity and the communication and transport links. Red McBryan of Hay River raised questions related to communities being able to run programs, the future government honouring land leases and ways of selecting senators. Marguerite Robinson of Fort Smith asked how the government document on constitutional development fit into the process.

More importantly according to Ballantyne, the federal minister of Indian Affairs and Northern Development, John Munro, and his officials were looking to see if leaders in the North could work together and agree on some principles. He suggested that the rest of the conference be spent on seeing if there was agreement on a process. Tom Butters objected that it was too early to begin negotiations on constitutional matters as the process of consultations was just beginning, citing the fact that many organizations and community representatives were not there. He also made the point that the issue of residency was something for the impending Charter of Rights and not likely to be determined in the North. Bob MacQuarrie added that although constitutional development in the North required the consent and goodwill of the Dene and Métis, many non-Native people also lived in the North and they had a right to be there. They might not accept some of the provisions in the Dene proposal. Similarly the federal government, which had recently passed Bill C-48, giving it control of large tracts of land for oil and gas development, might disagree. Clauses in the proposed constitution that gave provinces the ability to extend their northern borders and the mobility rights in the charter could create roadblocks. Hence, the Dene and Métis leadership needed to reconsider some of the items that were in the discussion paper.

On the third and final day of the conference, delegates made concluding remarks and attempted to set the course for future conferences by proposing motions of various types. For example Cynthia Hill, mayor of Inuvik, spoke in favour of an undivided North, indicating that she believed that people of all cultures could live together. McBryan suggested a committee be struck to continue work once the conference finished. Otto Romeike from Pine Point spoke in favour of holding conferences to work towards a government for the west and sought funding to assist municipalities to become knowledgeable and involved. Joachim Bonnetrouge asserted that, despite fear of change, change to the present government was exactly what was needed.

Georges Erasmus proposed forming a united front in dealing with the federal government. Delegates should agree in principle to the process contained in the Dene Nation proposal and continue to exchange proposals on constitutional changes. Further, the parties would continue to negotiate their proposals with the federal government while a committee would be struck of all the major groups, mandated to co-ordinate and improve the process of public consultation and involvement. Some delegates hesitated to support such a sweeping proposal. All of the municipal representatives and MLAS stated that they did not have a mandate to endorse such a resolution.

After much debate and attempts by Erasmus to explain his ideas, reluctance to support the process remained. Eventually Cynthia Hill proposed to set up a committee as Erasmus suggested and to seek funds for its work. This motion passed, but when Erasmus's more substantive proposal was voted on it was supported only by the Aboriginal delegates. The final vote was eleven to ten against the motion, with all the non-Native delegates voting no.

As chairman, I summed up the proceedings of the last three days. It had been a historic conference. When we called the meeting, we did not know if anyone would attend. There had been dialogue by all the western leaders, and though not everyone was happy with the results, it was a good start at dealing with a very difficult subject. The committee we established would continue this work and we would meet again.

A few weeks later the *News/North* wrote an editorial headlined "Bouquet for Sibbeston" for having done what it called a "credible job" in chairing the conference, and added, "Nick has been the target of the occasional slings and arrows from this space in the past. In our eyes, he's redeemed himself and has handled a very demanding job in an exceptional and fair manner."

In the ensuing months, the new committee met a number of times, and a series of pamphlets were printed and distributed widely throughout the North. These pamphlets were written in plain English with charts that showed clearly the differences between the existing government and what a future government could look like. Materials were also prepared in the various Native languages. For the delegates at the conference, we prepared what we called a green working paper setting out all the major issues contained in the Denendeh document.

Not everyone was supportive of the proposals being discussed at the January conference, especially the Denendeh plan put forward by Georges Erasmus. The response from residents and political leaders in Hay River was particularly vehement. At a meeting in early September 1982, numerous speakers demanded that the changes requested by the Dene be rejected out of hand as undemocratic, unconstitutional and unfair to non-Natives. Those attacking the proposals were careful to declare that they weren't racist or anti-Indian, but it was clear that

Nick Sibbeston at the age of three with his grandmother, Ehmbee, behind their house in Fort Simpson. Before being taken away to residential school, Sibbeston lived an idyllic existence with his mother and grandmother.

PHOTO COURTESY NICK SIBBESTON

CHARLES HANSEN   GEORGE SIBBESTON   Philip BONNETROUGE   WILLIAM CLI

1939

PHOTO COURTESY NICK SIBBESTON

Sibbeston's grandfather George Sibbeston (second from left) in 1939.

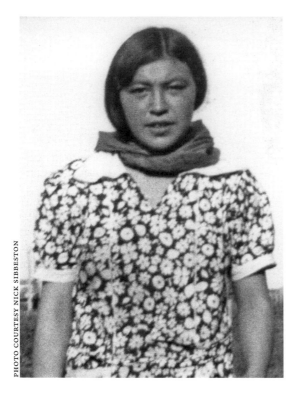

Sibbeston's mother, Laura, 1944. Due to her poor health and alcohol problems, Sibbeston saw little of his mother after he left for residential school.

Class photo from the residential school in Fort Providence, circa 1949. Sibbeston is the third boy from the right.

Sibbeston at the Fort Providence residential school, 1950. The loneliness and neglect he faced at school left a lasting mark on his mental health.

Sibbeston with his cousins, circa 1955. Left to right: Kenneth, Wendy holding baby Joyce, Nick, Dolly.

Sibbeston and Karen Benoit out on the town during their university years in Edmonton. Despite Karen's good influence, Sibbeston continued to party through much of his early university career.

Campaign photo from the 1970 election, when Sibbeston ran to become a member of the territorial council of the Northwest Territories.

The fully elected ninth Northwest Territories Legislative Assembly,
serving from 1979 to 1983.

The 1984 executive council, with Richard Nerysoo (bottom row, centre)
as government leader. At this time, Sibbeston (top row, left) was serving
as minister of local government.

Sibbeston speaking with characteristic passion as chair of the Western Constitutional Forum, created to negotiate the boundary for Nunavut's division from the Northwest Territories and develop the new territory's constitution.

Commissioner John Parker passes Sibbeston a gavel as Sibbeston, now government leader, replaces him as chairman of the executive council, 1985.

Family photo taken in 1986. From left to right: Karen, Nick, Jerald, Laurie (on floor), Janice, Glen, Randy and Murray.

Sibbeston and his wife, Karen, welcome Pope John Paul II on his trip to Fort Simpson in 1987.

Election night 1988, with campaign manager Paul Gammon.
Sibbeston was narrowly defeated in the race for government leader
by Dennis Patterson, who pushed him out of cabinet soon after.

Family photo at Sibbeston's swearing-in ceremony
on his appointment to the Senate in 1999.

they were concerned that Aboriginal people might change the status quo and gain some real control over their lives. MLA Bob MacQuarrie made a strong defence of the western constitutional process and persuaded the meeting, in the end, to support continued work and negotiation with Native groups on their proposals.

The second constitutional conference was held September 14 to 16, 1982, with many of the same delegates plus representatives from Cambridge Bay, Coppermine, Deline and Fort Simpson. As chairman, I suggested a format similar to that of the first conference: statements the first day, reaction and responses the second day, and conclusions and motions the final day. Since the last conference, the vote on division had passed and the newly repatriated constitution, with the Charter of Rights and Freedoms and guarantees of Aboriginal rights, had been adopted, lending a new urgency to our deliberations.

Georges Erasmus believed that the constitutional process could proceed at the same time as Aboriginal rights negotiations but hoped the land claims issue would be dealt with prior to resources and lands being turned over to the government in the North. Delegates needed to have honest exchanges to get into "the meat of what is bothering some people": contentious issues like the residency requirement and the proposed senate. "We have to get beyond communicating with each other by pamphlets and [create] a position that we all can live with." He hoped people would leave the conference "feeling like the Dene are not creatures from other planets."

Many delegates expressed the fears that non-Natives had about changes to the structure of government, land tenure within communities and the ability to form unions. A common question revolved around how the recent Charter of Rights and Freedoms would affect our proposals. The City of Yellowknife's position was outlined by Mike Ballantyne in a lengthy speech, focusing on guaranteed representation for Native groups, the need for consensus and the lead role for the legislative assembly, which needed to evolve into full, responsible government.

The delegates asked that an independent political scientist or constitutional lawyer be made available to inform discussion on the Canadian form of provincial government and advise how the unique features proposed by the Dene Nation would compare. The next day, Stein Lal, the GNWT deputy minister of justice, outlined the differences between a provincial and a territorial form of government. The executive power in the provinces was vested in the premier and cabinet, with the lieutenant governor having a ceremonial role, while in the Northwest Territories executive power rested with the commissioner who, by virtue of the Northwest Territories Act, was the chief executive officer. While there were now elected MLAs on the executive committee, they were subservient to the commissioner as chairman of the executive committee. As well, the legislative powers of the provinces were set out in Section 92 of the Constitution Act, 1867, while the powers of our territory were established in the Northwest Territories Act passed by the federal government. Public lands were controlled by provinces, which were therefore responsible for Crown lands and resources within their borders. In the Northwest Territories, these powers were vested in the federal government.

Lal's presentation led to a lengthy discussion on a range of topics, including the provisions of the new constitution that gave existing provinces a role in the creation of new provinces. The Yukon government was cited as an example of a fully responsible territorial government, which raised the issues of the role of political parties in a democracy and whether consensus government was an impediment to more responsible government. The commissioner's role in passing territorial legislation and the powers of the federal government to disallow it were also examined.

The green working paper prepared for the conference soon became the central focus of our discussion. The five principles of governance, such as those providing every level of government with enough power and resources to be effective, were quickly approved.

The Dene had proposed a senate as a means to protect Aboriginal rights; other delegates suggested the provisions of the new constitution, combined with a Human Rights Commission, would be sufficient. Historically, it was argued, treaties made with Native peoples had not been honoured. In more recent years, the James Bay land claims agreement had proven that once agreements were entered into, governments had a difficult time fulfilling and implementing them.

(Indeed, nearly thirty years of litigation finally led to a $1.4 billion settlement and a new agreement in 2008). After much debate, a sympathetic understanding developed that some sort of watchdog was needed to protect Aboriginal rights, whether that be a senate-type mechanism or a modified Human Rights Commission. When I saw that there was consensus on the issue, I proposed a motion to the effect "that there be a mechanism set up to protect the Aboriginal rights that are gained through claim negotiations."

The residency requirement for both voting and eligibility for office was the next major item on the agenda. There was some reluctance to support the idea of ten years, with Marguerite Robinson and Vince Steen suggesting three years would be reasonable. The matter of mobility rights in the constitution was also raised. After sufficient discussion, I suggested a motion "that we should extend the residency requirements for elections beyond one year to a reasonable time permitted by the Canadian Constitution." The motion passed by a vote of twelve to four. This conference was proving to be significantly different from the earlier one where there had been a reluctance to deal with issues.

On the third day, the delegates focused on two items: guaranteed representation and forming a government in the tradition and style of the Dene. In small communities, the issue of Aboriginal participation in government was no longer a problem, but in the larger centres Aboriginal participation remained low. With large developments in the works leading to an influx of southern workers into the North, the Dene were concerned about being overwhelmed by non-Native voters. However, Georges Erasmus conceded that the Dene proposal for a guaranteed 30 percent of seats on elected bodies might be a little high. What was reasonable? I asked simply if there was agreement that some form of guaranteed representation should be accorded to the Aboriginal people in any future government and, by a show of hands, the answer was yes.

Forming a government in the tradition and style of the Dene was next on the agenda. Joachim Bonnetrouge raised the example of the Town of Hay River having an inuksuk standing at the front of the town hall. As an Inuit structure, the inuksuk was "a disgrace to the

Dene people of Hay River. It is more than a slap in the face. It is ridiculous … a real ridicule to anyone with a sense of cultural pride." Red McBryan said that he had no difficulty in the identity of the Dene being incorporated into the future form of government.

At the beginning of the afternoon session I stated that there appeared to be consensus that the subject of tradition and style of government was exhausted and agreed upon, so we moved on to dealing with other topics. Mike Ballantyne moved that another conference be held within six months and that a working committee be struck to develop various mechanisms to achieve some of the basic principles we had adopted. Georges Erasmus concluded that we had made significant headway and that a certain level of trust had been created. I concurred that the conference had been a success. We had acted like real northerners, resulting in one of the best meetings ever between Native and non-Native peoples.

Following the conferences, the Western Constitutional Forum (WCF), along with a parallel organization for Nunavut, was created to negotiate the boundary for division—which was proposed in 1987 and adopted, with revisions, by plebiscite in 1992—and to develop a constitution for a new western territory. The WCF worked for nearly eight years, developing position papers and holding workshops, but in the end very little change resulted. Indeed, the changes I had forced in the assembly and subsequently to the system of government in the Northwest Territories during my years in cabinet have had more lasting influence than any of the work carried out in these constitutional conferences or by the WCF. I sometimes look back in wonder on how all that work by the WCF, all the goodwill that had been created between the GNWT, the Dene and other Aboriginal groups came to so little. The ramifications continue to be felt today.

AFTER THE SECOND conference, I continued to be active as an MLA leading up to the election in 1983. However, things after September 1982 were of a more routine nature and certainly didn't compare to the tumultuous events of that critical year. I had spent some time away from the assembly after the cup-throwing incident and, even after my return, was more concerned with issues in my own constituency. I and other leaders had been dealing with a number of tough issues like alcohol and the hunting along the highways. Both of these issues were divisive in a community like Fort Simpson because of the mixed Native and non-Native population.

Early in my term I had helped achieve a great success in limiting the flow of alcohol in Fort Simpson. It never once entered my mind at the time what ramifications these initiatives would have on my upcoming election. Similarly, I had played a role in having restrictions placed on hunting and shooting moose or any other game along the Mackenzie and Liard highways. People in my area were concerned about the number of big game being shot along the highways, especially by people from other areas like Yellowknife. A few people who lived along the highway cited experiences of being shot at. They were afraid to walk along the highway, lest they be accidentally targeted. The idea was to disallow hunting along the highway altogether, even for the Native people who had general hunting licences. We had many meetings about the issue and eventually there seemed to be consensus, so we got the government to restrict shooting of any big game one kilometre on each side of the highway.

Although these measures dealing with alcohol and hunting along the highway were made after many meetings and the concurrence of many people, I found when the territorial election came, those opposed to the restrictions blamed me. It would cost me many votes.

Chapter 11: Communities and Regions

I WENT INTO 1983 confident I would easily win re-election. I had been the most active MLA in the assembly, raising issues of concern to Native people. The last year of the ninth assembly had been turbulent, but I had been active and pushed the government to make changes in a number of areas. In my district, Deh Cho Gah (formerly Mackenzie–Liard), I was up against Bill Lafferty. Bill had served the riding from 1975 to 1979, but I had easily defeated him in the last election and I was sure 1983 would be no different.

I ran my usual style of campaign, travelling to every community and visiting people in their homes. In the small communities, I sensed that people were satisfied with my work on their behalf. I could see the efforts of my work in the new and improved houses people lived in. In communities like Fort Liard and Nahanni Butte, I had made special efforts to have houses built for those still living in tents. In those days, politics was mostly done face to face. Newspapers had little circulation outside the larger centres and, other than in Yellowknife, radio was limited to the CBC, so advertising consisted largely of posters and a few flyers. For those who only spoke Slavey, the personal touch was important, and my fluency in the Dene language was a great asset.

As the campaign progressed, I remained confident. Bill Lafferty was well-liked but not as well-known and he certainly wasn't campaigning as hard, limiting himself to quick visits and focusing on a few communities. He later said that he got some of his strongest support in places he had not campaigned. I began to see those trends developing as election day approached.

People will seldom criticize you openly to your face, even in the midst of a campaign, but I had begun to sense a certain coolness especially from non-Native voters. For four years as MLA, my focus had been on Native issues. In my efforts to help those who needed it the most, I lost the support of some white people. Further, my efforts for the closure of bars during certain events and the outlawing of moose hunting along the highway were divisive even amongst Native people.

Still, the final results were a shock. On election night, November 21, which also happened to be my fortieth birthday, I finished a mere fourteen votes ahead. It was a tense finish as results flowed in and the lead changed hands several times. Even with the count complete, the tension continued, as an official recount was needed for such a close result.

I had received, at the very least, a startling wake-up call, a reminder that politicians are hired by the people and can be fired by them, too. Having always won by large majorities, it was a blow to almost lose. A politician's stock rises and falls based on the issues, and obviously mine was at its lowest ebb. But the voters are always right, and I resolved to be more open and sensitive to *all* my constituents' needs.

Far more troubling than the close vote were some of the events that occurred on election night and the days following. During the course of the evening I received five threatening phone calls, which I believed came from people in the bars because I could hear a lot of noise in the background. I immediately phoned the RCMP about the calls, and they said they would put a trace on our phone. I never heard anything more about the matter from them.

A few days later, returning home from an evening out, Karen and I discovered eggs smashed against our windows. I called and reported the matter to the RCMP, but they seemed uninterested in investigating. Had they bothered to come and inspect the scene of the offence, they would have easily solved the crime. In the morning I followed footsteps in the snow from our house back to a house a couple of blocks away. It was obvious that the person who threw the eggs had come from there. I didn't bother telling the police, as I was satisfied knowing who did it. I'm not sure what I would have done if the person had come out and confronted me, but fortunately it didn't come to that.

I let the matter lie and chalked it up to unbridled election fever. Certainly, there were no further incidents of that type. Nonetheless, the next little while was unsettling as I waited for the results of the official recount. I was eager to get to work, but there was still the possibility that the result could be overturned. Finally, Judge Calvin Tallis of the NWT Supreme Court came to Fort Simpson to do the count. I was greatly relieved to see my margin of victory rise to seventeen votes.

The *News of the North* did a lengthy post-mortem on the results in their November 25, 1983 issue. Quoting anonymous sources they claimed, as I myself had suspected, that my near-defeat was a direct result of my "unapologetic push for Native rights and tradition… [including]…Native business development, Native jobs and mandatory Slavey programs in schools." Those issues, along with my advocacy for restricting the amount of alcohol that an individual could purchase from the liquor store at any one time, had certainly cost me votes, especially in Fort Simpson. While a few non-Natives may have considered me a "racist in reverse" (a charge I find more amusing than hurtful, given my marriage to a white woman and my long history of working closely and productively with non-Native colleagues and public servants), there were other factors at play, factors that had more to do with the way elections work in consensus government than they did with me.

My biggest drop in votes came in the small mining community of Tungsten, where my count plummeted by ninety-eight votes from the previous election, a huge drop given that the population was less than five hundred souls including children too young to vote. Tungsten is on the very western edge of the Northwest Territories and had long complained about the lack of government services. I had made a number of trips into the community and did as much as I could to help them by raising their issues in the assembly and writing ministers about their concerns. However, in a consensus-style government, voters can't vote for or against the government but only for their local representative. Even though I had been a vocal Opposition critic, the voters in Tungsten, as I was told in subsequent visits, decided en masse to vote against me as a way of drawing attention to the lack of government services.

The one element of the newspaper's analysis that I disagreed with then and now was that Natives, especially elders, were "appalled by [my] brash assembly tactics" and that my "methods weren't always understood or supported." As I've recounted previously, I frequently consulted my constituents and was always encouraged, especially by the elders, to keep on fighting on their behalf.

I spent a quiet Christmas at home with my family, recovering from the strains of campaigning and preparing myself for the coming session. I had decided I would try to get on the executive council. I felt sure my years of hard work on the Opposition side of the House had earned me a shot at becoming a minister, but the close call I had had the previous month taught me to take nothing for granted.

EARLY IN JANUARY I travelled to Yellowknife where all the elected members were gathered to choose the new Speaker and the eight people who would serve in cabinet. I had been one of the most active members during the previous assembly, playing the role of Opposition and critic. While I savoured that role and a lot of good came of it, I didn't want to continue it forever. My brash tactics, as the newspaper called them—throwing cups, hitting a colleague, speaking Slavey to shut the assembly down and stripping off my suit and tie—combined with the regular work of questioning the government and speaking out against their policies, had achieved results and gotten me attention. Still, I was in Opposition without any power, and that's not why one enters the political fray. I thought it was time for fresh blood and for a stronger and more assertive cabinet. I wanted to be a minister, to have a hand in government and to make changes from the inside. I wanted to use ministerial power and authority to pursue my own lengthy agenda.

Despite the humbling experience of the election, I assumed I would be a shoo-in for a ministerial position. I was well-educated and had been one the hardest working and most effective MLAs. Despite public set-tos, I had privately nurtured good relationships with my fellow MLAs.

I got the surprise of my life. The assembly consisted of twenty-four members with officially fourteen from the west, although Nellie

Cournoyea considered her Tuktoyaktuk-area constituency part of eastern caucus. You would think that with a western majority, the west would control the selection of ministers and determine who would be chosen to cabinet. However, the west was not united. There were many differing interests and too many wanting to get into cabinet. I quickly grasped that the lobbying efforts were already well underway and tried to get into the eastern caucus meeting to get their support. I had friends from the east, and the Inuit interests were similar to the Dene, for which I was a strong advocate. Like my election, it was a humbling experience. As it happened, I even had difficulty getting into the meeting room.

John T'Seleie, MLA for Sahtu, and I were standing outside the Nunavut caucus door, knocking, trying to get in and being told to wait outside. John supported me in my quest to become a minister, and his attendance was intended to show I had support from Dene members. We stood outside the eastern caucus room waiting for hours, it seemed, so I could make my case for their support. I felt embarrassed and worked hard to control and hide my feelings.

Once we were in the room, the first question asked of me, not by an Inuk but by one of the white members, was whether I was stable enough to be a minister. I could hardly believe what I was hearing. The very intelligence and passion with which I approached issues, and which had been so successful, was being called into question, as though I was somehow mentally unbalanced and irrational.

At this time in my career, I felt healthy and was ready to move from the ranks of an ordinary member to being a minister. I thought it would be a lot easier being a level-headed minister than a hard-working, passionate Opposition member and less frustrating, too, with the power to make decisions rather than wresting concessions from the government. To think, plan, gather information and organize one's self to tackle an issue is a lot of work. I would spend days planning, researching the issues and organizing my speeches in preparation for the start of the assembly. I was emotional at times about issues, sometimes going to extremes such as with my carefully orchestrated striptease, but my outbursts were unplanned and arose in the course of events. Sometimes, especially in the face of stonewalling or unreasonable resistance to change, one just has to throw a cup or slam a desk to get attention. I've often said that you don't get anything done by writing nice letters and speaking calmly. You have to slam the table and often raise your voice to get your point across.

As for the question put to me in caucus, I reassured the gathered members that, yes, indeed, I was stable and rational and would be a good minister. There wasn't much more discussion, though from the smiles and body language of the Inuit members, I knew that I would be supported at least by them.

THIS SITUATION OF the east controlling the west had persisted throughout the years I was MLA, with few exceptions. It wasn't obvious to the public, but behind the scenes there was a lot of manipulation going on by the Nunavut caucus to control politics in the North. One outcome of this scheming was the eventual agreement that four executive members would be from the west and four from the east, despite the fact that the west had a much higher population. A caucus process was put in place to choose, by secret ballot, first the Speaker and then the eight members who would become ministers. All of this occurred in private, behind closed doors. Each member vying for a position was given an opportunity to make a short speech giving their reasons and qualifications. My speech stressed my Opposition work during the past few years, showing how I fought for changes that improved the assembly and government. Now, I said, I was ready to go to the other side and work as a minister.

I was chosen along with seven others: Tom Butters, Richard Nerysoo and Bruce McLaughlin from the west, and Dennis Patterson, Tagak Curley, Nellie Cournoyea and Gordon Wray from the east. The runoff for leader, which occurred immediately after the cabinet was chosen, was between Richard Nerysoo and Nellie Cournoyea, with Richard coming out the winner.

It was important in the consensus style of government that the members retain control and keep the cabinet accountable to the legislative assembly. The term of the assembly was four years, too long a period without some kind of review of the performances of the ministers. It was decided that after two years, all positions from the government leader to the ordinary ministers would be reviewed. Of course, if the conduct of a minister at any given time was unacceptable, the matter could be handled by a motion in the legislative assembly.

A few days later all the ministers were called to the government leader's office. We waited in an adjoining room like school students called to the principal's office. I was one of the first into the room where Richard Nerysoo and John Parker were seated. After a few pleasantries, I was asked by Richard to take on the portfolios of Local Government and Culture and be the associate minister of the Aboriginal Rights and Constitutional Development Secretariat. I gladly agreed, pleased that Richard had trusted me to take on those demanding portfolios. The Department of Local Government was one of the most important, having the biggest capital budget in government. I came out of the office with a big grin, not telling my colleagues what I was given, leaving them to find out for themselves what I and others received as their assignments.

I WAS NOW a minister of the GNWT, a government I had spent eight years of my life criticizing and cajoling to improve. From now on I wouldn't be the one asking questions and urging ministers to make changes; I could make those decisions myself. My position had fundamentally changed. It did seem amusing to be called a minister. In my experience, the term meant an Anglican Church priest. Those ministers wore white collars and were devoted to serving God. I would be devoted to serving the people.

In the ensuing weeks I launched into work, learning everything about the departments for which I was responsible, and going through thick binders of documents covering the budget, spending plans and policies. I was determined to have a hands-on approach to running the departments, having effective control for all matters under my responsibility. Some of my predecessors, from lack of knowledge, determination or hard work, did not have real control of their departments. Deputy ministers still had power over their departments; ministers, despite public appearances, were often mere figureheads. True ministerial government requires full control over all aspects of one's department.

My deputy minister Michael Moore, who had extensive Arctic experience, would be invaluable to me. He and I began mapping out the things that I hoped to accomplish in the years ahead. Primarily, my focus would be to get local governments well established, to have regional councils organized in all regions and to find a solution for the communities in the west that had difficulty reconciling band councils with community governments. Our departmental capital budget contained millions of dollars for municipal water and sewage systems and recreation facilities, and I was committed to making the best use of these monies to improve people's lives throughout the North.

The first time I sat down with the senior management of local government, I was introduced to the chief of finance, the chief of policy, the chief of recreation and so on. I said, "See, that's the problem with this government. Too many chiefs and not enough Indians." It drew a laugh, albeit a nervous one. I then made it clear that I respected them and looked forward to working with them. For the most part they served me and the public very well over the next few years. Nonetheless, a few months later all the titles were changed from "chief" to "director."

One of my early discoveries as a minister was that even when you give directions and orders, things don't readily change. Of course small things do, but the bigger issues take time and a lot of pushing and prodding. It was easy enough to move an item in the capital budget from one year to another, but giving communities a bigger say in creating the plan was a long, slow process that in the end stretched over the mandates of several successive ministers.

I've always found that injecting a bit of humour into situations was a good way to get people to work together but I was also ready to talk tough when needed, especially when it came to serious social issues. Early in my term as minister, I told residents in Fort Providence that they shouldn't come to Yellowknife drunk if they wanted to ask for anything from the territorial government. Some people were offended, but News/North concluded, "He may be rude but he's right." Many communities struggled with alcohol, but I knew that the first step to solving local problems was for local leaders to take responsibility. That meant they needed to be sober, both at home and when meeting with territorial civil servants. Having faced and overcome my own issues with drinking, I knew it could be done.

TO BE A hands-on minister, I had to know the situation in the communities and regions. The department was spending millions of dollars on civil servants' salaries and even more on capital projects. I undertook to travel within the first six months to all the regions to learn first-hand what those dollars were doing. I remembered Stu Hodgson making forays to the regions; that was his way of getting the government known and to a certain extent bringing government to life amongst the people. I could not be the Santa Claus that he had been, but I felt I could do a great deal to show how the newly elected government and its ministers were ready and available to work on behalf of the peoples in all regions.

For some reason, I particularly enjoyed travelling to the Baffin region. It was like going to another planet. The terrain was so different, but I found the people friendly and responsive. They were the farthest away from Yellowknife and the seat of government, but I wanted to make them feel the government was available to them. In many ways, the Inuit were the same as the Dene people, struggling with complex issues and making the move from igloos to living in a modern society.

In my trips to Baffin and the High Arctic, I relied heavily on regional staff to plan and organize my itinerary and handle the logistics. Michael Ferris, the regional superintendent of local government, who in later years served as a deputy minister in Nunavut, was particularly adept. During one trip we visited twelve of thirteen communities in the Baffin region (missing only Sanikiluak) in a mere six days, flying by Twin Otter. Mike had arranged two meetings a day with hamlet councils and residents, and everything went off without a hitch. When a tailwind brought us in to our last stop, Cape Dorset, an hour early, I teased Mike about his poor planning.

In my travels into the Inuvik and Central Arctic communities I felt fortunate to meet with many Inuit leaders whom I had gone to school with in residential schools in Inuvik and Yellowknife. This helped me forge good relationships and made my job fruitful and enjoyable.

Trips weren't always trouble-free. Once during the fall, I was in Pond Inlet for meetings with the hamlet council when a storm brought freezing rain, coating the roads and the airport in ice. For a few days, no vehicle could move in the community and Caterpillar tractors were used to bring water and dispose of sewage at the hotel where we stayed. Peter Fraser, the MLA for Sahtu, was my guest on this trip, and with playing cards and jokes he helped while away the time. Charles Dent, the mayor of Yellowknife and president of the Association of Municipalities was also with us, benefitting from seeing what far-flung communities had to contend with. We visited the schools and had more thorough meetings with the community, practically having to skate to some of these events. It was several days before a plane made it in from Resolute Bay to fly us out. It could have been worse. A few years earlier, one government employee was weathered into a community for sixty-three days. The minute he stepped off the plane in Frobisher Bay, he quit his job and headed south.

MAKING THE TRANSITION from being an ordinary MLA to being a minister was an interesting and complicated process. One day you're standing in the assembly asking questions, criticizing the government or making motions to get the government to do something. The next you're in cabinet, part of the government and in a position of power to make decisions. Now you had to answer the questions, not ask them. It was as stark as night and day.

Cabinet government was still in its infancy in the Northwest Territories. Although we had a government leader, the executive council—as the cabinet was officially called—was still chaired by the commissioner, John Parker. He also retained control of the Department of Personnel, a significant lever of control over government operations.

The federal government was in the process of transferring responsibility to the territorial government in the first of several rounds of devolution, a process that is still going on to this day. During the next four years, we would take over responsibility for community airports, highways and, most important of all, health.

As ministers acquired more power and responsibility, the relationship between the cabinet and other MLAs began to shift. We were certainly all aware of this; it was the main reason the legislative assembly had insisted on a two-year review of ministerial appointments. They were wary of losing their hard-won control over decision making. We were struggling to find a balance between consensus government based on northern and Aboriginal traditions, and the Westminster process of ministerial accountability. We had no political parties, and individual cabinet ministers had their own and often quite different political views, so in effect the cabinet was a permanent minority co-alition government. We were constantly mindful that any decision we made had to be supported by the assembly to be implemented. It made for interesting discussions around the cabinet table and de-manded careful navigation of both aspects of our government.

As one result, I needed to separate my role as minister from my responsibilities as an MLA. Particularly in 1984, I continued to raise matters of concern to my own constituents in the legislature. Clearly, I could have made my points privately—and sometimes did—with my colleagues in cabinet. However, by making my requests in public I hoped to make it clear that all MLAs—even those privileged to be ministers—still had to fight and sometimes lose battles for their con-stituencies. Sometimes the other ministers seemed surprised to have to field questions from a fellow cabinet member, but several of them subsequently followed suit when it was my turn to defend my budget, so I think it was a useful innovation.

At the same time, I was concerned that MLAs have as much input to the process of budgeting and law-making as possible. We had a sys-tem where the Standing Committee on Finance was able to comment on draft budgets—something that was unheard of in provincial and federal governments at the time though it is now quite common—but it was still somewhat limited, especially with respect to the capital plan. One innovation I proposed was to allow MLAs to see the five-year capital planning documents that the executive council was using rather than only the current year. This allowed greater MLA input but also moderated their demands, as they were able to see that many community needs were being accommodated over time.

Nonetheless budgets, especially for capital, were the greatest area of contention during my time as minister of local government. My department had the largest capital budget as we were responsible for providing basic infrastructure to local communities. From sporting facilities to airports, municipal offices and garages to water and sewer systems, I was responsible for the development of more than sixty communities spread over a territory larger than Quebec and Ontario combined. Demand always exceeded the supply of money, and finding regional and community balance while having the flexibility to meet sudden emergencies was a constant challenge. Most communities in the North didn't have a tax base, as there was little private property. Even the seven tax-based communities faced significant funding issues, with only Yellowknife being sufficiently large to finance the bulk of its needs.

The provision of clean water and the disposal of sewage was a particular challenge, especially in Arctic communities. You might think a land of ice and snow with endless lakes and numerous rivers would have no difficulty supplying fresh water, but such was not the case. In all communities in the Arctic and in the small communities in the west, it was not possible to put water and sewer lines in the ground. Lakes and rivers were often shallow and froze solid in winter. Moreover, surface water was often contaminated with sediment or organic material. Even when a community had a good reliable source of potable water, transporting it to people's homes was complex, especially during long stretches of forty-below weather. Trucks were the most common delivery system, especially in smaller communities.

It didn't help when engineers made mistakes, which fortunately didn't happen too often. Still, there was the case of Resolute Bay, one of the few small settlements with piped water. There, a new row-housing complex had been constructed and attached to the system. All the pipes ran above ground and were well insulated and heated. Unfortunately, the pipes in the complex itself were less well-protected and moreover, were placed along the north wall of the building. During the first winter they froze and burst. For many years, the complex sat empty, a silent testament to bad planning. Another community had a long pipe designed to carry water from a nearby lake situated on a plateau to the community; it too froze solid during its first year of operation.

FORTUNATELY, WE HAD far more success stories than failures. Pangnirtung, the second-largest community on Baffin Island, was a case in point. Sitting on the banks of a fiord that leads to Auyuittuq National Park, the hamlet obtained its water from a small river in the summer, and in the winter from a lake more than twenty kilometres distant on a plateau several hundred metres above the community. There were tremendous problems and expenses in maintaining the road and trucks under harsh conditions, and eventually another solution had to be found. Our department built a large reservoir lined with thick plastic and filled from the summer water supply. The reservoir was deep enough not to freeze in the winter and large enough to supply the entire community for eight or nine months, while having sufficient capacity for emergencies such as firefighting. I was present when it was finished and was happy the community had a good and reliable source of water.

Emergencies could happen any time and in the least expected places. In early 1984, for example, a study of the sewer system that served the central part of Yellowknife indicated a complete failure could occur at any time. Indeed, there had already been several small collapses. The cost of replacing the system was estimated at eight million dollars, a considerable sum of money at the time and more than could be found in the normal budget process by either the municipality or the territorial government. I approached the federal government—which had installed the original line thirty-five years before—for additional funds, and between the three levels of government we were able to make repairs before a disaster occurred. It may have helped to carry a short section of the dilapidated sewer pipe to Ottawa and put it on the minister's desk to make our point about the seriously rotten state of the sewage system. Maintaining infrastructure was always a challenge in the North, and I don't envy current governments who face increasing pressures caused by climate change and melting permafrost.

AS ONE MIGHT imagine, the constant fighting over limited resources created a certain amount of tension between ministers and MLAS. In early 1985 I proposed a hockey match between the cabinet and the rest of the MLAS. I was after all minister of Sport and Recreation and it seemed a good way to bring us all together while dealing with the winter doldrums. We ministers labelled ourselves the Sixth Floor Flyers (the sixth floor of the Laing Building was where our offices were located), and I gave everyone from both sides appropriate hockey nicknames. I was "Quick Nick" Sibbeston and we also had Tom "Boom Boom" Butters and "King" Richard Nerysoo and so on. On the other side were Ted "Rocket" Richard and Sam "The Slam" Gargan. It was all in good fun and the game, quite intentionally, ended in a 5–5 draw. It improved the mood in the assembly for some time.

I also recognized the need for good communication if the work I was doing was to be understood and accepted by MLAS and the public. I wasn't entirely satisfied with the bureaucratic style of my staff and toward the end of 1984 asked Mike Moore if he could find me someone who could write well and had a good understanding of the department's programs. He directed my attention to the Baffin Region. Hayden Trenholm, from Nova Scotia, had spent two years there as the senior municipal officer and was looking for a change. He was well-educated, had served as the president of the union local and had shown himself to be an excellent communicator. I asked about him on my next trip to the Baffin and Mike Ferris, whose opinion I greatly respected, recommended him highly, so I made arrangements to meet him. Hayden told me later that he had prepared for a lengthy interview, but I cut it short and hired him on the spot. He served me for the rest of my time as minister and when I became government leader, became my executive assistant. We stayed in touch over time and, a few years after I became senator, he agreed to come to Ottawa and serve as my policy advisor.

MY PERSONAL HEALTH was also going through ups and downs despite ongoing counselling and other efforts. I continued to suffer from the effects of residential school, which often left me depressed and uncertain about my role as husband and father. Occasionally I had lapses that later overwhelmed me with guilt and remorse.

In the summer of 1984, Pope John Paul II made his first visit to Canada. He wanted especially to meet with Aboriginal peoples, and Karen argued that Fort Simpson would be an ideal location for a meeting. I was skeptical that the pope would ever visit the North, let alone the tiny community of Fort Simpson, but Karen and other local women prevailed and were instrumental in persuading the officials who were organizing the pope's trip that Fort Simpson would be a good location for a large gathering.

On September 18, 1984, Aboriginal peoples from all over Canada converged on Fort Simpson to witness a visit by the pope. Thousands of people arrived in every imaginable way: motor vehicles from the south, planes from all areas of the country and boats from along the river. Campsites were set up in every available space, even on the small secondary airstrip on the far side of the community. People visited from camp to camp, sharing food cooked over open fires; in the evenings, smoke covered the town. A large log teepee with a podium was built on the flats where the pope was to meet with Aboriginal leaders. A replica of a beaver lodge and a drum was built with a place for a campfire at the entrance where the pope was to stop and pray before he made his way to the podium. A large circular arbour was built for drum dances and gatherings. The RCMP, who were responsible for the security, came by the hundreds and could be seen everywhere.

The night before the pope's arrival there was a large dance at the drum circle. Thousands of people attended, filling the circle with dancers and observers. I met lots of friends, including a woman I knew from earlier in my life. Caught up in the revelry and excitement, after a couple of dances, I invited the woman for a ride in my van. We drove out to a secluded area and sinned.

The next day, I was part of a delegation that included Bishop Piche, the governor general and local leaders and elders who were gathered at the airport to meet and welcome the pope as he stepped from the plane. We arrived in the dark and waited in the vehicle that would drive us out on the tarmac at the appointed time. As daylight came, fog lay across the runway so thick you couldn't see a foot in front of you. We remained hopeful as the bishop began reciting the rosary and led us in prayer. We thought our prayers had been answered when the Popemobile was rolled out onto the tarmac and we heard the plane circling overhead. Eventually, however, the sound of the plane receded as the plane diverted to Yellowknife. Our welcoming party returned to the community to wait with the people on the flats. As we drove back to town, we could see RCMP officers crawling out of culverts and coming out of the woods all along the highway where the pope and his entourage were to travel.

In town, the people were gathered patiently on the flats, the elderly huddled in blankets and warm coats. Fog permeated the area. It was hours before it finally cleared, and by then the pope was already on his way to Vancouver and his next scheduled event. As the people slowly made their way from the flats, I cried, thinking of their disappointment and wondering if my previous night's sinning had in some small way had a part in causing the fog to descend and spoil the occasion.

PERSONAL DIFFICULTIES ASIDE, there was still much to do for the territorial government to work for all its citizens. We had to overcome the divisions between the parliamentary system favoured by non-Aboriginals and the traditional ways of making decisions used by Natives.

With my combined portfolios of Local Government and Aboriginal Rights and Constitutional Development, I was able to tackle this governance issue on two fronts. I had been impressed by the Baffin Regional Council (BRC) during several visits to Frobisher Bay. The BRC was made up of representatives from all the municipalities of the region, including the Town of Frobisher Bay, all ten hamlets and the settlements of Resolute Bay and Grise Fiord. It was more than an organization of municipalities, however. The BRC dealt with a range of issues including wildlife management, social services and economic development. Technically advisory, with funding support from my department, the BRC had a lot of influence over the regional administration. Though a far cry from a real regional government, they did pass resolutions and received reports on progress from all the senior territorial bureaucrats.

I believed that elements of the BRC could be transferred to other regions and over the next couple of years I encouraged the creation and development of similar bodies throughout the North. In the Kitikmeot and Keewatin, this proved fairly easy. The Inuit were relatively new to organized communities—many had been created only in the fifties and sixties—and had little experience with the Department of Indian Affairs. They didn't come under the Indian Act so there were no reserves and no band councils; it was relatively easy for them to adopt the model that was so successful in the Baffin.

The situation in the west was quite different. Many of the communities were well established, and Aboriginal people had a long history of local government through band councils. When the territorial government tried to create municipal governments, they were viewed as an intrusion and an imposition. Most places ended up with both types of local government, competing with each other. The municipal councils had the money but the band councils had the legitimacy, especially in those communities where the population was 80 or 90 percent Aboriginal.

One approach to resolve this separation was to encourage the creation of charter communities, where the band and municipal councils were merged into a single governing body. They would receive funding from both levels of government and their powers would be broader than either alone. I had hoped it would be a way to bring Aboriginal and non-Aboriginal people together in places like Fort Simpson, but it didn't work out that way. Only a couple communities pursued it, mostly in the Sahtu, but we did recognize and establish them in the new Municipal Act that was being developed.

We were exploring a great many other ideas at that time, too, such as sources of municipal revenue that were more broadly based than property tax, as well as ideas like guaranteed seats for minorities (Aboriginal in large communities, non-Aboriginal in smaller ones) on community councils. Although most of these ideas were never incorporated in legislation, some seeds were planted: the Tli'cho, for example, took the idea of guaranteed Aboriginal representation even further in the self-government agreement they negotiated and adopted in 2005. While all permanent residents of each of the four

Tli'cho communities can vote for the local councils, half the seats are reserved for Tli'cho citizens. At the senior government level, where the Tli'cho exercise powers similar to that of a province, half the representatives plus the grand chief must be Tli'cho. This will remain true no matter what changes occur in the future—the agreement is protected by the Canadian constitution.

The situation was even more complicated in the Beaufort Delta region, with a number of Inuvialuit communities to the north and several Dene (Gwich'in) villages to the south and west. In the middle was Inuvik, where both groups mixed with a largely non-Aboriginal population. The town did not have any Aboriginal councillors, and I pointed this out as one of the deficiencies of the system. Local Inuvialuit leaders had been negotiating for years to form the Western Arctic Regional Municipality (WARM), which was meant to be a true regional government, largely independent from the one in Yellowknife. Little progress had been made. The federal government, for one, was not yet ready to discuss that level of self-government. I encouraged the local leaders to form a regional council, at least as a first step. It was opposed from both ends of the spectrum: the town of Inuvik dismissed it as another layer of bureaucracy; Aboriginal leaders were opposed to its advisory nature. Exasperated, I said that they should smarten up and start taking control. Regional councils might start as advisory but, as I had seen in the Baffin, once they started flexing their muscles and gained experience at making regional decisions, they could have a major effect on the territorial bureaucracy. Once again, *News/North* agreed with me, reporting on May 3, 1985, "It seems a group of communities can't lose when they are offered more power than they now have." However, these communities never did take me up on the offer, and regional government continues to be a challenge even after years of further self-government negotiations.

IN 1984, THE Committee for Original Peoples Entitlement (COPE) representing the Inuvialuit reached a historic land claims agreement with the federal government. The territorial government was not a party to these negotiations, but participated as part of the federal team. The Inuvialuit received surface rights to a large tract of land and subsurface rights to a smaller area within it. They also received cash and co-management rights over renewable resources, land and water for the entire settlement region. Over the years, the Inuvialuit have taken great advantage of this settlement to improve the social and economic lives of their people.

During this time I was active as chairman of the Western Constitutional Forum (WCF), which was the group set up to negotiate the boundary between east and west after territorial division and to develop and promote a new government for the west. The dividing line between the two territories was particularly contentious. The Nunavut Constitutional Forum wanted to include all the Inuit in the same territory, including the Inuvialuit in the Beaufort. Oil and gas was of course an issue, and I remember Larry Tourangeau, a Métis from the Sahtu, once punning when the debate was getting heated, "We'll have the oil and gas and you'll have Nunavut" ("none of it").

The WCF argued that division should follow natural transportation links and common economic interests. The Inuvialuit were tied to the west by common economic history and established road, air and sea transport routes. Family links were also strong between the Inuvialuit and the Central Arctic, and I made several trips to the Kitikmeot trying to convince them to stay in the west as well. I recall that a large community meeting in Coppermine became contentious as the debate went back and forth between us from the west and those favouring Nunavut. Peter Ittinuar, the MP at the time, went so far as referring to "Bloody Falls," where a number of Inuit were slaughtered by Dene travelling with Samuel Hearne in his overland trip to the region in 1771, as a reason why the Inuit should not remain with the Dene in the west.

COPE was using its organizational skills and recent land claims settlement as a lever against both sides to obtain the best deal for their communities. I was reasonably open to making concessions, provided COPE was willing to become part of the WCF and negotiate for greater autonomy within that forum. I wanted similar things for Dene regions and saw the advantage of having COPE as a power block in the west, rather than going off to Nunavut or worse yet becoming a separate territory as some like Charles Hoagak were demanding. In

January of 1985, we reached a tentative agreement to divide the territory on a more or less north–south line rather than along the treeline, with Cambridge Bay and Coppermine deciding whether they would be in the west or the east. The Inuvialuit communities would all stay in the west.

That agreement broke down some months later and a slightly different border was eventually drawn, though the Inuvialuit communities did remain in the Northwest Territories rather than going to Nunavut.

These debates, as well as those on the shape of a new western government, were still unresolved in the fall of 1985 when the time for the leadership review arrived. Although there had been some difficulties and criticisms of several ministers, including Government Leader Nerysoo, I expected the status quo to hold and that the issues I had pursued for the last two years would continue to dominate my agenda. It was not to be.

Chapter 12: Taking the Reins of Government

THE GOVERNMENT WAS midway through its four-year mandate, the previously agreed-to time when a review of ministers was to take place in October 1985. All eight ministers submitted their resignations to the commissioner and the selection process was repeated. In consensus government, ministers are accountable directly to the MLAs. In the absence of political parties, where the party leader becomes premier and chooses the ministers from within his caucus, MLAs in the Northwest Territories retain control over the selection of both the ministers and the leader.

Once again, the twenty-four caucus members gathered and all those interested in being ministers gave short speeches, after which secret-ballot voting took place. With the stipulation that there be four members each from east and west, the eight members receiving the most votes became ministers. The outcome was shocking. Both Government Leader Richard Nerysoo and Nellie Cournoyea, the minister of Renewable Resources, were dropped from cabinet. In their places Michael Ballantyne, the former mayor of Yellowknife, and Red Pedersen of Kitikmeot West were chosen. It was another case of the unpredictable nature of secret ballots and the unintended consequences of playing politics.

Although Richard Nerysoo had performed reasonably well, members were dissatisfied with Richard's performance as government leader. No particular issue brought him down; rather, members felt that he had not dealt with some issues in a strong enough manner.

Richard's position had been made even more difficult by the actions of Nellie Cournoyea, who was working hard in the background to discredit him. Her plan was to oust him so she could take over the job. The solid bloc of eastern MLAs and a few disgruntled members from the west led to Richard's dismissal. At the same time, western MLAs were determined that Nellie not profit from her political activity. If the east would not support Richard for leader, the western caucus was equally determined not to support Nellie. As a result, both were off the executive council and out of the running for government leader.

Who then would become government leader? Prior to the vote, it had never occurred to me to seek the position. I suppose I thought that with either Richard or Nellie in the chair, I would continue on much as I had before. Everything had changed.

The selection of cabinet occurred on a Friday, so I had the whole weekend to ponder the matter before the Monday vote for leader. For the next two days Karen and I talked ceaselessly about whether I should seek the position of government leader. Our family of six young children was uppermost in our minds as Karen and I considered the matter.

In the end Karen left it for me to decide. The compelling reason, I thought, was I had always espoused Aboriginal people taking responsibility and getting into positions of power, and there were only two Aboriginal members on the executive: Tagak Curley and myself. In all my years as an MLA, I had been in the forefront of fighting for responsible government, advocating a fully elected assembly and wresting power from the commissioners and the unelected executive council. Should I now, when there was a chance to take over the reins of government, grasp them, or would I hand the reins over to someone else?

I called a few of my friends and then began contacting MLAs I thought might be supportive. As I made the rounds, I realized I had significant support. Dennis Patterson from Frobisher Bay would be my opponent, and while the eastern caucus had the solidarity and determination to control cabinet selection, the west still had the majority, as we had recently demonstrated when Nellie was voted out.

On Monday morning I met with the rest of the western caucus and urged everyone to vote for me. I put it in the context of a fight between the west and east; because we had the majority, we could control the outcome. It felt that we were united, but one can never be sure when a secret ballot is cast.

When the full caucus met, there was excitement in the air. Dennis and I each made a brief speech. I emphasized my two effective years of work in cabinet, my transition from being a rambunctious MLA to being a responsible minister, my education, legal background, vision and dedication to lead the government. Dennis then made his pitch and the vote was held.

After a brief break the clerk, David Hamilton, re-entered the caucus room and announced that I had been chosen as government leader. It was exhilarating, with everyone, even the eastern members, congratulating me and slapping me on the back. I phoned to let Karen know and then I went out to meet the press. The media seemed surprised at my win. Toward the end of the press conference, one of the reporters asked if I was still apt to throw a cup. I replied that I didn't need to anymore as I was the leader, and everyone laughed.

MY TRANSITION TO government leader was not an easy one. Even though I had been a minister for two years, I still had the instincts of an Opposition member. As well, I had no role model of an elected leader who had really taken control of things. I had advised Richard to be more assertive; I now had to follow my own advice. I viewed my new role as a serious obligation to make the kinds of changes that I had been demanding for years: complete control of the instruments of government by elected officials and advancement of Aboriginal people into positions of authority in the territorial bureaucracy. There were a lot of pressing issues but none more pressing in my mind than taking the final steps in creating a truly responsible government.

During the next few days I met with Commissioner John Parker, who was available to provide advice. The transition to an elected cabinet had gone smoothly to this point in the North's political evolution. The remaining step was to replace Parker as chairman of the executive council and head of the Department of Personnel. In the Yukon, a lot of conflict had arisen with Commissioner Ione Christensen over this issue; Yukon's cabinet eventually began meeting early in the day so that by the time the Yukon commissioner showed up, all the decisions had been made.

Fortunately, we didn't face that same problem. John was very encouraging and co-operative and never resisted the transfer of power. Under the Northwest Territories Act, he had to seek the approval of the federal minister of Indian Affairs and Northern Development in order to step down, but he did so promptly and with enthusiasm. Minister David Crombie approved, and in January 1986 the Chair of Cabinet and responsibility for personnel were formally transferred to the government leader. We held a ceremony, opening up the cabinet room to the media for the event. I thanked John for his support in the development of political leadership in the North and called him "a friend of democracy." We marked the occasion by exchanging gifts: I received a gavel carved by Métis artist Sonny MacDonald, and John was given a portrait of himself as a young man.

My next task was to assign the cabinet portfolios, a job I took very seriously and carried out on my own. The CBC falsely reported that the commissioner had played a significant role, an error I felt obliged to correct in the legislative assembly. It was one of only a handful of times I felt it necessary to chastise the media for incorrect or biased reporting.

All the ministers were doing a good job in their portfolios, and I wanted to maintain a degree of continuity. At the same time, there were two new ministers, and as government leader and new Minister of Personnel, I needed to give up my other portfolios including Local Government. In the end, four ministers stayed where they were: Butters in Finance and Government Services, McLaughlin in Health and Social Services, Curley in Economic Development and Energy, and Patterson in Education and Constitutional Development. I also made Dennis Patterson the deputy leader. Red Pedersen was given responsibility for Renewable Resources and the newly created department of Culture and Communications.

My original desire was to keep Local Government, with its large capital budget and responsibility for communities, in the hands of a western minister. Mike Ballantyne, whom I had picked as Justice Minister, had been the mayor of Yellowknife and seemed ideal for

Local Government as well. He was happy with the assignment. However, Gordon Wray was pushing for that department, which he argued was a perfect complement to his current portfolio of Public Works. It could have become a serious conflict but Mike took the initiative and suggested a compromise. He would give up Local Government and take over the Housing Corporation, which also had a significant budget. Gordon, who I think wanted to keep all three, reluctantly agreed to the arrangement, and that was how the final assignments were made.

Although I remained the Associate Minister of Aboriginal Affairs and Constitutional Development, I did resign my position as Chair of the Western Constitutional Forum and declared I would henceforth be neutral on the issue of division.

One of the first things I did was appoint a new Deputy Minister of Personnel. Jake Heron from Fort Smith was the first Métis and the first northern-born Aboriginal to serve in such a senior position. Jim Bourque, who had served as Deputy of Renewable Resources since 1982, was a Cree from northern Alberta so, though most people still think of Jim as a true northerner, the role of pioneer really went to Jake. Early in his career while Jake was working in the Department of Economic Development and I was an MLA, I had received a letter from a territorial official stating that Jake didn't "know where his loyalties lay—with the government or with Indians"—so I knew he would be my kind of civil servant. Imagine a senior territorial civil servant denigrating an employee for having sympathy for Native people! But such was the bureaucracy at the time.

The population of the Northwest Territories was more than 50 percent Aboriginal, but only 17 percent of the civil service was Aboriginal. It had always been my goal to increase that percentage so the government could better represent the people it governed. There had been roadblocks to achieving that goal, not the least of which was the attitude of many Native people that working for the GNWT was not quite honourable. They would rather work for Native organizations where they felt more comfortable assisting and advancing their cause. With me as government leader and Aboriginal people at senior positions, that attitude had started to change.

Another roadblock to the goal had often been the Department of Personnel. Jake's appointment wasn't without controversy, of course, but it did lead to an increase of Native employees from 17 to 26 percent in just two years. We also brought a number of strong Aboriginal people into senior positions, scouring the horizon for all the best Native people then occupying positions in Native organizations, other governments or agencies. During my time as government leader, we appointed Joe Handley, an Aboriginal from Manitoba and later premier of the Northwest Territories, as deputy minister of Education, Ethel Blondin-Andrew (later an MP and federal cabinet minister) as assistant deputy minister of Culture and Communications, and Helen Adamache as regional director of the Kitikmeot region. Fred Koe was taken from the Inuvik regional office to become the assistant deputy minister of Economic Development and Tourism. Both Charlie and Bobby Overvold joined our government from Native organizations; Charlie became the executive director of Aboriginal Affairs in the Department of the Executive, and Bobby a special advisor to cabinet. I tried hiring George Tuccaro, who was working for the CBC, to be the press secretary operating out of my office, but he declined.

In making these appointments, I was always looking for qualified people who could be effective and bring about real change. I didn't believe in quotas or tokenism; I wanted Aboriginal people to succeed, so I certainly wasn't going to put them in positions they couldn't handle. Merit crossed all lines and was well-distributed between Natives and non-Natives, and between men and women.

Although it was well-known that I believed children were better off if women stayed home to raise them, it was less well-known that I also knew this wasn't always possible and I believed that women in the workplace deserved the same opportunities to advance as men.

When an opportunity to demonstrate that belief presented itself, I seized it. I had inherited a deputy minister of the executive from the commissioner. Bob Pilot was a former RCMP officer who had served as assistant deputy commissioner under Stu Hodgson. He was looked upon as part of the old guard that we were replacing, and so when an opening became available in Ottawa as the Northwest Territories liaison officer, I offered the position to him and he agreed to go. He spent several years assisting us with our relationships with federal departments before retiring.

I decided to hold an open competition for the vacant deputy position—the first time that had ever been done in the Northwest Territories—but I was determined that if a qualified woman applied I would hire her. As luck would have it, there were two excellent female applicants. I interviewed both as well as a strong male candidate. Louise Vertes, who had worked in Public Works and most recently as secretary to the Priorities and Planning Secretariat of cabinet, became the new deputy minister of the executive, a position she held until 1991.

With the expanded role I had claimed for government leader, I needed more support in my own office. I got Public Works to enlarge my office to provide for a meeting area and three additional office spaces nearby for staff who would serve me. I hired Hayden Trenholm as my executive assistant; he occupied an adjacent office with a hidden door through which he emerged whenever I needed him. He was a brilliant person with a master's degree in political science and had worked for me earlier when I was minister of local government. Just outside my door sat my secretary Darlene Powder, whom I hired from the Fort Smith Regional Director's office. I initially hired reporter Pat Scott as my press secretary, but he left after a few months to return to the CBC. I then hired Cindy Clegg, also a former reporter with the CBC, who stayed with me throughout my term. Finally I hired Mike Whittington, a political science professor from Carleton University, as principal secretary and constitutional advisor; he also stayed with me till the end of my term. Mike provided great advice to me and to the cabinet, especially when we were dealing with the Meech Lake Accord. He later became the chief federal negotiator for the Yukon land claims, spending eight years guiding it to completion.

Getting my team together took several months; it wasn't until April or May that everyone was in place. Meanwhile, the business of government couldn't wait. There were many issues that required immediate attention—the implementation of the Official Languages Act, Expo 86 and the involvement of the Northwest Territories in national political and constitutional meetings—as well as the day-to-day business of running and financing a government.

John Parker had always been a good chairman of the executive council and served as a good model. Organized and fair, he never tried to dominate the debate. Discussions were kept reasonable and I don't recall many heated arguments or contentious votes on major issues. Once he had been replaced as chair, he soon moved away from the main table, sitting at a side table reserved for advisors. Halfway through my term he stopped coming to cabinet meetings altogether.

As chairman I tried to keep a similar tone, and for the most part I succeeded. Cabinet meetings were business-like. Everyone contributed to the discussion to reach a consensus outcome. Big issues during my tenure, such as implementing the Native employment policy and decentralizing the Fort Smith region to area centres in Fort Simpson and Rae-Edzo, were approved without much dissension. Few if any contentious issues even required a vote.

Not that our meetings weren't lively. All the ministers had strong personalities and some were quite aggressive. Gordon Wray was boisterous and loud like a little bull in china shop. Mike Ballantyne was also loud, but big and quite manipulative. He was like a poker player, keeping a straight face but scheming and playing his hand to win.

Tom Butters was our elder, with the most years in cabinet. He was generally calm and gave good advice, though he was always firm when it came to spending money. Tom kept unusual hours, going to sleep early in the evening and coming to work at three or four in morning. We used to tease him that he stood on guard for us and ran the government at night while we slept.

Bruce McLaughlin was easygoing and often injected a note of humour into the meetings. Tagak Curley was full of energy and enthusiastic about Native employment, economic development and especially the Northwest Territories Pavilion at Expo 86. Dennis Patterson and Red Pedersen were always well briefed and calm in their approach.

We met three times a week—Priorities and Planning Committee on Tuesday, Financial Management Board on Wednesday and full cabinet on Thursday. I always began meetings—which ran from nine to about noon—with a prayer and then we got right down to business. We would start most meetings with a brief *in-camera* session to deal with sensitive issues. The only non-cabinet member present, as a rule, was principal secretary Mike Whittington, though John Parker sometimes sat in during the early days. Once the regular meeting started, Dick Abernathy, the cabinet secretary, would enter the room and start to take notes. He was like the fly on the wall who heard and witnessed everything that was ever said in cabinet.

I was responsible for setting the agenda, which was handed out a few days earlier with briefing notes and supporting materials attached. I made sure I read all the cabinet materials at least the day before. Ministers had to defend their submissions before the other members; they would make opening remarks while deputy ministers and other officials, who waited outside until their item came up, were available to answer any questions. Nothing went through cabinet without careful analysis and scrutiny.

I recall the issue of the poor maintenance of highways. I called the deputy minister to task, saying, "We've been building roads in the North for decades. Why haven't we figured out how to build proper roads so they don't heave or need constant repairs?" I guess the same question could be asked today. I was constantly after the Housing Corporation, as well, about foundations. I wanted them to put houses on proper foundations and not up on blocks or metal piles as they were in the eastern Arctic. Some officials found the meetings stressful, and once a person even had to be taken away in an ambulance when he collapsed during a grilling.

I HAD ONE more major change to make to the structure of government in the Northwest Territories. Each region of the North—Baffin, Keewatin, Kitikmeot, Inuvik and Fort Smith—had been organized in such a way as to have some degree of autonomy. This was a holdover from the days of Commissioner Hodgson, who had appointed regional directors as kind of mini-commissioners. Officially, the regional director job was to coordinate the administration of each region and implement policies made at headquarters. In reality, they exercised a great deal of control over all aspects of government operations and often seemed to have more power than ministers. As we implemented fully responsible government, it was clear they had to be reined in.

As minister of local government I had promoted regional and tribal councils as a means of transferring some power to communities and away from the bureaucracy. However, they could never be more than advisory and could not be allowed to interfere with ministerial accountability. Moreover, clever regional directors soon realized they could use the councils to shore up their own autonomy. In the fall of 1986, I instituted a review of all regional and tribal councils with a report due a year later.

The chair of the review committee was George Braden, who had been the first elected member to serve as government leader back in 1979. The purpose of the review was to find a way to have strong regional consultative processes while maintaining central accountability. The report was tabled in the legislative assembly just prior to the 1987 election, and its recommendations guided the development of regional operations in the years leading up to division.

However, I wasn't prepared to wait years before making immediate changes. By giving ministers greater control over their departments, including the appointment of their deputies, and by encouraging them to get out to the regions to deal directly with local leaders, I was able to systematically reduce the influence of the regional directors and gradually ensure that they were subservient to ministers and deputies. Stu Hodgson had a practice of appointing retired military or RCMP officers as regional directors. They took orders and didn't question his authority. We shuffled or retired them and put in men and women who were in tune with our new type of representative administration.

A more pressing matter was the reorganization of the Fort Smith region. When the GNWT first moved north in 1967, people in Fort Smith assumed that their community would be chosen as the new capital. It was a well-established community about the same size as Yellowknife and had better links to the south. However, Yellowknife was both more central geographically and the centre of the mining industry, and it became the capital. As a consolation prize, Fort Smith was made a regional centre, and eventually also became the home of Arctic (later Thebacha) College.

On the face of it, the organization of the Fort Smith region seemed ridiculous. Communities such as Fort Simpson and Rae-Edzo, north of Yellowknife, were far removed from Fort Smith and had no direct communication links. People who wanted to deal with the regional administration often found it necessary to go through Yellowknife to get there. I had long been a critic of this set-up and now was in a position to do something about it. I knew there would be some resistance but I also knew I was right.

To deal with the issue, I obtained cabinet approval to hire Ewan Cotterill, who had previously done work on the establishment of the GNWT, to study the Fort Smith region and make recommendations respecting its future. Cotterill found that the region had the highest percentage of middle managers in the North and that much time and resources were wasted on communications and travel. Although cabinet didn't accept all his recommendations, the key elements were adopted in the fall of 1986 and I went to Fort Smith to personally announce the changes that would take place. I hired Gary Black, former regional director of the Fort Smith region, to implement the changes.

Twenty-four positions were removed from Fort Smith, and area offices were set up in Rae-Edzo (to deal with the Tli'cho communities) and Fort Simpson (to manage the Deh Cho area). Fort Smith was reduced to an area office to serve the communities south of Great Slave Lake. This general structure has remained in place ever since.

THUS BY THE end of the summer of 1986, I had made or initiated major changes to the face of government. It had not been easy, and I had suffered a great deal of stress and occasional bouts of depression. I wasn't the only one in cabinet to experience the strain, and when I suggested we have stress-management workshops and retreats, the other ministers agreed. The workshops helped me through many rough patches and allowed me to devote my full energy to the tough work ahead.

Many of us were new to government, and we had been placed in demanding roles; initiating change was bound to be stressful. I quickly learned that with power came great tension. I had made tremendous changes in government during my two years as minister and now as government leader. The reviews had generally been good, with the *News/North* praising me as a master of compromise and many commentators applauding the changes we had made to the public service. Still, it was sometimes hard to forget I wasn't still the brash young critic of government. I recall visiting Fort Providence, where there were many people critical of new property taxation rules for houses built on band land. I suggested that perhaps they shouldn't pay, that they should stand up to government. As I warmed to the topic of how government needed to be fought at every step, Mike Whittington leaned over and whispered in my ear, "Nick, you *are* the government!" He was right, of course.

I and my cabinet colleagues were the government now, and if we wanted to accomplish things, we simply had to roll up our sleeves and get to work.

Chapter 13: An Evolving Territory

WHILE A MAJOR focus for me was on changing the nature of government in the North, we were also being affected by numerous external events.

The division debate was still raging, and the issue of where the boundary would be drawn was a hot topic. The Inuvialuit claim had been ratified and was being implemented. The Dene and Métis of the west and the Inuit in the eastern Arctic were making significant progress on their negotiations, and there was every reason to think that a pair of settlements would be reached covering the entire Northwest Territories. I had always viewed the settlement of land claims as critical to the future economic and social well-being of Aboriginal people. It provided for ownership of lands, resources and monies to invest. It would also provide a degree of certainty to permit businesses to thrive in the North.

Although we could not foresee it at the time, the Dene and Métis claim would ultimately founder. An agreement-in-principle was reached in 1988 and a final one was initialled in April 1990, but it was not universally supported. The critical issue proved to be extinguishment of Aboriginal title. Those regions close to the Inuvialuit could see the benefits they were already reaping and were worried about being left behind. They wanted to reach a settlement even if it included extinguishment. Southern Métis, too, were willing to go along with the agreement-in-principle. The Dene of the south, however, felt that they could get a better deal through further negotiation. In July 1990, at the Dene Assembly, the final agreement was rejected. In response the minister revoked it and announced his intention to pursue agreements on a regional basis. The Gwich'in of the Delta settled in 1991 and the Sahtu followed suit a year later. The Tli'cho eventually reached a final agreement on both a land claim and self-government in 2005. The agreement didn't include an extinguishment clause (more recent agreements have avoided that language) but does have one stating that they will not assert rights that aren't covered in the agreement, which provides an adequate degree of certainty to government and industry. Unfortunately neither the Deh Cho (my home region) nor the Akaitcho region, south and east of Yellowknife, have settled their claims and some communities have even broken away to reach their own deals.

There can be little doubt that the breakdown of the Dene and Métis claim had tremendous consequences for the development of government and the growth of the economy in the western Arctic. The complexity of the regulatory system is due, at least in part, to the patchwork implementation of land claims. As well, those regions without settled claims were more likely to be opposed to economic development or even if not opposed, less capable of taking advantage of the opportunities presented to them. Though of course that was not the only factor.

Also much of the work that the Western Constitutional Forum was doing on the structure of a future government for the west after division was predicated on a single unified claim covering all of the Dene and Métis. Such a comprehensive claim would have strengthened the hand of the Aboriginal peoples of the west, who would be in a slight minority following division, and would have put them in a position to demand a government system that more closely represented their traditions and interests. Regional claims, or no claims at all, shifted the balance of power in favour of the GNWT, who had access to much greater resources. I take some solace that many of the changes I had supported in the GNWT—to make it more respectable for Native people to take part as politicians and public servants—helped ensure that the government continued to evolve in a way that was inclusive of Aboriginal values. In particular, the expansion of support for Native languages and the inclusion of Aboriginal culture in such things as the assembly or the naming of geographical places demonstrated that the GNWT was open to all northerners.

WHILE THIS WAS going on, big changes were being made to the powers and jurisdiction of the territorial government. When the government had moved north in 1967 it had, over the subsequent five years, taken over responsibility for many provincial-style programs, such as education and municipal affairs. However, many programs were still operated by the federal government including forestry, transportation, health, prosecutions and the management of land and resources.

After the election of 1983, a further round of devolution occurred: the transfer of authority from the federal to territorial government. Over the next four years, and especially during my time as government leader, this process accelerated. By 1987 we had taken over highways and community airports from the feds as well as forestry (primarily fire suppression) and health. We also acquired a bigger role in land and water management, though jurisdiction remained federal. Health was of course the biggest one, and the negotiations to acquire adequate funding and personnel were tough. We didn't get all we wanted, but we ultimately decided that we could do a better job locally with fewer resources than the federal government could with more money but with all decisions being made back in Ottawa.

We faced a lot of opposition from Aboriginal organizations, who were concerned about the effects of federal–territorial devolution on self-government. In April 1986, I signed a memorandum of understanding with all the northern Aboriginal organizations, approving devolution in principle (including the devolution of land and resources) and assuring them that it would proceed without prejudicing their claims. We slowed things down to permit ongoing consultation, but in the end much of devolution—though not control over land and resources—occurred, and most people in the North would agree that the territorial government, while not perfect, was a big improvement over what came before.

Devolution of land and resources in the Northwest Territories finally occurred on April 1, 2014 with the agreement and participation of some though not all Aboriginal groups. I hope people can look back on what we accomplished in the 1980s and see devolution as a positive thing.

CONSTITUTIONAL DEVELOPMENT WAS not only of concern in the North; it was a major component of political life in Canada, too. The Canada Act (1982) had repatriated the constitution and introduced the Charter of Rights and Freedoms, but there was still unfinished business, especially with respect to Aboriginal people. The 1982 constitution contained a clause recognizing and affirming existing Aboriginal and treaty rights without defining what these rights were. Between March 1983 and March 1987, four federal-provincial First Ministers' Conferences to define and implement these rights were held. I attended two of these as associate minister of Aboriginal Affairs and Constitutional Development and another as government leader.

In those days, the territorial government had a very limited role at First Ministers' Conferences; we were technically viewed as part of the federal delegation. Generally, we did not sit at the main table except when we were given a brief opportunity to make a statement. The Aboriginal conferences were different in that the government leaders of both the Northwest Territories and the Yukon were able to participate fully in most sessions along with the leaders of the five national Aboriginal organizations, though not in the private sessions held between the prime minister and premiers. In fact, the territorial leaders were not even recognized as premiers, though both Tony Penikett of the Yukon and I began to adopt the term informally in our own speeches and public comments.

Our government tried to make positive interventions in the process, though it was sometimes difficult. John Amagoalik, who represented the Inuit, viewed the GNWT with suspicion and never missed an opportunity to suggest that we were dragging our feet on division. I didn't take it personally. I had always been supportive of division, even if I had been a tough negotiator on the placement of the boundary. I also sympathized with John; after all, the west had not voted strongly in favour of division and Yellowknife, where most territorial bureaucrats lived, had been strongly opposed. In his place, I would have been suspicious, too.

Some premiers, especially those from Quebec and some of the smaller provinces, were supportive of our interventions. In those days, only Quebec and the Northwest Territories had had real-life experience with the impacts of land claims on their governments and societies, and we could both see the benefits of recognizing Aboriginal rights. Overall, my experiences at the conferences were positive, even though I often sensed the prime minister and some premiers from larger provinces were impatient and inattentive whenever either of the territories raised a point.

In any case, the process eventually failed, despite serious efforts from dozens of elected leaders and thousands of officials in government and Aboriginal organizations. No agreement was reached on further changes to the constitution, though the matter would come up again in the Meech Lake Accord a few months later in 1987. It was left to the courts to interpret what Section 35 of the constitution really means, and numerous decisions over the last twenty-five years have gradually defined the extent and limit of those rights.

IN ADDITION TO the Conferences on Aboriginal Rights, I took part in the annual First Ministers' Conferences in November of 1985 and 1986 and Premiers' Conferences in August 1986 and 1987. Whenever I was given a chance to speak, I used it as an opportunity to educate southerners about the North and to impress upon other governments the important role the territorial governments could and should play in national debates.

These days, no one would think to exclude a territorial premier or minister from intergovernmental meetings or from discussions affecting the constitution, the economy or any matter of national importance. However, in the mid-1980s, exclusion was still the norm, although signs of change had begun to appear. Territorial ministers were increasingly invited to observe and often fully participate at conferences, especially those dealing with provincial-type responsibilities such as education and local government. When I attended the premiers' conference in Edmonton in August 1986, neither territorial government leader was invited to any of the private sessions. We were able to make a ten-minute speech each during the one open session and we were invited to all the social events, but generally we were on the outside looking in. Even the official photograph had two versions—one where we were included and one where we weren't! Senator John Buchanan, who was the premier of Nova Scotia at those meetings, often reminded me that he saw me in those pictures whenever he walked up his stairs leading to the second floor of his home.

By the following year in Saint John, New Brunswick, things had improved somewhat. Our government had been active on a number of fronts, and at the 1986 conference, I had given a well-received speech on developing a new Northern vision for the economy. Although we were still limited in our participation in 1987, both territorial premiers—as we were now calling ourselves—were included in the private conference session dealing with the economy. (By 1991, territorial premiers were invited to all private sessions and beginning in 1992 were listed as full delegates with the other premiers.) It helped that the 1987 conference was hosted and chaired by Richard Hatfield of New Brunswick. As the premier of the only officially bilingual province, he was sensitive to the concerns of minorities and he knew that both the Yukon and the Northwest Territories were on the road to joining the bilingual club.

In any case, I was allowed to attend this private session on the economy with my executive assistant as my sole advisor. The discussion, which lasted about two hours, was wide-ranging but focused primarily on energy, the economy and the future of confederation, all topics of considerable interest to the Northwest Territories. Premier Hatfield was a very good chair and made sure that everyone got a chance to speak, including the territorial leaders. I recall that Premier Robert Bourassa, who seemed somewhat disengaged through much of the talk, perked up whenever the North was mentioned. He had a great interest in developing northern Quebec, primarily as a source of hydroelectricity, and was interested in how land claims and Aboriginal rights might affect that. Brian Peckford was as boisterous in private as he was in public and spent much of the meeting with a huge cigar clutched in his hand, though thankfully he didn't light it until the session was wrapping up. Howard Pawley, who was always calm in public, seemed surprisingly fretful in private, constantly pointing out the downside of any development. The late Joe Ghiz, although he came from the smallest province, Prince Edward Island, always had big ideas and contributed many thoughtful remarks. All in all, it was a fascinating experience, and marked one of the highlights of my time on the national stage. I made it a practice to stop in and visit premiers whenever I was in their capitals and remember well private office visits with Premiers Bill Vander Zalm and Joe Ghiz.

BY 1987, A new constitutional initiative had been put forward by Prime Minister Mulroney and the premiers after a private meeting at Meech Lake, from whence the accord drew its name. The territorial governments had not been invited to participate and we learned about it the way most people in Canada did: by reading the newspapers. Not surprisingly, territorial interests had been completely excluded from consideration. Under the accord, provinces would have an even greater say in the creation of new provincial jurisdictions, a power that had originally been exclusively federal. Although there was no strong desire to move quickly to provincial status, both territorial governments saw this as effectively preventing it from ever happening. Provinces would also be able to extend their borders northward without the consent of territorial legislatures or residents and were give a role in selecting senators and Supreme Court judges, a right denied to the territories. As well, Aboriginal concerns had fallen completely off the agenda.

While we didn't oppose other elements of the Accord, such as those that would have recognized Quebec as a distinct society or would have increased provincial powers, we were strongly opposed to the key elements affecting the territories. There was considerable debate in the assembly and strong support for the government to take an active role, not in opposing the accord but in seeking changes to it.

We began our campaign by taking out a full-page ad in *The Globe and Mail* outlining the GNWT's objection to the offending clauses. We travelled to Ottawa to lobby the federal government and our ministers took every opportunity to raise concerns with their federal and provincial counterparts. At one point, we were able to persuade Ed Broadbent, then leader of the NDP and a supporter of the accord, to raise our issues in the House of Commons. The accord was the main topic of my public speech at the premiers' conference in 1987, where I said, "My fellow premiers, I had come to expect more vision from Canada's leaders. We should all certainly welcome Quebec into its rightful place in the Constitution of Canada but I can see no legal or political rationale to justify crushing the hopes and aspirations of the people of the Northwest Territories and the Yukon to achieve this goal."

It was clear that our pleas were falling on deaf ears so in late 1987, as my term as government leader was coming to an end, a charter challenge to the accord was launched with my name put forward as the appellant. The suit argued that my rights were being discriminated against because I had been excluded from the opportunity of being appointed to the Supreme Court or the Senate. The irony of the latter is not lost on me today.

Of course, the territorial governments were not the only groups opposed to the Meech Lake Accord. Although the accord was initially supported by the public, the tide began to shift as more and more voices were raised against one or more provisions. The amendments had to be adopted within three years of the accord being signed, and a mere twenty days before that deadline, further meetings were held to try to change the deal. The territorial governments were initially invited, but a week before the conference, Prime Minister Mulroney decided they were too insignificant for full participation and the territorial premiers were reduced to attending by video conference. Some changes reflecting our concerns were made: our governments were given a role in nominating senators and Supreme Court justices and promises were made for further discussions around Aboriginal rights and the formation of new provinces. Regardless, a few months later the accord collapsed when Elijah Harper refused unanimous consent to proceed by raising an eagle feather in the Manitoba legislature and when Premier Clyde Wells of Newfoundland cancelled a free vote in his provincial legislature that seemed doomed to fail.

BACK IN EARLY 1984, John Munro, Minister of Indian Affairs and Northern Development in the dying days of the Trudeau government, came to Yellowknife to meet with the executive council. The federal government had decided to extend its policy on bilingualism to the North; they could and would pass legislation forcing our government to become bilingual and there was nothing we could do about it. However, their preference was that we pass legislation ourselves, and they were willing to add money to our base funding to cover the cost.

I had long been a defender of Aboriginal languages and frankly I resented the imposition of French on our territory for the benefit of a very small minority, while the majority of people in the Northwest Territories were Aboriginal. At this time, interpreter services were provided in the legislature and the courts, but the programs were underfunded. Aboriginal languages were also included in the school curricula, especially in the Inuit areas, but these programs too were underfunded and were provided on only a limited basis. Now French would be mandated throughout the territories, not just in the legislature and courts but in the provision of education and government services.

The Yukon government had simply agreed, but in the GNWT it seemed to me and to other ministers that there might be room to negotiate. After all, Minister Munro was gradually accepting greater control by northern politicians, and the federal government didn't want to be seen as the bad guys. Moreover, Munro knew that although the federal government could pass legislation, they would still need our cooperation to implement it. Eventually, the federal government agreed that we could determine the level of recognition afforded to Aboriginal languages as long as it didn't exceed that granted to English and French. It was also agreed that some funds would be provided for Aboriginal languages. Shortly after that the government in Ottawa changed, but the Mulroney government was equally determined to extend French into the North.

Cabinet debated at considerable length how to proceed and what shape the legislation should take, specifically what status would be accorded Aboriginal languages. Of course, I was pushing to have all Aboriginal languages in the North recognized as official on the same footing as English and French. Our legal and financial advisors told us that we couldn't do that and we should accept incremental changes for the time being. I didn't agree, arguing strenuously that we indeed had the jurisdiction over Aboriginal languages and we should make sweeping changes now when we had the chance. But I was alone in cabinet in holding this view, so I relented. The notion of incremental changes instead of forging full speed ahead bothers me to this day, as it seems an excuse to do little or nothing.

In the end, we passed an Official Languages Act in 1984 granting full official language status to English and French and official recognition to seven Aboriginal languages. All Aboriginal languages were equal and to some extent, notably in the legislature and the courts, they were treated similarly to English and French. However, the provision of government services in Aboriginal languages was only on a community-by-community basis, where numbers warranted and capacity existed. So services might be provided in Inuvialuktun in Paulatuk, South Slavey in Fort Simpson or Tli'cho in Rae-Edzo. There were also provisions but no guarantees for Aboriginal language education.

It soon became clear to me that the government simply didn't have the capacity to implement the provisions of the act on the schedule originally planned. Federal funds had been transferred but we had a shortage of French-speaking staff in headquarters and most regions, and it would take time to build up our capabilities. As well, I wanted to get a head start on the development of our Aboriginal languages programs. We had created a Department of Culture and Communications to handle these new programs, but it had capacity issues as well.

I went to Ottawa and met with Benoît Bouchard, then Minister of State for languages in the Mulroney government. The two main points I made to him were first that we didn't have the ability to meet the legislative deadlines in our act, and second and more importantly, the act focused on dry formalities such as the provision of translated legislation rather than on the living aspect of the French language, the way it was used in day-to-day life. He was very open to considering these issues and in redirecting funds for French into more practical areas.

In February 1986 I introduced amendments to the NWT Official Languages Act to extend the deadline for implementation by three years. A month later Minister Bouchard came to the legislative assembly and spoke to MLAS. I answered him in English, French, Inuktitut and Slavey. That same day, I tabled the report of the Task Force on Aboriginal Languages that was to guide government policy for some years to come and signed a five-year funding agreement with Minister Bouchard that would provide $16 million for Aboriginal language development.

At the time I had hoped we could raise the status of Aboriginal languages to the same level as French and English during the life of our government and indeed made such a commitment in the assembly that March. The task proved more onerous than I hoped and changes were not made until 1990, while I was still an MLA but no longer a minister.

THE ECONOMY IS always of central concern to any government and it was no different during my time as government leader. I had always had admiration for people who went into business—I viewed it and still view it as one of the toughest things you can do—and I always encouraged Aboriginal people to take that step. I had organized a co-op in Fort Simpson shortly after I returned there in 1970. I had even dabbled in business myself, both when I set up my law office in Yellowknife in the mid-1970s and on several occasions as a general contractor to build my own house.

Still I only really began to understand the role of government in supporting and stimulating the economy after I entered cabinet, especially after I became government leader. Tagak Curley, an Inuk from the Keewatin, was enthusiastic about the ability of the private sector. At the same time he saw a clear role for government, both through its own expenditures and through its support of the business community. I was much influenced by his arguments and when circumstances required me to take over the Economic Development and Tourism

portfolio in March 1987, I tried to bring the same energy and enthusiasm to the role as he had.

The territorial economy was heavily dependent on non-renewable resource development: mining, and oil and gas. Gold mining
was at the heart of Yellowknife, a city Indian Affairs Minister David
Crombie once described as "two gold mines separated by three lay-
ers of government." There were several smaller gold mines north of
the city. Pine Point had been a major lead-zinc producer (though it
was in the process of shutting down) and Tungsten on the far west of
the Northwest Territories operated on a sporadic basis producing its
namesake metal. Exploration for new mines was also a major component of the industry, and local bush pilots were kept busy flying
prospectors out onto the land in search of the next big thing. (Of
course, no one in those days thought the next big thing would be
diamonds.)

Oil had been produced at Norman Wells since the Second World
War and in 1986, despite what the Berger Report had recommended,
a small pipeline was built by Interprovincial Pipelines Ltd. to carry oil
south to Alberta. The company later changed its name to Enbridge.
The company had offered the Dene Nation a 10 percent stake in the
pipeline, which our government supported, but they had refused,
feeling it would compromise their independence and freedom to oppose the pipeline for environmental and other reasons.

Meanwhile, hundreds of millions of dollars, mostly taxpayer
money through the Petroleum Incentive Program (PIP), had been
spent in the Beaufort Delta looking for oil and gas. Large gas deposits
had been found there in the early 1970s and during the 1980s nearly
ninety wells were drilled. I recall flying in a huge twin-blade helicop-
ter out to Gulf's Amauligak oil rig with most of the cabinet in the winter of 1986. The rig was frozen into the shallow ocean and was a largely
self-contained community on the ice.

By the mid-1980s the Mulroney government was winding down
the PIP grants as part of the dismantling of the National Energy Program, and the economy in Inuvik was severely affected. Added to the
general downturn in the world economy at that time, both oil and gas
and mining were struggling to keep going.

The rest of the Northern economy was quite small by comparison, with government and related service industries playing a significant role in most communities. There was some tourism, and with Expo 86 our government was making a significant investment in trying to expand that sector. There was fishing in Great Slave Lake, and traditional economic activities such as hunting, trapping and arts and crafts played a small but significant role, especially in smaller communities. Forestry, farming and manufacturing were almost non-existent.

Faced with a recession compounded by federal spending cuts, our government made the decision to run deficit budgets in both 1986 and 1987, hoping to stimulate the economy by maintaining government services while building new infrastructure that would help develop communities and support economic activity. At the national level we lobbied federal and provincial governments on a number of fronts to see Northern development as a key part of Canada's future economic growth. During my speech at the First Ministers' Conference in November 1986, I called for a new Northern vision (similar to that of the late Prime Minister John Diefenbaker) that would settle Aboriginal claims and advance constitutional development in the North. Investments in transportation and other infrastructure would open up the North to greater resource development and integrate it into the Northern economy. We were already working closely with the federal government on some of these initiatives through a committee that included three federal ministers, both Northwest Territories MPs and a committee of territorial ministers, but I wanted to put the North on a national stage by reminding the premiers that every job created north of sixty produced tens of jobs in their jurisdictions. The speech was well-received in the North but I'm not sure how much resonance it had down south (though perhaps Stephen Harper, who has spoken in similar terms, came across it in his younger years).

It has always been difficult to get the attention of people outside the North, and matters of the economy were no different. We made our views known on free trade and regional development, but we always knew it would be a struggle to be heard or to have much influence. Still, I think that I and my colleagues always hit above our weight, as they say in boxing, and were able to achieve some significant results.

For example when the Mulroney government was making significant cuts to regional development funds, I obtained an exemption for the Northwest Territories.

One time we did make a significant impact on the south was during Expo 86, when the NWT pavilion was rated by visitors as one of the hits of the show. Although I and every other MLA supported the effort and each minister made a special contribution from their department (as minister of local government I created a display of community flags, many of which were commissioned specifically for the Expo), it was Tagak Curley who was the driving force. He threw his heart and soul into the project, working with architects, program staff and even the chefs at the restaurant to create a true northern experience for visitors. Former government leader George Braden was hired to manage the pavilion, which was designed to look like an iceberg, all glass and angles, and the staff was all from the Northwest Territories. Icicles, the restaurant in the pavilion, served traditional northern dishes like muskox, caribou and Arctic char and served drinks chilled with actual iceberg ice. It did well over a million dollars' business in the six months it operated. I visited several times as government leader and took my whole family during Northwest Territories Day in June 1986. It was an experience to make any northerner proud.

Chapter 14: Struggles and Scandals

THE PERIOD FROM 1983 to 1987 was one of great progress and achievement for the Northwest Territories. As a government, we had completed the transition, begun in the late 1970s, from being dominated by the commissioner to having elected politicians in control. We had achieved responsible government, accountable to the people through the legislative assembly. Working with my colleagues, I had accomplished much of what I had set out to do.

However, none of this was accomplished without controversy. MLAS and the media didn't always agree with my decisions or actions. It was a struggle at times to maintain consistency and integrity in cabinet, and we had plenty of ongoing disagreements with the federal government. All these things were stressful and yet for the most part, I never felt they were things I couldn't deal with and overcome.

But success did not come without a price. Throughout my time as minister and especially as government leader, I struggled with an anxiety disorder now recognized as post-traumatic stress disorder (PTSD), resulting from the traumas of my childhood. Eventually, I also suffered from mild depression brought on by years of trying to cope with anxiety. At any given time, 10 percent of Canada's population suffers from some form of depression, a mental illness caused by chemical imbalance in your body or by trauma suffered during one's life. I did not experience depression until I took on the responsibilities of being a minister in government, when I began experiencing anxiety, tension and insomnia.

The change from being an ordinary MLA to being a minister was pronounced. As an MLA, I had freedom to work at my pace and do my work as I felt like it. I dealt with a lot of issues and had periods when my work was intense, but I had some control and could engage intensely or withdraw as I felt. A minister's job was full-time with no respite; issues had to be dealt with regardless of my own feelings. I was acutely conscious that a Native person taking on such roles was new, and I felt compelled to succeed at any personal cost. I had been vocal in demanding change, and now that I was in a position to do something about it, I needed to be especially effective. Thus, I placed myself on a treadmill—running constantly with no end in sight. I felt as if the whole North was watching my every move. I felt compelled to be a super minister and accomplish super feats.

Being a politician was a noble undertaking with an opportunity to do good for people. For some reason I wasn't able to cope with the pressure and didn't have the resilience day in and day out to perform to the best of my abilities. The role of minister had its pressures, but the heightened fear and anxiety I experienced went far beyond the ordinary tensions associated with the work. I had the education, ability and experience to do the job, but I was anxious and nervous, and as each day came to an end, I could not let go and be confident that everything would be fine the following day. Instead of sleeping, I worried. It was painful getting up in the morning, feeling tired and knowing I had a busy day ahead of me. As I performed tasks, I would tell myself, "See how easy that was?" I had made mountains out of tiny anthills. I knew rationally that the things I had to do were within my abilities, but emotionally I was a wreck, and it often took sheer guts and determination to get me through the day.

I had already accomplished a great deal. As a teenager, I learned to play guitar well enough to play in a band and I also became a good hockey player. Although I had to repeat grade nine, I was generally an excellent student who got good grades. I had a bachelor's degree in political science and a law degree. I had married a wonderful woman and now I had a great family. I'd been a hard-hitting member of the legislative assembly, facing down government officials and raising contentious issues. I was a lawyer—the first Aboriginal lawyer from the North—and had started my own law practice.

Overall, I had faced a lot of big challenges—bears on the trail—and overcome them with little difficulty. And here I was facing mice and squirrels and being incapacitated by sheer fright. Years later my former executive assistant, Hayden Trenholm, who worked with me every day I was government leader and often travelled with me and my family, said, "I had no idea you were depressed. You were dealing with dozens of decisions every day, so of course you sometimes seemed preoccupied or irritable, but you always focused on the important issues and got things done."

I wondered what in my life might have contributed to this anxiety. Was I insecure because of not having a father? My mother and grandmother had raised me with lots of love and security and there were always uncles and other male relatives to round out my upbringing. I never went without food or suffered any discomfort or yearned for a father. A few times I was puzzled about why I didn't have a father like everybody else, and I sometimes wished that I had brothers and sisters. I was occasionally teased that I was a bastard, but this was mostly in my teens when I could deal with such things. I dismissed this as a source of my problem, at least for the time being.

I searched my mind for other causes. I had drank, partied and chased girls throughout my young adult life, and unfortunately this continued for a long time during my marriage. Dalliances occurred under the influence of alcohol. After a few drinks I was a happy guy, and women were part of the mix.

My wife, Karen, never drank, and there was never any liquor in our house. In my drinking days I drank only when I was away from home, but that was a lot of the time. In those days, I likened our marriage to a cage: I was a wild bird trapped inside, and whenever the door was open, I flitted around and enjoyed my freedom. In the aftermath of yet another affair I would wonder if the girl might be pregnant or if I might have caught a venereal disease that, worse yet, I might pass on to Karen.

As the spouse of an alcoholic, Karen was profoundly affected and began attending Al-Anon meetings shortly after my return to politics. One evening in Yellowknife I went along, planning to attend the meeting with her. The hallway to the Al-Anon meeting went right by another room where an Alcoholics Anonymous meeting was in progress. Karen nudged me into the room and continued down the hall to her own meeting. That is how I ended up at my first AA meeting, one of thirty people sitting around a table. It was intimidating at the start, but after a few sessions I became comfortable amongst these men and women who had experienced the same difficulties as me. I was surprised by who was at the meeting. There were men and women from all walks of life, and I knew just about every one of them. Each took their turn telling their story, beginning with the statement, "Hello, my name is so-and-so and I'm an alcoholic." When it was my turn, it took everything in me to say those few words, and that's as much as I was able to say that first night. It took a number of years but I was eventually able to reduce and then stop my drinking. By 1985 I was sober.

I began seeking more help, attending counselling sessions and healing workshops. Over the course of my term as minister of local government and as government leader, I spent many hours in Donna Dupuis's office at a family counselling clinic. One time, when presented with a bill of fifty dollars for our one-hour session, I told her that I'd gladly pay a thousand dollars as it was such a relief to be free of anxiety.

On the home front, Karen and I had to deal with our marital problems. We had first gone on a Marriage Encounter weekend in 1969 and it helped us tremendously at the time. Now we went on several more—six in total—to learn to communicate with each other again. When you first meet the person who will become your spouse, you spend hours on end talking. Gradually you can lose that interest and a wall can develop between you. The Marriage Encounter process has helped our marriage tremendously. Over the years we have spent thousands of dollars on family counselling and attending workshops, often including our children in the process, but it's been worth it as it has brought us so close together. Eventually, Karen and I spearheaded bringing Marriage Encounter sessions to Yellowknife and facilitated several ourselves.

But it was not enough to deal with my private life. I had to make changes in the way I conducted public business, too. Travelling to northern communities was a part of my job as minister and couldn't be avoided. I decided that wherever there was a Catholic priest in a community, I would ask to stay with him. I found that I could sleep a lot better in a rectory than in a hotel room, and I felt comfortable around priests. They were good company and kept me away from the temptations of drinking and chasing women. When in Ottawa, I rented a room at the Oblate Priests' Seminary at the University of St. Paul campus.

As I examined my life through counselling and self-reflection, my focus always returned to my years in residential school. I came to realize that those years had had a profound effect on me. I was five years old when I was sent away to school in Providence, and I was there for all those years without seeing my mother. Those six years in residential school were the most traumatic period of my life. I experienced loneliness, sadness, abandonment, helplessness, insecurity and many psychological and physical hurts. I was constantly teased because I was fairer than the rest of the boys. I was sexually assaulted by a bigger boy. I was treated cruelly by the nuns.

As an adult I spent many a night tossing, turning and sweating in frustration and agony over my situation. Sometimes I would wake Karen and talk to her to try to get to the bottom of my problem. We would get on our knees and pray to God, and I would ask "What's the matter with me? Where is my strength? Why am I afraid?" The answers did not come readily, but after many agonizing years, the core reason emerged. As a child in residential school, my innocence, my trust, my hope was lost. As a child I was so traumatized by the separation from my mother and grandmother and being thrust into a strange institution with loveless Grey Nuns that I had become an emotional and spiritual wreck. I had no resilience; I was like a leaf blowing in the wind. In contrast, the first five years of my life with my grandmother and mother stand out as happy times. Many times I have thanked God for those early years when I was loved and nurtured in my Dene language and identity. I don't think I would have survived in this world without the security of those early formative years.

After I became a minister, I could rationalize the situation and tell myself that the things I faced were not difficult, but I could not let go and feel confident that when the morning came I would be able to deal with them competently. Even Karen's love, her arms around me comforting me, could not undo the harm done. Nothing could give me the strength I needed to overcome the harms of my childhood. A negative thought pattern would run like a tape recorder through my head: "Nick, you're not going to sleep; you don't deserve to be happy," and so on.

After the residential school issue became public and healing programs were made available to survivors, the Return to Spirit program sponsored by the Catholic Church in the North dealt with exactly those negative thought processes that were formed through trauma in the minds of young children. Subconsciously, these thought processes become an entrenched part of one's psyche. It is very hard to erase or change them.

ALL MY EFFORTS at prayer, counselling and support groups helped, but I still struggled with a sadness that permeated every aspect of my life and remained with me throughout my years in cabinet. One Christmas my mother was staying with us in the government leader's house on Matonabee. She was always a help to Karen in the kitchen and with the children, but there always came a point when she wanted to go out and there was nothing anyone could do to stop her. Such was the case that Christmas Eve. She insisted on going to a bar, so I gave her some money and dropped her off at the Gold Range, knowing full well that she would get drunk.

Full of sorrow, I decided to park and walk around downtown. Yellowknife is a small city, so I recognized the homeless woman, Margaret Thrasher, who stopped me to talk. She didn't ask for anything—just said she wanted to wish me a Merry Christmas. I felt like giving her something for Christmas so I gave her a twenty-dollar bill. She was happy to receive an unexpected gift and thanked me with a big smile. As I walked away I couldn't help but see the contrast between us. Here I was, the government leader with a home, money and family, but I was not very happy. Margaret was a street person with very little, yet she seemed a lot happier than me.

My mother was picked up by the police later that night while she was knocking on doors in our neighbourhood trying to find our house.

DEPRESSION CAN DEBILITATE a person to the point of suicide. Darkness and hopelessness can envelop you like a fog, rendering everything bleak. You don't see the blazing northern lights or feel the warm comfort of a Chinook wind. The pain can be so excruciating that, for some, the thought of death is a relief.

I didn't want to die. I wanted to live. Depression cast me into darkness, but I wouldn't succumb and fought my way into the light. When all I wanted was to be alone, hiding in a shadowed room, away from everyone, I forced myself to be present for Karen and my children. I made myself go jogging or out into the public, and it was always beneficial. A ptarmigan, squirrel or friendly word from a neighbour could lift my spirits. Just seeing people having fun would divert my attention from my sad state to something heartening. These little steps led me towards some semblance of normalcy and well-being.

In the end I was saved by two things: Karen's love and forgiveness, and my faith in God. The ordeal of depression was, for me, a fight between good and evil. I believed goodness could overcome all evil. My faith in God came from my grandmother Ehmbee, from whose knees I first saw the world around me. Though I was born of my mother, Ehmbee was the person who truly gave me life. Ehmbee was constantly present to talk to me, caution me, teach me and nourish me. As I grew, I went to church and sat with her in the very back pew observing everything. She didn't know a word of English or French, but she faithfully attended church every Sunday and lived a life of kindness, gentleness and love.

The importance of faith in maintaining my well-being may seem odd given my history. The Catholic Church was a presence in my life from my earliest years. The mission in Fort Simpson was large, with a church, hospital and farm and all the related buildings. I often saw the priests and brothers in their long dark cassocks and the nuns in their grey robes and black bonnets moving about the hospital and grounds as they carried out their duties. I attended church with my grandmother and from the security of her lap observed the mass. Still it all seemed distant—like another world—to my child's eyes.

That changed dramatically when I was thrust into the arms of the nuns and sent off to residential school. Those were the most horrible years of my life. True, I was provided with food, clothing, bed and housing, the essentials that would maintain my body, but there was no emotional nourishment. There was no love or affection shown us, none of the cuddling, hugs or kind words so essential to a child's development.

I have asked myself a thousand times why the sisters didn't hug us, touch us or even smile at us. After all, we were little children and they were women, left to care for us in place of our parents. They were also sisters devoted to God and committed to lives of kindness and charity. How much effort does it take to pat a child on the head or give him a hug? I left residential school hating the sisters for their unkindness and for the many punishments they meted out.

My experiences with the church varied as I grew older. My time in Fort Smith at Grandin Home was very positive and happy. Still, I grew up angry at the church, and for a number of years stopped attending altogether. I felt that religion had been forced on me and on the Dene people. I had many questions about the history of the church in the North: Why was the church not more Dene? Why didn't we have Dene priests? Why was the church so insistent on following a set way of holding its mass? Couldn't they have created a more northern and Native version of mass and other services?

On the other hand I wondered about our ancestors and wondered why they had not resisted the imposition of the Catholic faith more vigorously. Were their beliefs so weak and meaningless that they succumbed to the priests' teachings and let the church run roughshod over them? Why didn't they insist on more of their practices and beliefs being incorporated into the religion? All of these questions swirled angrily in my mind. For a number of years I was contemptuous of church authority. As the government began to deal with the matter of residential schools, I found the church's unwillingness to acknowledge and recognize their responsibility infuriating. At one early workshop, there were a number of priests and a bishop in attendance. They were at the workshop as observers and did not want to become involved in the discussions. Whenever they did interact with us, they tended to be dismissive and downplay the trauma caused by the residential schools. When I compared my story of early life in residential school to the way that Jews were treated in concentration camps, a priest was aghast that I should compare my experience to the Holocaust, but I told the bishop that he didn't have a corner on the truth.

Over time, I've come to understand and even forgive the nuns. They were not happy to be sent to the North to care for children but did so out of duty. They, too, were torn from their homes—usually in Quebec—sent to live in harsh conditions in the far north and put in charge of dozens or hundreds of children. My aunt who lived in Edmonton visited the old nuns in their retirement home, and many said that they regretted how they had treated children. I recall visiting the Grey Nuns' mother house in Montreal, a huge institution, where hundreds of girls trained before coming north. I've often reflected how unsuited these women were for the tasks they were assigned. They had left the world, renounced the ideas of marriage and children for a higher calling. Their vows of poverty and chastity required them to cover themselves from head to toe as a shield against the world and its sensual ways. How could they show much of their own personalities, let alone provide the physical affection that children need? Their maternal natures—their kindness and natural love—were covered up as they were trained to be distant and stern. Everything a child needed from a woman was made unavailable to us beneath those heavy robes.

Many of the sisters changed later in life. Sister Hébert, whom we had called The General in Inuvik, spent her later years in Fort Providence working with mothers and children as a catechist. As an MLA, I often visited her and Sister Pearson and found them to be the kindest and happiest of people. Even in the later years of residential schools, especially under the guidance of more enlightened priests, nuns were more outgoing and kinder. Sister Trembley helped supervise the junior girls at Breynat Hall when Karen and I worked there, and she was loving, happy and dynamic. The girls under her care were clearly happy.

As an adult, my friend Al Paquette from residential school visited Sister Letourneau in Montreal where she was living at the Grey Nuns' retirement residence. Sister Letourneau was one of the meanest, strictest sisters who supervised boys in Providence when I was a student there. At the time of Al's visit, Sister was very old, but she still had a good memory. The first question she asked Al was "Was I mean in disciplining you boys?"

Al said he didn't have the heart to tell her anything except "I guess we deserved it" and let the matter lie.

NOT ALL MY conflicts during those years I was a minister and then government leader were internal. I sometimes was criticized for decisions or actions I took by MLAs, the media or members of the public. Other times I had to take on the federal government or clean up the messes that other members of cabinet had made. Oddly enough, these situations didn't seem as difficult to deal with as facing my inner demons and functioning on a day-to-day basis.

Fighting the bureaucracy also occupied much of my time. As US President Harry Truman said, "My biggest surprise was when I gave an order and nothing happened." There were policies and rules that governed every aspect of the operations of a department. The civil service was huge and loath to change. It operated at the speed of freezing water. To achieve anything I first had to make northern citizens and northern bureaucrats understand who was in charge.

I knew that, if we were truly to transform the GNWT into an elected responsible government, I needed, as government leader, to replace the lasting influence of the commissioner in people's minds, if not hearts. I needed to make my office the face of government, not just for myself but for all those who would follow me. The commissioner had always had an official residence, so when I became government leader, I immediately moved into a government house. This in itself was not controversial—Richard Nerysoo had lived in the same place—but I saw that the building was inadequate as a home for my family and as a place to carry out any official functions. I ordered an extensive renovation, which was carried out by Public Works without delay. There were a few grumblings but, since I was still in the honeymoon phase of my new position, not as many as I expected.

The commissioner had always held a winter ball, an elaborate affair with military honours, a southern orchestra and fancy imported food. My first year as government leader, I staged a similar event but with drum dancers, fiddle music and northern dishes like caribou, muskox and Arctic char. Again there was little public criticism; it was a continuation of a Yellowknife tradition. Every MLA was given tickets for themselves and their spouse and two more for constituents. The only complaints came when I reserved an extra twenty tickets for my own constituents and supporters. I defended myself by saying I had had no earlier opportunity to celebrate my election to the position of government leader, but really I was trying to make it clear that an elected person had supplanted the commissioner. Seeing myself perched on a throne in an editorial cartoon in *News of the North* didn't hurt my feelings at all.

Travel was another issue that was sometimes raised during my time as minister and government leader. I made numerous trips, usually with my staff and with regional officials, and in later years I often brought my wife and occasionally my children, but only when there were empty seats on our charter aircraft. I was cognizant as well of the need to cover any additional expenses from my own pocket. Still, one headline in *News/North* read "Baffin Holiday for Nick?" even though the story was mostly about a working trip I had made early in my mandate. The title came when I mused about the possibility of returning to Baffin Island in the summer for a combination of work and holiday. As is often the case with political coverage, it was the offhand comment, rather than substance, that generated the headline.

As I struggled to repair and maintain my family life it was, of course, important to me and to my ability to do my job that I have them with me. However, personal concerns were not my main reasons for travelling as much as I did. Again I wanted to reinforce the idea that the commissioner had been replaced with an elected person; in the regions people needed to turn to elected MLAs and ministers for help rather than regional directors, who often were like mini-commissioners. In 1986, on the night before July 1, I made a point of flying with a few staff from Yellowknife to Fort Good Hope to Coppermine to Baker Lake. In the morning we went on to Eskimo Point and Chesterfield Inlet, finishing that afternoon in Rankin Inlet, so I could make an appearance in various Canada Day celebrations, a feat that would have made Stu Hodgson proud!

I had also learned during my time as minister of local government the tremendous value of seeing the different situations on the ground in the diverse northern communities and of talking face to face with the people who lived in them. As government leader, responsible for a wider range of issues, this was even more important so I never missed an opportunity to listen to people and leaders on their home turf. I encouraged my colleagues in cabinet to do the same thing, and many did follow suit.

Political considerations also played a role in my travels. Although I had supported territorial division in my earlier days, as government leader I had promised to stay neutral on the matter. Still I knew that division was some way off and in the interim it was critical that people in the eastern Arctic remained connected to and involved in the GNWT. If eastern MLAs had adopted a "wait until Nunavut" position, it would have been very difficult to get anything done. As well, I knew that some of my actions—the Fort Smith decentralization and affirmative action, for example—would cost me support from the once-unified western caucus. I needed eastern acceptance, if not enthusiastic support, if I were to maintain my authority.

Although I travelled broadly throughout the Arctic, it is the trips to the Baffin region that I remember most. The land and terrain were so different that I often said trips to Baffin were like going to the moon. Perhaps it was the majesty of the landscape, the icebergs, the towering rock and ice-filled harbours far above the treeline or the hospitality of the Inuit people, but it was always an inspiration. It was on a five-community visit to Baffin in May 1986 when I first "dreamed of being premier," as Ed Struzik described it in an article in the *Edmonton Journal*. My experiences with the Baffin Regional Council as minister and as government leader encouraged me to promote similar bodies across the North.

I particularly remember the trip I made one summer with Karen and four of my children. I and my staff would spend our days touring community facilities or in meetings with leaders or residents, hearing their concerns. In the long sunlit evenings (Baffin Island had twenty-four-hour daylight at that time of year), we would wander the hills and shorelines or participate in community feasts and dances. It was on that trip, too, that my executive assistant learned the meaning of "other duties as assigned." A few days before departure, my daughter Janice, then about eleven, fell from the playground monkey bars and broke her leg. Hayden, in addition to taking notes and writing letters, spent much of the trip carrying Janice on his back. Whatever criticism I may have received about my trips—and most people supported them—memories of that Baffin tour certainly made it all worthwhile.

NOT EVERY ACTION I took was treated gently by MLAs and the media. In September of 1986, I gave a speech at the annual Native Women's Association Assembly in Yellowknife that generated a flurry of negative press and letters to the editor. I recall standing before the delegates and holding up my prepared remarks, saying, "My staff aren't going to be happy but I have a few things to say that aren't in this speech they prepared." I didn't need to glance over at them to know there were dismayed expressions on their faces.

The issue was daycare. It was my view, and it remains my view, that children are better off if they are raised at home by one of their parents. In the 1980s that generally meant the mother—though nowadays men sometimes play that role—and I suggested that staying home should be the first choice of women when it came to child-rearing. I even compared daycare to sending kids off to residential school. "Sibbeston Opposes Daycare" read one headline; "Leader Gives Women Advice: Stay Home" read another. The letters the following week were even more dramatic, calling my statements "appalling."

What wasn't reported, at least not prominently, was what I said next—that I was being theoretical, speaking of a perfect world. If women wanted to work or had to work to support their families, then daycare should not only be provided but should be of the best possible quality, and our government would support it. I also went on to talk about the significant progress being made in providing women equal opportunities for advancement in our government and that I was committed to the equality of men and women in the workplace. Shortly after that speech we added women's equality to the GNWT's affirmative action policy. Such is the life of a politician—more often judged by what we say than what we do.

It was in the area of appointments to the civil service that I faced the greatest criticism. No one objected to me choosing deputy ministers or other senior officials. Other Canadian jurisdictions used a mixture of competitions and direct appointments to head up departments; in the Northwest Territories, the commissioner as head of personnel had always exercised that prerogative. In fact, the first-ever open competition for a deputy's job had taken place under my watch.

Direct appointments to lower positions in the public service also occurred when it was obvious there was only one person suited for the job. In those cases, the recommendation would come to cabinet from the deputy minister of personnel or sometimes from another deputy. A case would be made by the official, and generally we would approve it with some debate; on occasion we would order a competition. In any case, whether with a competition or a direct appointment, members of the public service could file an appeal if they felt they had been unfairly treated.

Increasing the number of Native people in government jobs had been an issue for me from my first days as MLA. Now that I had the power to make changes, I certainly wasn't going to back down no matter who objected. Normally the appeals process for appointments was open only to aggrieved public servants, but the legislation did provide the minister of personnel the option of reviewing an appointment and providing for an appeal even in the case of external applicants.

I made considerable use of direct appointments to bring talented Aboriginal people into the service, though this happened less frequently once the affirmative action policy was strengthened and began to be used effectively. An important part of that policy was requiring that job descriptions reflected the actual skills needed and not artificial requirements designed to ensure that the best jobs went to existing civil servants while excluding talented outsiders. I was always of the belief that job requirements and qualifications were exaggerated and made to look impossible to fulfill by an ordinary person. Many jobs were simple and could be done by using common sense, but put in writing it looked like the person was required to build a rocket ship. An example of this was a requirement for applicants to be familiar with the financial information system (FIS) of the government to become a manager. Clearly, a manager needed to understand accounting or financial management, but requiring specific knowledge of the FIS excluded people who weren't already employed by the government.

This was at the heart of the issue on one of the few occasions I exercised my discretionary powers. A position in the Department of Education had been filled internally, despite there being candidates from outside the service who were better qualified. The sticking point was experience with the FIS service. One of the external applicants, Jeannie Marie-Jewell (who, incidentally, some years later became a minister in the government) came to me with a complaint. I ordered that the process be redone with a less biased job description.

The response from several MLAS, from the union and from the press was immediate and substantial. The press implied that Marie-Jewell and I were close friends because she referred to me as Nick, which I guess meant I was good pals with every reporter in the North since they often referred to me by my first name (ironically, in a head-line on the very same page of *News/North* that covered the appointment controversy). I certainly knew of Marie-Jewell, as she had been active in Métis and territorial politics, but we had no prior personal relationship.

I explained myself in the legislature and refused to promise Yellowknife MLAS Ted Richard and Bob MacQuarrie that I wouldn't do the same thing again if the situation warranted. The power was in the act governing the civil service, approved by the legislature, and it was nonsense to give a minister a power and then ask that he never exercise it. Technically, at that moment the power was still vested in the commissioner (and had been used frequently by past commissioners). A few weeks later, when amendments were introduced to transfer the power of approving all appointments to the minister, there were further claims of partisan interference in the process and union pickets outside the assembly.

I publicly wondered if the same criticism would have been made had I been non-Native. That idea was reinforced when a newspaper editorial referred to me as Papa Sibbeston—a reference to Papa Doc Duvalier, who was then in the news for his tyrannical rule of Haiti—and implying that recent announcements in a number of areas were cases of arbitrary and individual action. Though I rarely responded to the media, this time I felt that I had no choice. I sent a lengthy rebuttal both to set the record straight with respect to my actual, and limited, role within a consensus cabinet and to decry such a blatantly racist attack. Eventually the matter died down as the process of hiring Aboriginal people became more accepted and routine.

MANY TIMES, IT is necessary to take positions or actions in government that others disagree with. In 1983 the Mulroney government agreed to permit American testing of cruise missiles and low-level flights by NATO jets over the North. Both were objectionable to people in the Northwest Territories for a range of reasons—opposition to nuclear weapons, concerns over the effects on wildlife and hunters, matters of safety in the event of a crash (one cruise missile did in fact crash)—and, responding to motions in the assembly and by Aboriginal organizations, I wrote a number of letters to the prime minister protesting these activities. My letters had little effect on Canadian military policy, but they did create a certain amount of friction in our other dealings with the federal government, though not as much as our opposition to the Meech Lake Accord.

Similarly, we occasionally had conflicts with various Native organizations when they objected to the devolution of federal powers from the federal to the territorial government. The old cry of "this is not our government" hadn't completely died away, despite the larger role of Aboriginal people in politics and the public service.

THE BIGGEST CRISIS our government faced occurred during the budget session of 1987. Tagak Curley, minister of Economic Development and Tourism, was facing some strong criticism of some of his programs. In the course of debate, he sent a note to MLA Sam Gargan that could be and was interpreted as threatening to projects in Gargan's own riding. Gargan (in later years Speaker of the assembly and grand chief of the Deh Cho First Nations) tabled the note and demanded that the minister resign. Tagak apologized both privately and publicly on several occasions, and I made a speech asking that the assembly accept the apology of an otherwise exceptional minister.

However, MLAs were not appeased and a motion calling for Tagak's resignation passed. He had no choice but to step down and was replaced on the executive council by Ludy Pudluk.

Ludy was a fine man with a great concern for the Inuit people and a terrific sense of humour. However, his English wasn't the strongest and he lacked significant management experience. I couldn't give him the important portfolio of Economic Development. Gordon Wray very much wanted the job, but, as he already held Public Works and Local Government; that would have made him by far the most powerful member of cabinet. As well, recent allegations of improper tendering of contracts in his home region of the Keewatin had somewhat tainted his reputation. Although the matter was eventually blamed on weak rules and careless actions by bureaucrats, I had lingering doubts.

In the end, I decided to take on the job myself for the remaining six months of our term, acquiring an additional executive assistant, Rose Marie Karnes, who had served in that capacity with Tagak. I had gained a great appreciation of businessmen in the previous few years and very much enjoyed my time working with them on the economy of the Northwest Territories. Still, I missed Tagak's presence in cabinet; he had been one of my strongest supporters from the east, especially on the issue of Native employment.

After two years as government leader I approached the coming election with considerable optimism. I felt I had done a good job and hoped it would be recognized both at the constituency level and in the decisions of the next assembly when they chose the new cabinet.

Chapter 15: The 1987 Election

POPE JOHN PAUL II's return visit to my hometown, Fort Simpson, in September 1987 was a spectacular event. Thousands of people again descended on the village, waiting on the flats where he was taken to meet the Aboriginal peoples of our country. I was part of the entourage at the airport when the pope walked down the steps of the plane and kissed the ground in his customary manner. Karen and I were in the line of dignitaries behind the governor general, Madame Sauvé, and were privileged to shake his hand and welcome him on behalf of all the peoples of the North. In preparation for the visit, the organizers had erected a beaver house monument and a large teepee with a raised floor on which ceremonies took place and a mass was held.

The visit was magnificent, with a few thousand people in attendance from all over the North and from southern points. After early morning drizzle, the sun broke through and all the events, the mass, the prayers and the meetings with Aboriginal leaders from across the country went off without a hitch. Karen and I were part of the delegation at the airport that saw the pope get into the plane and fly south into the blue clear sky.

The territorial election of 1987 was held on October 5, a few weeks after the pope's visit. An air of congeniality and well-being still permeated the region. I think this may have helped me in the election. Jim Villeneuve, the other candidate, and I visited communities, sometimes crossing paths and exchanging friendly banter; it hardly seemed like an election campaign at all. In the end I won the election by a huge margin of 80 percent of the votes cast.

I attributed my electoral success to my work as MLA and my elevation to minister of local government and then government leader, from which positions I was able to assist the communities with many of their problems. I also sensed that there was a certain pride in one of their own becoming prominent in government. While I believe people appreciated my previous role as an active critic, raising many issues that were important to them, they now saw that as a minister and government leader I was doing a credible job for them and for the whole North.

The election brought forth some new members: Steve Kakfwi, former president of the Dene Nation, representing the Sahtu; John Pollard, former mayor of Hay River; Jeannie Marie-Jewell, who had been at the centre of the controversy over hiring practices, representing Fort Smith; Don Morin from Fort Resolution; Peter Irniq from Rankin Inlet; Titus Allooloo from Pond Inlet; and Henry Zoe from Rae-Edzo. Both Kakfwi and Morin would later serve as premier of the Northwest Territories, while Irniq eventually served as commissioner for Nunavut.

I wasn't sure whether I would run for government leader again. I knew there would be pressure to have someone from the eastern Arctic because people from the west had held the position since 1979. As the weeks wound down to the time for all MLAs to gather in Yellowknife to start the assembly, lobbying for cabinet and the leadership intensified. I was approached by Steve Kakfwi and Richard Nerysoo to run for government leader. Richard, whom I had replaced two years earlier, said, "I think I can swallow my pride" and promised to support me. A few days later I decided I would run, and I met with the other Aboriginal members—Jeannie Marie-Jewell, Sam Gargan, Don Morin and Henry Zoe—all of whom expressed their support.

I also approached a few Inuit members but they were noncommittal. When I approached other western non-Aboriginal members like Mike Ballantyne, Ted Richard, Brian Lewis and John Pollard, they were most decidedly not supportive. It was obvious that they had put their lot in with Dennis Patterson. Others like Gordon Wray and Nellie Cournoyea wouldn't even talk with me. I could see that I didn't have enough support, but I didn't think Dennis should win by acclamation so I trudged on.

The caucus meetings took six long days with a lot of the time taken to decide on the process of choosing the ministers and the leader. Up to then, the executive council members had been chosen first, then the government leader was chosen from amongst them by all the MLAS. It was proposed that this should be changed to vote for the leader first.

Ted Richard (a Yellowknife lawyer who left politics in 1988 to become a judge on the NWT Supreme Court) was one of those who favoured the selection of the leader first. He then went further to suggest that the leader be given the power to choose the cabinet. This would give him complete control over management and discipline of ministers. Most of the members did not like this idea, as it would take power away from them. They still wanted to have a hand in selecting all the ministers.

Eventually, after much debate and argument, it was decided that the leader would be chosen first and the remainder of the cabinet chosen afterwards by all of the MLAS. While there had been rumours of others seeking the position, in the end it came down to me and Dennis. The process was not open to the public but speculation on the outcome was certainly a favourite topic of conversation and news reports. Some commentators likened the few days of choosing a cabinet and the government leader to the Vatican secret conclave used in selecting a pope, but without a chimney emitting smoke. David Hamilton, the clerk of the assembly, said, "When they get together to vote, it's a very dynamic atmosphere where almost anything can happen. There is certainly nothing like this process anywhere else in Canada." In the end, Patterson came out on top, though I was told by those counting the votes that it was a very close race.

The election of cabinet ministers occurred the following day. A full slate of fifteen members, nearly two-thirds of the legislature, sought cabinet posts. The cabinet consisted of eight members, including the government leader, so more than half would be disappointed. Each candidate gave a short speech, after which we held the secret ballot vote. When the tally was completed, there were three first-time members: Steve Kakfwi, Jeannie Marie-Jewell and Titus Allooloo. Nellie Cournoyea, Gordon Wray, Mike Ballantyne and I rounded out the group. Notably missing were long-time ministers Tom Butters and Bruce McLaughlin and one-term ministers Ludy Pudluk and Red Pedersen. The caucus did not provide for a review midway through the four-year term as we had done during the previous assembly.

Over the next few days Dennis was gracious, and in our private discussions said that he wanted me to be deputy government leader. When asked for my portfolio preference, I told him I was interested in education or alternatively, justice. That was the last of any cordial discussions.

For a number of weeks ministers from the previous government retained their old portfolios for the sake of continuity. I continued my work as minister of economic development, focused on nursing the economy out of the downturn that had begun in 1986. We had made some progress through a judicious use of capital spending to stimulate local economies and by negotiating a new economic development agreement with Canada. I was happy enough to be doing the work and was pleased with the media coverage of my accomplishments.

Still, I had a growing foreboding about the assignment of permanent portfolios that was to take place in March 1988. I often saw Mike, Nellie and Gordon going in and out of Dennis's office. Their camaraderie was obvious. As the weeks went by before Dennis assigned portfolios, I sensed a gulf developing between us.

When it came time to receive our assignments, my meeting with Dennis was terse. No pleasantries were exchanged about the weather or how I was doing. This was counter to my own experience, both from my original appointment by Richard Nerysoo and from my time as government leader, when the assignment of portfolios was both serious and pleasant. Fitting ministers to the right portfolio is a delicate undertaking requiring careful consideration of the needs of the government and the abilities and dignity of the ministers.

Prior to becoming leader, I had been minister of local government, one of the biggest and most important departments. I had been involved in the intricate and politically sensitive role of chairing the

Western Constitutional Forum. As government leader I handled two major departments: personnel and later economic development. I had engaged in constitutional talks with premiers and the prime minister. Hence when Dennis said my portfolios would be government services and the Housing Corporation, I was shocked. These were the least important portfolios, the bottom of the barrel. Government services was a department dealing with petroleum products, drivers' licensing and a grab bag of technical areas. Housing was likewise way down the scale of importance; with a board of directors governing the agency, the minister responsible for the corporation was largely a figurehead with little power. So there I was, coming down from being the leader responsible for running the whole of government, to two insignificant portfolios. What was I to do?

I told Dennis that I didn't accept his assignments and that I would think over whether I would remain in cabinet. I also told him I was no longer interested in being the deputy leader, not that he had offered it to me again. I left the room without any further discussion and went almost straight home to discuss the situation with Karen.

It occurred to me that I was now expendable in the eyes of Dennis, Michael, Gordon and Nellie, the inner clique. Steve Kakfwi, although newly elected, had been given Education, one of the more important portfolios; he would be the Dene person in cabinet who would give credibility to the government. I was not needed, particularly since I was much more able and likely to challenge them. I later heard that Dennis offered me the crumbs of departments to force me out. Steve Kakfwi, later premier himself, reported that Patterson had said, "He's a proud man; he'll leave."

I spent the weekend considering my options. I could refuse the portfolios on the basis that it was inappropriate, given my experience, education and status, to be given such minor departments. But I didn't think the caucus and northern public would understand my point. People in the North had insufficient experience with ministerial government to realize that in any government there are departmental rankings based on their strategic importance. In the federal government, for instance, the departments of finance, defence, foreign affairs, and industry are weightier and have a higher status than heritage, fisheries or corrections. You would not expect a former prime minister in a new cabinet to be given one of the latter. Former Prime Minister Joe Clark, for example, was then serving as foreign minister in the Mulroney government.

My other option was to accept the portfolios, make the best of things and see how I felt after six months or a year. I chose this option, though I felt distraught about being the bottom man in the new cabinet. Dropping from government leader to being a minor minister was going to be a humbling experience. I reminded myself that I had had a great political career to this point in my life. I'd come from the bottom to the top, and I did not relish the thought of languishing unhappily as a junior minister for the next four years. Nonetheless, on Monday morning I swallowed my pride and went to Dennis's office to tell him that I would take the departments he had assigned.

I was puzzled by Dennis's treatment of me. When I was government leader, I consciously treated everyone fairly and had a cordial and open relationship with all the ministers. Indeed, on one occasion when Dennis had gotten into some trouble, alcohol being a factor, I met with him and helped to resolve the issue.

For the next six months I stayed on the job but my heart wasn't in it. Far from it: I was stressed, not sleeping properly and deeply unhappy. I determined that I had to leave cabinet, and that meant I would want to move out of our government-supplied house. We had lived in Yellowknife for the past five years, first in a government house and later in a house designated for the government leader. It was time to have our own home again.

I had built a house in Yellowknife ten years earlier, so I began planning to build again. I knew the drill: I bought a lot, ordered a Nelson Home package and began putting in the foundation and basement. John Vogt, a friend from Fort Smith, came over to help and with a small crew, he and I worked all summer to put up the house. When John had to leave, Karen's brother Chris came up from Lloydminster and put the roof on for us. By the time fall came and the snow started flying, Karen and I were putting on the siding and arranging to have the interior work finished. Actually, building the house was easy compared to contending with the city building inspectors, three of whom were continually monitoring construction. One day Karen and I worked until dark high up on some scaffolding. When we returned the next morning, a white paper was tacked to the wall we had just finished. The words on the paper were few, but created a lot of concern: "Improperly installed, remove." I met with the inspectors and fortunately was able to resolve the issue without having to take down all the siding.

By the time there was a foot of snow on the ground, we had moved in and I was independent of government with our new home. In September of 1988, when I felt the time was right, I tendered my letter of resignation to Dennis. Again, it was a dry, emotionless exchange; he didn't query why I had decided to leave or thank me for my years of service in cabinet. I publicly stated I was leaving the government because I was not happy and felt I had been unfairly demoted; I refused to coast through the next three years doing trivial things. Patterson of course dismissed my concerns, stating that in a consensus cabinet every minister plays a role. That's like saying every player on a hockey team, even the ones sitting on the bench, assisted in the score.

My future felt uncertain beyond the need to continue to work on improving my family life. But I was a lawyer and had previously made a living at it, and I could return to practise law. I had been an elected member for thirteen years by then; by the end of my term in 1991, I would have served the public for sixteen years. Perhaps it was the right time to get out of politics and get on with other things in life.

I went through a grieving process. I grieved for what could have been a positive experience but wasn't. Fortunately, I quickly overcame that and got on with my work as an ordinary MLA, raising issues as I had done before I became a minister, speaking out on obtaining better health benefits for Métis or ensuring that Aboriginal people benefitted from mines or oil and gas development. I fought—and often won—for capital projects in Deh Cho communities and generally criticized the government when they deserved it. As the end of my term approached, I made a strong pitch for the new western territory to be called Denendeh, a campaign I continued after I became a senator. I admit to not having the same passion and intensity as before, but I think a big part of that was because I had already dealt with many of the more pressing issues, and changes had been made. It was time to leave politics.

Part Three:

POST POLITICS,
AND
ON TO THE HILL

Chapter 16: Post Politics

BY THE TIME I was finished with politics, I felt pretty beat up and was relieved to be done. I looked forward to life away from the spotlight, but I knew the only way I would be totally free and independent was to move south somewhere I was not known. Moving back to my hometown in Fort Simpson would not have worked. Karen and I decided to move to Calgary in the fall of 1991. I would take some refresher law courses to bring me up to date after ten years away from the law. In particular, the adoption in 1982 of the Charter of Rights and Freedoms had brought into existence a whole new dimension of rights that had a bearing on many aspects of law, particularly criminal law.

I received approval for funding from the Students' Grant Program. The program was available for all northern people and though I was clearly eligible, I felt uneasy about it as I was getting a pension from my years as MLA. But with children still in school, I needed the money.

We sold our house in Yellowknife and moved all our belongings to a rented home in Calgary. I started auditing two courses, criminal law and environmental law. For some reason, what should have been a stress-free and enjoyable exercise proved immensely difficult. What could be hard about getting up each day, riding a bus to the university, sitting in classes for a couple of hours and returning home? There weren't even any exams, as I was only auditing the courses. All I had to do was listen, read and study the materials for my own benefit and interest. Nonetheless, I suffered an intense amount of anxiety.

The first fall that I was away from the North, I was asked by CBC in Yellowknife to be a commentator on their television coverage of the territorial election. Normally, anyone would see this as a positive experience, but I agonized through many sleepless nights before I agreed to do it. What is normal and easy for one who is healthy can be intensely difficult for someone suffering depression. Depression makes it difficult to do anything.

EARLY IN THE summer of 1991, I had met Wayne Grigsby and Barbara Samuels, who were in Fort Simpson collecting information for a television series that they were trying to get filmed for CBC TV. They asked if I would be one of their advisors for the new show, *North of 60*, and when we moved to Calgary in the fall I began going out to their film set near Bragg Creek. I was the cultural advisor and Dene language coach for the series, which premiered in December 1992. I went out to the site once or twice a week and spent the day reading the script and advising the producers. The fictional town of Lynx River was supposed to be a small Dene community in the Deh Cho. My job was to make the show as authentically northern as possible. This included making sure the local Dene language was used, so I worked with the various actors teaching them the pronunciations of the words that they were to speak during the shooting sessions. The one whom I worked most with was Wilma Pelly, who played the role of Teevee's grandmother and the community elder, Elsie Tsa Che. Others like Dakota House (Teevee Tenia), Tina Keeper (Michele Kenedi) and Gordon Tootoosis (Albert Golo) would also utter the odd Dene word. (Tina Keeper later became a colleague in the Liberal caucus as an MP from Manitoba between 2006 and 2008.)

The set at Bragg Creek had a Hollywood atmosphere with directors, writers, producers and actors moving about the sets and scenes that were being shot. I was told more than once to get out of the way by the cameramen as I stood near the actors making sure they pronounced the Dene correctly. I tried to get some of the interesting characters from the North into the show, but was told that there was no money for bringing people down. Also, people from throughout the North would sometimes comment about the number of love scenes in the show, saying that it wasn't like that. I told the producers that the romance and sex depicted on the show were exaggerated. Although such behaviour did occur, especially when people were drinking, it would be both unlikely and improper to be so open about it in a northern community. I was told, "This is not an anthropological documentary; it's show biz." My advice on cultural matters clearly didn't extend to morality or how people would actually behave.

I also had my debut as an actor. I played Bapteese in two episodes. My career consisted of two short scenes in which I blurted out a few words of Dene at a band council meeting. Neither appearance lasted more than a few seconds. My acting career ended rather abruptly when I took the liberty of ad libbing a longer phrase, thinking it would add to the cultural part of the show. The director conducting the shooting seemed fine with it, but when the rushes came back the next day the producers were not happy with my improvisation and thereafter cut Bapteese out of the show. I discovered that in television production, every word or pause is measured, and any addition can disrupt the flow and pacing of the scene. I wondered whether I might have had a few more episodes if I had looked more Dene, with long, flowing black hair. Still, it was a great experience, and it amuses me to receive a small cheque, sometimes as little as four or five dollars, every year as residuals since the show went into syndication. It was a fun job, and as the show got underway on national television, it was nice to see my name scroll along each week with all the actors and producers.

My life in Calgary in some respects was one of semi-retirement, having only my two university courses and part-time work at *North of 60*. Despite this, I continued suffering from insomnia and many stretches of depression. Ordinary tasks loomed large and small matters became mountains. The notebook I kept of this time is riddled with passages of "can't sleep," "tired," "tension" and "going to the gallows." I agonized over every planned event, and when the time came to attend it I felt as if I was being taken to the gallows to be hanged. I sought out psychiatrists and sleep disorder doctors and continued taking weekly workshops and counselling sessions. I tried everything I could to deal with my depression, part of which was to attend mass almost daily and undertake a weekend-long cursillo, which is an intense praying experience.

During the second year of our stay in Calgary I became increasingly aware that one of the things weighing most on my mind was an affair that I had had years before while I was government leader. I had put it at the back of my mind, but it had pushed its way to the front and I felt plagued with guilt. I was torn between keeping it secret and being continuously troubled by it, or telling Karen and bearing the consequences. I decided I would tell Karen and get it out of my life.

One night I lay wide awake, tortured by guilt and anxiety. I woke Karen and told her what I had done. It hit her like a bolt of lightning. She shot up out of bed crying, hitting me with her fists, angry and anguished. For days afterwards Karen cried. I feared she would leave me. I apologized profusely and repeatedly, telling her I would be willing to do anything to make amends.

After a few days Karen suggested that we go for Christian counselling at Elijah House outside Coeur d'Alene, Idaho. We arranged to spend a week at the centre as soon as possible, and soon were driving south. The counselling was intense as we shared intimate details of our life together and individually. I talked about how I had learned about sex through my mother's *True Romance* magazines, Father Lesage's anatomy text and Uncle Charlie's birds-and-bees talk. In addition, I had become aware that when my mother didn't come home from her weekend drinking binges, she was sometimes with men she had met at parties. As I grew up to be a young man, drinking, partying and having sex with girls was common practice. Everybody I knew did that, wherever and whenever we had the chance. Karen's background was radically different, as she grew up in a large farm family with strong moral values. For her, sex was to be preserved for marriage. While my Aboriginal background and carefree attitude towards sex may have explained my behaviour, they couldn't justify it—not if I wanted to keep my family.

The counsellor said I needed to lay everything on the table if Karen and I were to move forward in our relationship. Only then would I be free of the guilt and the secrets that added to my depression. I spilled everything, telling Karen the names of all the women I had had sex with during our marriage. It was shattering for Karen. She even knew some of the women. "How could you do that? Why? Wasn't I good enough?" I could see that her womanhood, her self-worth and her confidence were shaken to the core. At times, I did not know how we would ever get through it. I prayed for God's help.

The pain that Karen went through was intense. My infidelity devastated her. The counsellor told us that infidelity was similar to parents suffering the loss of a child; it would take at least two years to overcome all the hurt and trauma. As the spouse who was unfaithful, I had to be patient and make a constant effort to reassure Karen of my love and affection. Blessedly, Karen was able to forgive me, as she has done a number of times in our marriage, and I renewed my commitment to be true to her, a vow I have kept ever since. We made our way back to Calgary, pained but with renewed hope. With no more secrets clogging my heart and mind, I was at last able to sleep.

IN 1993 WE moved back to Fort Simpson. I had had my break from the North, my fill of the city, and I was ready to get involved in some job or project again. Actually I did both. I got a job with the GNWT as a justice specialist, working with the communities to set up justice committees so they could handle their own court and sentencing, and I spearheaded a business proposal to build an office building in Fort Simpson.

In my role as a justice specialist, a big focus was on restorative justice, which brought non-violent offenders together with the victims of their crimes. Rehabilitation and reconciliation rather than punishment were the keys, and we involved elders and other community representatives in the process. I would go into a community such as Wrigley, meet with the chief and band council and explain it was possible for the community to deal with people who got into trouble, particularly young people and offences that were not too serious. I encouraged and cajoled them: "Why have the police and court officials do your dirty work?" They could and should do it themselves. Once I got the community's consent, I set up workshops and training sessions and worked with them to form a justice committee and a justice circle to deal with the offenders.

I had the cooperation and full support of Sergeant Paul Gamble of the Fort Simpson detachment, who travelled with me. With Paul's presence, the community was assured that the circle-sentencing approach to dealing with justice issues was supported by the police and justice system. It wasn't just "Nick and his wild ideas."

We held practice sessions in each community to prepare for the circle sentencing. During one such practice in Wrigley, quite a number of local people gathered in the community hall participating in, watching and listening to the proceedings. Our mock case presented a young man who stole a marten from another person's trapline. The "thief" sat as part of the circle along with the police and the circle sentencing members. The audience watched with interest as the young man was questioned and spoken to by the circle members. Halfway through the proceedings a couple of elders were so engrossed that they forgot that it was just a practice session and stood up, asking, "When did this happen?" We all laughed as we saw how real and effective the circle sentencing approach could be in a community wanting to deal with its own justice matters.

Interestingly, one month later I received a phone call from a local organizer, Stella Pellisey, telling me that Wrigley had its first circle sentencing case of a young girl caught stealing a jacket from the co-op store. The young girl was repentant, and the elders in the circle, while admonishing her, encouraged her to grow up to become a good person. This approach of dealing with offenders in communities is much more effective than the approach of a court party coming into a community and the judge handing our fines or brief periods of jail time. After two years as a justice specialist, I managed the Deh Cho Health Services for a year, training and setting up a functional board in that time.

My simultaneous project during those years was developing an office building in Fort Simpson to lease to the GNWT. With all the government positions that were to be moved from Fort Smith, there would be need for office space in the community. I met with the band and Métis leadership to pitch the idea that we should work together to build an office building. Our little town had never seen anything like it. I suggested that we partner with Seamus Henry, a businessman from Yellowknife who would later become an MLA. Together we set up a company called Nahendeh Developments Ltd. with a shareholders' agreement establishing the structure and the shares to be held by each of the partners. The band negotiated for 50 percent of the shares with the Métis, Seamus and me holding the remainder. The agreement provided an option for the band and Métis to buy out Seamus's and my shares in three years, giving them the opportunity to own the building if they wanted to do so.

It was a year-long process of land purchasing, meeting with government officials, seeking tenants and getting the financing in place with a bank. As we were finalizing the financing, the bank required the partners to come up with 25 percent of the equity needed for the building. With a 50 percent share of the company, the band had to come up with the biggest portion of the cash. The rest of us were surprised when instead the band voted to withdraw from the partnership, stating that they did not wish to jeopardize the monies they had available. We tried to convince them that it was a good long-term investment, but to no avail. The Métis, Seamus and I redistributed the shares, came up with the necessary equity and finalized the financing with the bank. Construction began in the fall of 1993, and by the following summer the two-storey building was ready for occupation. It was a gratifying success.

I've always felt badly about the band pulling out of the partnership, as the office building occupies a prominent location in the community and has been a good investment. It took many years to realize a profit, but I've always been proud that as Aboriginal people we could undertake such a business project. Seamus has been a good partner, lending his expertise in negotiating with the government and financial institutions to get us the best deals. What I learned from Seamus is that in business you have to be hardnosed in negotiating for the best possible deal; it's not an insult to tell a potential buyer that his offer is too low or a lender that his rate is too high.

I HAD ANOTHER business venture on the go during those years. Back in 1989, I had bought fifty-four acres of land along the Liard River a few kilometres from Fort Simpson along the Mackenzie highway. As a young boy I used to see Allen Tosh go by boat up the Liard to land he had cleared and used to grow potatoes and vegetables. Henry

Deneyoua, who helped Tosh harvest the vegetables·in the fall, said they could take at least four hundred bags of potatoes from those gardens; the soil was excellent. When Allen retired to the south, he sold the land to Phil Walton of Edmonton. Walton was a trucker who hoped to use the land as a staging area when the Mackenzie Valley pipeline was being built, but the pipeline project never materialized. When I saw signs posted in town offering the land up for sale at the same time as I knew I would be leaving politics, I got in touch with Walton and bought the land. It was most unusual in the North to have such a large tract of titled land available for sale, so I felt fortunate.

After our first winter in Calgary, I spent the summer of 1992 back in Fort Simpson clearing our land. I set up a tent and Janice, my eldest daughter, and I spent most of the summer living in it while we cleared bush for a road from the highway and cleared an area where we would eventually build a bed-and-breakfast establishment. When I told Charlie Hansen about the land, he said the area was called Peter's Place after the man who had originally cleared a small part of it and lived there. Charlie himself had lived there for a couple of years before establishing himself as a contractor in town. Wop May, the famous northern bush pilot, flew in a bunch of chicks for him and Charlie raised chickens on the land. When we cleared bush to build a house, I could see there had been a cellar dug and there was still some chicken fence strewn around in the bush.

In 1995, with blueprints drawn up by an engineer friend in Grande Prairie, I went to the Economic Development office in Fort Simpson to see if the government would contribute some money to the bed and breakfast I was planning. I didn't need government funds to go ahead, as I had arranged financing through a bank in Yellowknife, but with the additional money I could improve the quality of the facility with top-grade finishing features, making it an attractive facility for visitors. The civil servant at the Fort Simpson Economic Development office wasn't convinced. He said our B&B would be a market disruption for the existing hotel and motel in the community and turned a deaf ear to my argument that our B&B would actually attract *more* people. In addition to business from summertime tourists, Fort Simpson would benefit from groups we attracted during the winter for meetings and workshops. With a small conference room as part of the facility, I would be filling a niche. He wasn't convinced, though I couldn't fathom how his negative policy would make it possible for any local person to get help to start a new business.

Back in Yellowknife, I met with John Todd, the minister in charge of Economic Development, and he approved a grant without any hesitation. I finalized the financing for the B&B with Gordon Van Tighem, the manager of the Bank of Montreal and later three-term mayor of Yellowknife. When everything was in order, we arranged for Karen's brother Grant to construct the building and on October 18, 1995, excavation began.

By April 1996, Bannockland Inn was complete, and within a month we were open for business. We received our first guest in May and right away we learned something about running a guest house: expect the unexpected! When I went out to the airport to pick up our first guest, he had a dog with him. Our B&B was to be pet-free, so the dog ended up staying in the shed, though it yelped for a good part of the first night until it got used to being away from its owner.

Our business did very well. For the first month of operation, we were full practically every day. After that it was a few years before we replicated that first month of operation, but Karen and I worked hard to build up our clientele. Through the years we enjoyed trying to be the best B&B in the North. We made special efforts to provide a real northern experience by serving caribou sausages, bannock and wild cranberry sauces and jams with every breakfast. For the first few years Karen and I shared the cleaning and the cooking of hot breakfasts. We eventually hired my cousin Marie Lafferty, and she ran the business for us for a number of years.

Many of our summer guests were there to canoe on the Nahanni River, which emptied into the Liard River south of Fort Simpson. We would tell them intriguing stories about the "dangerous" Nahanni, ending by asking, "So what should we do with your luggage if you don't come back?" Our business did sufficiently well that we paid the whole mortgage off in less than two years, well ahead of schedule. Bannockland Inn operated under our family until it finally closed in 2005.

Despite these successes, I still had recurring bouts of depression and struggled with insomnia, tension and anxiety. In 1997 I went to Nats'ejée K'éh Treatment Centre in Hay River for a thirty-five-day program. At the same time, Karen availed herself of the programs for spouses to deal with her own issues. It was at about this time I reconnected with my son, Shane McNeely, whom I fathered so many years before in Fort Smith. It was a positive experience for both of us. Having grown up without knowing who my father was, I knew something of what he had gone through. We have continued to meet from time to time, and he is now an accepted part of my family.

Chapter 17: The Senator and the Demons

BECOMING A SENATOR is not something you plan. After all, there are only 105 senators in a country of more than thirty million. Nor does it simply happen; it is a product of the achievements and contributions you've made to some aspect of Canadian society. Politics is part of it, of course, though many senators have no history of political activity before their appointment. Certainly, I had never thought of becoming a senator.

The creation of Nunavut on April 1, 1999, added a new senate seat. Willie Adams, who had been the senator for all the Northwest Territories before division, became the senator for Nunavut, meaning a new senator for the Northwest Territories would have to be appointed. It had been known the position was coming open since 1995, and Jim Bourque was reputed to be the front runner. But he had died unexpectedly in 1996, leaving the way open for other candidates.

Over the summer of 1999 I was living back in Fort Simpson, running the bed and breakfast with Karen and doing some work for the Canadian Human Rights Commission. Ethel Blondin-Andrew, a Dene MP and a cabinet minister in the Chrétien government, told me that she had advanced my name to become senator and was quite optimistic about it. There were others who wanted the job, of course; it was rumoured that Nellie Cournoyea, who had also served as premier of the Northwest Territories, was actively campaigning in Liberal circles. In fact, an editorial in *News/North* in late August mentioned her interest and qualifications and suggested that, "Ottawa's gain would be the Delta's loss."

Then on September 1, 1999, I had been working outside at the B&B and when I went back in, my cousin Marie told me that a man had called from Ottawa but hadn't left a name or number. That evening Percy Downe called from the prime minister's office and told me I was on a shortlist of people being considered for the Northwest Territories senator position. Would I accept such an appointment if it were offered to me? I told him I would, and he said he would call me the next day.

Karen was in Edmonton with our daughters, so I phoned her right away and told them the news. That night I slept out on the deck, watching the skies with all its stars and wondering whether I would be able to manage the job if it were offered. I had been out of politics for almost ten years. Would I be able to cope with public life again?

The following morning Downe faxed some information about the Senate, and at approximately 9:45 I received a call from the PMO. A voice asked me to hold, please, as the prime minister would like to speak to me. After a pause, Jean Chrétien came on the line.

"Hello, Nick," he said, as if we were lifelong friends. He said that he remembered me from earlier days when he was the minister of Indian and Northern Affairs and used to make trips to the North. I was the MLA asking him tough questions! He asked what I was doing these days and I told him about our B&B.

After some further talk he asked if I would like to be a senator. Immediately I said, "Yes, I would be honoured."

He indicated that he needed my support for a number of bills that were going through the Senate, and I assured him he had it. Wishing me well and saying he would be seeing me in Ottawa, the prime minister ended the call.

I talked to some of his officials to give them a bit of a biography, and at about two o'clock that afternoon the announcement was made on CBC Radio. It was a good thing I had already called Karen and told her the news, because the phone immediately began to ring. A number of friends called from Tuktoyaktuk, Rae-Edzo, Yellowknife and of course locally, and it was really heartening to hear how happy everyone was for me. Then the media called—*News/North*, CBC and some southern papers and stations. We had three phones in the B&B,

and Marie and I were laughing because one phone would ring and as we answered it another one at the other end of the house would start ringing. It was as if our house was jingling with joy, and we were running from one part of the house to the other to answer the phone calls. In reporting the news, *News/North* applauded my appointment as an excellent choice.

The next day I went down to Willow River to see Joa Boots and tell him the news that his friend Jean Chrétien had made me a senator. Joa referred to Jean Chrétien as his friend as he had met him on several occasions and often talked of him when issues close to his heart arose. As an example, when gun registration was an issue, Joa told me to tell Jean Chrétien that he had hunted with a gun since he was ten years old and never hurt anybody. Joa was happy for me and we topped off the day by going down the river with his boat to visit Jim and Terry Villeneuve at their cabin.

Over the next few days, Karen and I made plans to travel to Ottawa with all our family to be introduced into the Senate. My oldest son Glen was in the military, flying Sea King helicopters at the time, and he came from Halifax to attend. Randy was up in Iqaluit with his wife, Stephanie, doing a rock sculpture, and they were able to come. My other four children also travelled to Ottawa to take part in the ceremony and see me introduced in the Senate. There were documents to be signed and oaths to be taken, and on my first day I was escorted into the senate chamber and introduced by Senators Willie Adams and Bernie Graham, the leader of the government in the Senate at the time.

I was back in the familiar political realm. It would be easier than an elected position, with no campaigns to run and limited constituency work, but I had been out of politics for eight years. I was also still plagued by depression, so although I felt honoured to be chosen by the prime minister and was excited about the appointment, I was only cautiously optimistic that I could handle the job.

As a senator I had the opportunity to go home every weekend if I wanted, but it was not practical to fly across the country to get home on Friday and have to leave again on Sunday. Instead, Karen and I usually stayed in Ottawa for a month before coming home for a week.

I enjoyed living in Ottawa during most of the winter and spending the summers in Fort Simpson. It was good to leave with the ducks in the fall when the snow started flying, but when spring came I longed for home and wanted to fly with the geese on their long flights to the North.

ONE WOULD THINK that as a senator I would finally feel happy. I now had a good income, and I would be secure in my position until the age of seventy-five. Yet daily life in Ottawa was not always happy for me. Many times I questioned what I was doing in Ottawa far from my family, friends and home in the North. Depression is an insidious disease, not obvious to anyone on the outside. You may look and act normal while inside you are sapped of enjoyment, feeling no zest for life. During the day it's like living in a haze, having just enough energy to carry out your duties and routines, and the nights are horrific: sweating, tossing and turning. You're constantly exhausted because you can't get proper rest and sleep. This was life for me for the first few years as a senator.

As I had done earlier in my life when faced with similar bouts of depression, I sought counselling, went to mass as often as I could and sought medical help. Regularly, my family doctor prescribed anti-depressants and in 2000, I went to The Haven on Gabriola Island in British Columbia for a one-week workshop on depression.

During this time, I also suffered from pain in my back and neck. I had never experienced that sort of physical pain, and I used to tell my friends that the Senate job must be tough as I had all these unusual ailments. But in April 2000, severe pain sent me to the doctor, who diagnosed appendicitis. I had my appendix removed, and within a few months all my neck and back pains went away.

In February of 2002 I reached my lowest point. Karen and I were staying in the Palliser Hotel in Calgary. In my dark state of depression, I told Karen that I wanted to leave her. I told her I was unhappy and thought separation was the answer. Karen was horribly upset. She cried and kept saying, "Where do I go?" We talked things out and in a couple days we reconciled, but her words haunt me to this day.

I WAS APPOINTED to the Standing Committee on Aboriginal Peoples, and I was chairman in 2005 at the time the Tli'Cho land claims settlement bill was going through. I was proud to have the Tli'Cho leaders come before the committee to tell us why the land claims agreement was so important to them. Elders like Alexie Arrowmaker, Joe Migwi, Louis Wedawin, Francis Williah and James Rabesca were watching intently, having spent their lives advancing the claim. The committee process went well and we were able to move Bill C-14, the Tli'Cho Land Claims and Self-Government Act, along in record time to get it back into the Senate for final vote at third reading. Still the night before the bill was to be voted on in the Senate, I had difficulty sleeping and went through my usual ordeal. Finally, in desperation, I woke Karen and said that if it continued, I was going to go to the hospital and check myself into the psychiatry ward. We knelt together in prayer and I eventually managed to fall asleep.

The next day, February 10, the Senate's public gallery was filled with about forty Tli'Cho people, the leaders, the staff who had worked on the agreement, the elders and some well-wishers. All eyes and ears were on me as I reported that our committee had reviewed and approved the bill and it was ready for third reading. It was a Thursday, and normally we would have had to wait until the following Tuesday to give final reading to the bill, as the rules call for a one-day delay between reporting and third reading. That delay would have been a great inconvenience to the Tli'Cho people attending but much to my surprise Gerry St. Germain, the Conservative vice-chair of the committee, asked for unanimous consent to permit the bill to pass that day. Gerry told me later that he did not give advance warning to the Conservative leadership that he would be taking this bold step because he thought his best chance lay in springing it unannounced on his colleagues. I think the request caught everyone by surprise and no one objected, so we proceeded to give the bill third reading.

I stood up and gave a speech in both Dene and English about the Tli'Cho people, praising them as a progressive group of Dene in the North who had worked for ten years negotiating their agreement. They were to receive ownership of 39,000 square kilometres of land plus $152 million, a share of royalties from resource development and the right to set up their own government. The Tli'Cho people had traditionally had strong leadership and had embarked on an education program so they could be "strong like two people." The bill passed, and before the Senate concluded I told all the senators that the Tli'Cho, in appreciation of the passage of their land claims bill, would like to perform a tea dance in the foyer.

The foyer outside the senate entrance has a marble floor and pillars and huge paintings of queens and kings hanging from the walls. Word about the bill's passage quickly spread throughout parliament, and before long the foyer was filled with MPs and senators mingling and congratulating the Tli'Cho people. The drums were taken out and soon a big circle had formed and a tea dance was underway. As I joined the dance, I looked up at the paintings and couldn't help but think in amusement that the pictured kings and queens were probably turning in their graves about what was going on in the senate foyer.

As the dance wound down I met with Ethel Blondin-Andrew and Sue Barnes, who was the parliamentary secretary to the minister of Indian Affairs and Northern Development, and we decided to seek Royal Assent immediately. The process involved getting either the governor general or a Supreme Court judge to sign the bill. Governor General Adrienne Clarkson was not in Ottawa at the time, so we sought to have a judge sign the proclamation. Phone calls were made and soon the senate clerk and I were walking into the Supreme Court of Canada building, where Madame Justice Marie Deschamps signed the bill. It was thus proclaimed into law. I returned to the hotel where everyone was gathered to tell them that their land claim agreement had received Royal Assent, and the cheers and claps resounded. It is the only Northwest Territories land claim settlement that I was directly involved in passing, though I still hope to see one for my home area, the Deh Cho, before I retire.

THE TURNING POINT in my dealing with depression came in 2006. I had seen a number of psychiatrists and doctors and had been given medication for short periods of time, but I did not feel that they helped on a long-term basis. The depression was still with me.

I attended a meeting of people dealing with depression. In some ways it was like an AA meeting given that it was a support group of people having the same problem. But I didn't find the meeting helpful; most of the people just complained, and there was no talk about the spiritual side of their lives. The AA program, which is considered to be the most effective program in the world for dealing with alcohol addiction, depends on believing in a higher power that will help you overcome alcoholism. Members share stories not just of problems, but of the spiritual growth that has helped them overcome those problems and the actions they took leading to that growth. Most of the discussion in the depression meeting was about the medication they were on and their dealings with psychiatrists and social service agencies.

In my own experience, while medication is important, equally important and necessary are the counselling sessions, the workshops and the vitality of your spiritual life. As my belief in God increased, so did my ability to let go and think positively. Healing does not happen in one big swoop or event; rather, it comes in baby steps, occurring over a period of time. Whenever I took healing workshops, went on spiritual retreats or was at home in the North, I got relief and would have stretches of peace and well-being until the depression returned again.

In May of 2006 the *Ottawa Citizen* ran a front-page story about Margaret Trudeau and her struggle with bipolar disorder, otherwise known as manic depression. There was an accompanying story in *Maclean's* magazine. She described how she had admitted herself into the Royal Ottawa Hospital, and with proper medication and therapy was able to stabilize the fluctuations she experienced between extreme euphoria and severe depression. Later she became a spokeswoman for those dealing with depression: "I have my life back and I'm here to champion the cause." She lauded the treatment she received at the hospital, saying there had been great advancements made in treatment of depression and similar mental illnesses. Although my depression was not as serious as hers, I too wanted to be healed. I was inspired by Trudeau's story and made arrangements to see a psychiatrist at the Royal Ottawa Hospital. That was the turning point for me. Not only did that doctor prescribe antidepressants, but together we began to look at the roots of my problems. I began to feel better within a few weeks, and over the next months I continuously improved and began to enjoy life again.

By coincidence, later that summer I had the chance to meet Margaret Trudeau when she came to Fort Simpson to speak at a conference on the protection of water resources. I told her how she had inspired me, and she ended up coming to meet Karen and staying at our B&B. At the conference's concluding feast and drum dance I was honoured to start off the dance with her.

EVEN DURING MY darkest days I had continued to carry on with my work and represent the Northwest Territories in the upper chamber. Karen's love and support helped tremendously. She almost always travelled to Ottawa with me and she attended many of the events senators are expected to participate in.

I've also been fortunate to have good staff to help me in Ottawa. Over the years I've had several executive assistants: Cindy McAvour, Carole Hupé and most recently Renee Allen. Long-time northerner and Liberal insider Claire Barnabe helped me get established and along with Peggy Blair, whom I knew from the Human Rights Tribunal, provided policy advice. I also made some use of contractors such as Lutra Associates in Yellowknife and Mike Whittington, my former principal secretary, who lives in Ottawa. Then in 2001 I rehired my old assistant from my days as premier to be my full-time policy advisor. It is an interesting story of how chance can change your life.

Hayden Trenholm had left the North for Calgary in 1991 to pursue a career in the arts. I had seen him from time to time while I was back in Calgary renewing my law degree. After I became a senator, we spoke a few times when he was in Ottawa on business. On September 13, 2001, I phoned him from Fort Simpson. I had been in the bush and was only vaguely aware of the terrorist events in the United States of a few days before. He, on the other hand, had been scheduled to go to a writers' conference that was cancelled when flights were grounded. When I called him he was in the midst of a conversation with his wife about going back into public policy in light of the changes that 9/11 would inevitably bring. He told me later that it was too big of a coincidence to ignore, and a few months later he was on his way to Ottawa.

Chapter 18: The Senate Years

I CONSIDER IT one of my most important roles to educate people in the south about the realities of life in the North. In the Senate, where laws are passed, I realize it is my utmost duty to speak and ensure that the realities of people of the North are taken into account. I realize that many laws, particularly criminal laws, are made with the people of large cities as the main consideration. I try to remind people that life in the North, whether in Yellowknife or in small communities, is different from life in large southern cities. It is not simply a matter of climate or isolation; people have different values and different approaches to problems. A good example of this is shown in a speech I made in the Senate about the controversial gun registry.

Guns are central to the traditional way of life practised by Aboriginal people for generations. We use them to hunt for our food and to protect us from predators not only in the bush but also in our communities. In my hometown it is not uncommon to see bears cross our yards throughout the summer, so for safety it is necessary to have a gun handy. Guns are not a problem in the North; they are part of the solution, because preserving our traditional way of life is vital if we are to overcome the social problems we face. The gun registry was designed for southern people with southern problems. It may be that they need it. In the North, however, it has been a failure. It interfered with traditional lifestyles and generated anger and defiance.

The failure of the designers of the gun registry to take into account the rights of Aboriginal people or the reality of life in northern communities made the issues of gun safety and crime prevention so divisive that inevitably the gun registry failed. I was proud to oppose the registry when the Liberals were in power and glad to vote to end it under the Conservatives.

Not that government learned from these lessons. In 2011, speaking to the Conservative government's omnibus crime bill, I pointed out they were making the same mistake, trying to write one-size-fits-all legislation that imposed solutions for southern problems on northern communities—legislation designed to deal with big-city problems that took little account of the realities of life in small communities in the North. Our problems in the North are not criminal but social. With high unemployment rates, overcrowded housing and a lack of activities for young people, most crime is "driven by despair and fuelled by alcohol."

WHEN THE CONSERVATIVE party won the federal general election in 2006, I could no longer raise northern issues in caucus directly with ministers. Instead I started to ask more questions in the senate chamber. I had few expectations of getting clear answers—it is, as the old adage puts it, question period not answer period—but it is one of the few tools we have to make our concerns known. It also served as another way to educate my colleagues and the public about the North. In a 2010 question about stimulus funding for infrastructure, for example, I reminded the government that southern rules and processes don't always work in the North. The North being what it is—remote and distant, with some areas subject to summer sea lift, winter ice roads and short summer work seasons—it is challenging to start and finish construction projects. I asked the minister for assurance that planned projects in the northern territories would receive all the promised funding and that small, remote communities and financially strapped territorial governments would not be penalized if the reality of northern construction was in conflict with federal government–imposed timelines. In this particular case, the minister responded that the government recognized the specific needs of the North and had taken measures to ensure that planned projects could be completed.

Of course, the best way of learning about a place is actually to go there, and I never missed an opportunity to encourage the prime minister, ministers, MPs and senators to go to the Northwest Territories and experience first-hand the challenges (and opportunities) that the North presented. Over the course of my time in the Senate I have been able to persuade senate committees to hold hearings or send fact-finding delegations to northern communities to study a variety of issues. When possible I have sat in on hearings held in the North, even if not actually a member of that committee. That's one of the privileges of being a senator: you can attend and ask questions, even if you can't vote, at any senate committee hearing. I recall sitting in on a meeting of the Social Affairs Committee in Yellowknife when they were studying the issue of poverty. It was a tremendous learning experience for me. Until then, I hadn't really been aware of how serious poverty and homelessness was in the North, especially in Yellowknife.

One of my first actions as a senator and member of the Senate Aboriginal Peoples Committee was to get the committee to strike a working group to look at northern parks and their effect on Aboriginal people. I travelled north with two colleagues and Library of Parliament researchers and produced a 2001 report called "Northern Parks—A New Way," which resulted in new management approaches by Parks Canada when dealing with local people and communities.

On another occasion in 2009, the Energy, Environment and Natural Resources Committee made an extensive visit to the Northwest Territories and Yukon, travelling to Yellowknife, Norman Wells, Inuvik, Tuktoyaktuk and Whitehorse over the course of a week to hold fact-finding meetings on issues concerning Arctic sovereignty and northern development. These meetings were supplemented by public hearings held in Ottawa, and all the work culminated in the report "With Respect, Canada's North." It came to the same conclusion I had about government policies: they had to be adapted to northern realities if they were to do any good north of sixty. The report made nine recommendations in all, dealing with infrastructure, regulatory reform and climate change. The most important of these called on the government of Canada to enhance local consultation and decision-making and to recognize it is the people who live in the North that are the greatest claim Canada can make to Arctic sovereignty.

On a less official level, I organized several trips by groups of senators to visit the Northwest Territories and experience it for themselves through a combination of tours, meetings and social events. In 2003, 2005 and 2007, groups of two to seven senators from both major political parties accompanied me on trips to Yellowknife and in 2005 to Fort Smith, where they met with local leaders and community members. We tailored the visits to the interests of the participating senators and included meetings with local politicians, business leaders and community activists. Each visit included a trip to one of the diamond mines—Ekati or Diavik—and concluded with a dinner and cultural event that gave senators a real taste of northern life. It was great fun to see my colleagues throw off the stuffiness of the Senate and participate in an old-fashioned square dance! I remember Senator Viola Léger's visible delight as she looked out the window of a small plane a group of us were on as we were leaving Yellowknife on a trip to a diamond mine. It was a glorious, crisp, cold morning, and she said, "I wish every Canadian could see and experience this."

That was the exact experience I had hoped she would have.

After the government changed in 2006, it became increasingly difficult to get senators to participate in these kinds of trips as the emphasis shifted from being informed to saving money. Still, I continued to encourage senators to travel north at every opportunity and perhaps before I'm done I'll get one more northern tour organized.

ON TOP OF representing the Northwest Territories in the Senate, I have also been one of a small number of Aboriginal senators who have served in parliament over the years. Although I've sometimes said I don't want to be the senator for all Aboriginal people, I do take my role as a representative of Native people very seriously. The Aboriginal Peoples Committee is the only one of which I've been a member for my entire senate career, acting as both chair and deputy chair for a number of years. While I've enjoyed serving on other committees, this is the one to which I've devoted my greatest time and energy. Whenever I get a request to meet with Aboriginal people in Ottawa, I make every effort to accommodate them and to facilitate the work they are doing. I've travelled to many communities both officially and as an individual to learn more about the Aboriginal experience across Canada.

So in addition to being "northern" when I speak in the Senate and its committees, I am also conscious of being Aboriginal. I've tried both to represent my own experiences as a Native person and to re-mind senators that there is a diversity of views between regions and communities; not every Aboriginal person is the same; not every Ab-original group has the same interests and approaches. I believe it is important for Canadians to remember that there are more than two founding peoples (English and French) in Canada. Indians and Inuit had strong viable societies long before Europeans ever arrived.

In 2004, during the discussion of a technical bill to harmonize com-mon law and civil code (Quebec), Senator Serge Joyal, the sponsor of the bill, spoke of the recognition of a third legal tradition, Aboriginal law. I was inspired by his remarks and took the opportunity to make some impromptu observations of my own, relating my experiences as a lawyer defending Native people and commenting on the growing recognition of this legal tradition: "When we talk about Aboriginal law, this is what we are talking about—the practices and traditions that Aboriginal people have carried from generation to generation. They are embodied. They are based on common sense and rules for good living on the land, that is, the handling of people, animals and the land. Those are the traditions and practices that apply, and slowly they are being recognized."

On another occasion, when the rules of the Senate were being changed to allow senators to speak Inuktitut (in recognition of Sen-ator Adams, who spoke well in Inuktitut but sometimes struggled with English), I spoke of the importance of recognizing all Aborig-inal languages and told of our struggles in the Northwest Territories to make Aboriginal languages official. From time to time, to prove the point, I will speak briefly in both the Senate and at committee in Slavey, my own language. It is always well-received.

People, especially those from the North, often ask me what I do as a senator because the position and function are not well-known, certainly not as well-known as that of Member of Parliament. MPs are seen more often, and people get to vote for them every few years.

Although I try to make it out to communities throughout the North-west Territories on a regular basis, there is less urgency to do so since I don't need to remind them to vote for me. My visits tend to be more low-key and less political as well, more an opportunity to check in on local issues and gather information I can use in my work in Ottawa. From time to time, I will prepare newsletters or pamphlets and circulate them to people in the North, though my budget is limited for this type of communication. In recent years, I've added a website and even tried my hand at social media as a way of letting people know what is going on and getting feedback on issues.

Generally, my brochures were well-received even when they dealt with controversial issues such as my opposition to the expansion of the Nahanni Park. I think most people like to hear another view of a situation, especially since being a senator means I'm able to speak my mind without fear of reprisal. That is one advantage of an unelected senate; you really can operate according to your conscience and do what you think is best for the region you represent.

When asked what I do, I explain as best I can that there are 105 senators who represent the regions of our country and that we act as the upper chamber of parliament, giving sober second thought to the bills. We study the bills in committee, often making observations about areas of concern and from time to time making amendments to fix things the government and the House of Commons missed. Both the House and the Senate must give three readings to every bill, and have to agree on amendments, after which they are signed by the governor general and become law.

I am often teased by people in the communities that as their senator, I sit in a house of old men where everybody is grey, and asleep half the time. Not true, I reply glibly, it is a house of old men and women. (The Senate has a higher percentage of women than any legislature in Canada.) To this I add that we're not like the House of Commons and their rowdy question period where there is heckling, loud shouting back and forth and everyone behaving like excited children. The Senate in contrast is an orderly, quiet place; we don't raise our voices lest we scare the other senators awake. I tell them that we have a nurse on stand-by and a health clinic in a nearby room in case anyone keels over. The young men and women who serve as pages, bringing us water and notes, also check our pulses if we seem to have been asleep for a while.

Prior to 1965, senators were appointed for life, and there are stories of senators being wheeled in on their deathbeds to vote in critical situations and afterwards dying out in the lobby, having done their duty. Since 1965 senators, like Supreme Court judges, must retire at age seventy-five.

Senators have a lower profile in Canada than do MPs and rightly so. I have always fought for elected people to have a greater say than those appointed. Right from my very first day as a member of the NWT Legislative Council in 1970, it was my view that the people— through their elected representatives—should dictate to appointed officials, not the other way around. It would be hypocritical now not to defer to elected representatives. Indeed, I have been supportive of the idea of an elected senate, but I honestly feel this can only be done through a constitutional amendment that also deals with the powers of the Senate, its regional makeup, the term of office for senators and the method of election. It is interesting to note that there are over sixty bicameral legislatures (that is, having two houses) in the world, but not one of them uses the same method of selection for the upper and lower house. Someday Canadians will be ready for further constitutional reform, and significant changes will be made to the Senate at that time.

The least important thing I do is going to the senate chamber to ask questions or participate in debates. In my view, asking questions in the Senate is like play politics. It's all in the realm of fantasy, wishing something real would come of your efforts. I do it, of course, because it is part of the job and it occasionally provides an opportunity to bring issues to the forefront that might otherwise remain unknown. At least my colleagues sitting in the Senate hear me and are either interested or amused about the things I ask or say. There are very few reporters in the Senate and unless someone, perhaps a civil servant, reads the debates, my efforts could go unnoticed. I tell my colleagues, especially when we are in caucus and being frank, that it certainly is not like the real politics carried out in the legislative assembly or the

House of Commons where you ask the ministers in charge of departments about issues within their control and responsibility. A slip-up
there can embarrass the government and even cost the minister his
or her job. In a minority government, as we experienced from 2005 to
2010, there is always the chance the government will be defeated and
forced to call an election.

In the Senate, all of the thirty minutes of question period is spent
directing questions to the government leader. Because she sits in cabinet as the leader of the government in the Senate, she is deemed to
know the government's position on any given matter. Of course, she
could not possibly know the position or decisions of all the ministers
in cabinet. Unless she is briefed and guesses correctly what the issues
on any day are likely to be, all she can do is give a partisan non-answer
or take the question on notice and provide a reply days or weeks later.
In 2013 the government leader in the Senate was left out of cabinet,
further reducing the relevance of question period.

Moreover, the Senate is not a confidence house. Were the government to lose a vote in the Senate, the consequences are not severe. A
bill might need to be retracted or the government might need to make
a report, but ministers' jobs are not at stake and the government cannot be brought down.

Having been in what I call the front lines of politics—a minister
in a legislative assembly and the head of a government—I find the
process of question period in the Senate a bit of a sham. At least we
only have to do it three days a week, usually only sitting from Tuesday to Thursday, with a rare Monday or Friday session thrown in. My
staff always laughs when I come to the office and say, "Thank God it's
Thursday!"

As the senator for the Northwest Territories, my most useful
work is done in the committees I sit on. I'm currently on the Aboriginal Peoples and the Energy, Environment and Natural Resources committees. The work of senators in committee reviewing bills
and conducting studies on relevant important areas of public policy
is effective and is generally highly regarded, so that is where I've focused my energies over the last dozen years. With four committee
meetings a week to prepare for and attend, I often spend more time in

committee than I do in the senate chamber itself. When we travel to different parts of Canada to hold hearings, committee meetings may extend from early morning well into the evening for three or four days in a row.

Over the years I've dealt with dozens of pieces of legislation in committee and participated in almost as many studies or special reports. Some issues were dealt with over a matter of years; others came and went in a few weeks. No matter how obscure some things might seem to most Canadians, in every case the issues we dealt with were vitally important to some people, affecting their lives and their livelihoods in profound ways. Aboriginal rights, political and economic development (especially in the North), the environment (especially climate change) and issues of social justice were all areas where I feel I made—and will continue to make—some contribution during my senate years.

EXISTING ABORIGINAL AND treaty rights are recognized and affirmed in Canada under Section 35 of the Constitution Act (1982), the same legislation that repatriated the constitution and introduced the Charter of Rights and Freedoms. The act also lists the Aboriginal Peoples of Canada as being Indians, Inuit and Métis and promises that nothing else in the Act will "abrogate or derogate" from those rights. Like all legal enactments, this one has been subject to interpretation, generally by the courts, though sometimes by government policy or legislation.

Gradually over the last thirty years, the Supreme Court has, through a series of decisions, determined the nature and extent of existing Aboriginal and treaty rights and determined if and when they might be breached by the government while preserving the "Honour of the Crown." The courts have also begun to define the Crown's duty to consult, and, in many cases, accommodate (or compensate) Aboriginal peoples over matters that affect their rights.

Rights arise either because of underlying Aboriginal land title that existed prior to settlement or through specific agreements (treaties) that established relationships between the Crown and Aboriginal peoples. There are numerous pre-Confederation agreements, especially in eastern Canada, that are still binding on Canada and have shaped such things as fishing rights in Atlantic Canada.

Eleven treaties were also signed between Canada and First Nations peoples between 1873 and 1921, covering much of northern Ontario, all of Manitoba, Saskatchewan and Alberta and portions of British Columbia, Northwest Territories and the Yukon. These so-called numbered treaties guaranteed certain rights and benefits to Indians in exchange for occupancy rights for Europeans. In some cases Aboriginal title was surrendered by the numbered treaties, but in others it was not. Historic treaties did not cover the majority of British Columbia and no treaties were made with the Inuit.

Since 1973, Canada has negotiated a number of modern treaties or comprehensive land claims agreements that now cover all of northern Canada, including northern Quebec and Labrador, and that provide certainty about land tenure to the government in exchange for clear title to blocks of land, cash settlements and management rights over things like land, water and wildlife within a public government structure. A few more settlements have been reached with First Nations in British Columbia through the BC Treaty process.

Canada has also recognized, through policy, an Aboriginal right to self-government and has negotiated a number of self-government agreements, some of which are constitutionally protected, though a few are not.

Generally speaking, it has been my observation that comprehensive land claims and self-government agreements have been extremely effective at improving the lot in life of the Aboriginal people that come under them. At times, the federal government has been lax in fulfilling some aspects of these claims, but progress continues to be made. However in southern Canada, the ability to negotiate these claims is complicated by the existing treaties and the involvement of provincial governments.

In addition to comprehensive claims, there is also a category of land claims called specific claims. These arise where the government has failed to live up to the terms of historic treaties or where federal officials have made mistakes or even committed fraud with respect to Indian lands or monies. The process of proving such claims and then negotiating them has always been time-consuming and expensive, and until recently there was a huge backlog of these claims either within the bureaucracy or before the courts.

Some of the most important work I've done in parliament has been on the issue of Aboriginal rights. A lot of this work has been carried out in the Aboriginal Peoples Committee but some I've done as an individual senator or in partnership with my Aboriginal colleagues.

The negotiation of comprehensive claims is a complex and lengthy process, and by the time they arrive in parliament they are in most respects a done deal. The Aboriginal communities, the federal government and in some cases provincial or territorial governments have all agreed on the provisions of the settlement, and the final agreement—often running several hundred pages—could not be changed without reopening the entire negotiation. The Aboriginal group has already voted to ratify the agreement; parliament, and the affected provincial legislature, are expected to pass legislation to put the agreement into law. Amending the implementation legislation, not to mention the agreement itself, would be nearly impossible.

The fact that lengthy negotiations have gone on before the agreement reaches parliament doesn't stop some parliamentarians from raising questions about agreements or even opposing them. The debates have sometimes been fierce, especially when the agreements include elements of self-government. Some of my first speeches as a senator were in support of the Nisga'a agreement. I said at that time, "I believe the Aboriginal peoples of Canada can best achieve their goals and create a strong independent society by having full and responsible self-government. As for delegated powers, what we have now in the Indian Act is not working. The status quo is not working. It is simply not good enough. Full responsible government is what is called for." That was my position then and it remains my position to this day. I'm happy to say, in the case of the Nisga'a and so many other Aboriginal communities, my belief has proven true.

Of course, negotiating and signing a claim is not the same as implementing it, and there have been lots of complaints about the federal government not fulfilling the spirit of the agreements, or in some cases even the letter. These complaints have been made not only by claimant groups—either in parliament or often in the courts—but were also raised by Auditor General Sheila Fraser in a number of reports during her tenure of 2001–2011. At my urging, the Aboriginal Peoples Committee undertook a study of claims implementation and found many flaws with how the government acted. Some improvements were made subsequent to our recommendations, but the matter of claims implementation remains contentious and subject to frequent litigation (which usually results in an out-of-court settlement by the government).

During the Chrétien government, in 2002 Minister of Indian Affairs Bob Nault introduced a number of bills to replace or update sections of the Indian Act. This suite of legislation proved controversial and led to months of demonstrations, including temporary encampments on Parliament Hill long before the Occupy movement or Idle No More had the same idea. The legislation to reform governance on reserve stalled, but another bill to create a tribunal to deal with resolving outstanding specific claims did make it through parliament, though it was never proclaimed and was eventually dumped by Paul Martin.

The legislation would have replaced a mediation body, the Specific Claims Commission, with one that could make final decisions on claims when a negotiated settlement couldn't be reached. The legislation was flawed in many respects, notably because of the continued role of the minister and the limits placed on the size of claims that could be arbitrated.

After hearing testimony from many experts in the field and from First Nations and their organizations, I proposed a number of amendments, seven or eight as I recall, which would have substantially improved the bill. I and four other Liberal Aboriginal senators were determined that changes be made. Eventually we had a meeting with Minister Nault—just the Aboriginal senators, a few of our staff and a few of his.

Bob started the meeting by saying, "Look, we're all Liberals here," and then went on to explain why our recommended changes couldn't be made. When it was clear that we were determined, he agreed to look at them. Later Senator Jake Austin, the bill's sponsor, came to me with a counter offer: four of the amendments—all slightly watered down—would be accepted by the government. It wasn't much but it was something, so I introduced the amendments at the next committee meeting and they were passed both there and in the Senate. The amendments then had to go back to the House of Commons, where the government quickly agreed to pass them.

As I noted, the bill never came into effect, but it was a good lesson for me. I've never hesitated to suggest amendments to legislation whether introduced by Liberal or Conservative governments, when I thought I could improve it. I haven't always been successful, but occasionally I've managed to get one or two changes approved. Even in Opposition I've noted that a concerted effort can change the thinking of government members.

The matter of specific claims came before us again a few years later in 2007, when Jim Prentice was appointed Minister of Indian Affairs and Northern Development in the Stephen Harper government. Prentice had been a long-time member of the Indian Claims Commission and knew as much about the problems with the specific claims negotiation process as anyone in Canada. With his encouragement, our committee undertook a study of the system and made numerous recommendations for improving it.

The legislation, developed in cooperation with the assembly of First Nations, closely reflected our report, and the Specific Claims Tribunal Act was introduced in 2008 as a rare senate government bill and passed into law. Though it is too soon to say that it has solved the problem once and for all, it has by all accounts helped reduce the backlog and provided a more satisfactory mechanism for resolving disputes.

NOT ALL THE Aboriginal rights issues I've dealt with have been nearly so clear-cut as claims or self-government. One that occupied an inordinate amount of my time for several years was the matter of non-derogation clauses in federal legislation. It's such a technical legal issue that I hesitate to raise it for fear of putting readers to sleep, but it also offers useful insight into the inner workings of the legislative process and the duties of a senator.

A non-derogation clause in legislation is a statement of parliament's intent that is meant to assist the courts in interpreting legislation that could abrogate or derogate from Aboriginal and treaty rights—a fancy way of saying damage or diminish them. The clauses were originally meant to direct the courts to be respectful of Aboriginal and treaty rights in interpreting specific legislation. In the Sparrow decision, the Supreme Court agreed with that expectation. In addition, Aboriginal people (and other citizens) must be assured that Aboriginal rights are not being ignored or treated casually. Non-derogation clauses were meant to provide both comfort and certainty.

Non-derogation wording had originally been modelled on Section 25 of the Charter of Rights and Freedoms but over the years different, less robust, versions appeared in legislation. The change in wording of non-derogation clauses created confusion with respect to both legal and political implications. Between 2001 and 2003, other Aboriginal senators and I made efforts to revert to bills' clauses to the original wording. Eventually, the matter was referred by the government leader in the Senate to the Standing Committee on Legal and Constitutional Affairs, which finally issued a report in December 2007 that largely agreed with our conclusions. Minister of Justice Rob Nicholson promised to consider their recommendations seriously but nothing came of it, so the matter of varying non-derogation clauses continues to arise to this day.

MY INTEREST IN economic development, which began in my university days when I was back in Fort Simpson for the summer in 1970 and helped organize a local co-op, increased over the years and has been a central theme in much of my work as a senator. I have been actively promoting the economic well-being of the North and encouraging the involvement of Aboriginal communities across Canada in business.

It is my view that if Aboriginal people are going to lift themselves out of poverty and provide security for future generations, they have no choice but to be involved in business, both individually as entrepreneurs and collectively through development corporations. It is not easy—business is one of the hardest things to do well—but there is no other choice. Government cannot be relied on to meet all the needs of communities. Traditional economies are insufficient to support growing populations and are often quite marginal. Only through wealth creation can sustainable communities be built.

There is a wide range of economic activities at which Aboriginal people can and have been successful. Resource development, construction, real estate, transportation, tourism, agriculture, manufacturing, arts and crafts, and entertainment—there is no sector of the economy where a highly successful Aboriginal business can't be found. Aboriginal people had vibrant economies before European settlement—they fed, housed and clothed their people, engaged in trade and transportation of goods, supported cultural activities— but colonization and the strictures of the Indian Act destroyed those economies and kept Aboriginal communities from accessing the settler financial systems. They had no opportunities to use their land and resources or to raise capital for business ventures.

Things have changed dramatically in the last thirty years. Now there are many Aboriginal success stories and for every struggling community, like Attiwapiskat, there is a highly successful one like the Osoyoos First Nation. Improved leadership and governance and access to capital through land claims or resource revenue sharing have led to many successful Aboriginal businesses. Some, like the Cree of northern Quebec and the Inuvialuit of the Northwest Territories, have grown into some of the largest corporations in Canada. Over the years I've had the opportunity to visit many successful First Nations—Membertou in Nova Scotia, Westbank near Kelowna, BC, and Lac La Ronge in northern Saskatchewan. They have seized whatever opportunities were available to them to improve the lives of their citizens.

When I was chair of the Aboriginal Peoples Committee, I wanted to investigate why some communities were succeeding while others struggled. We undertook a study of Aboriginal economic development that spanned several years and two governments and resulted in a comprehensive report entitled "Sharing Canada's Prosperity—a Hand Up, Not a Hand Out," which was tabled in March 2007. Numerous recommendations were made and I'm pleased to say at least some of them informed the government's approach to Aboriginal economies for some years thereafter.

DEVELOPMENT OFTEN REQUIRES hard choices between environmental protection and economic needs. In the North we have been very concerned to ensure that land and water are protected for future generations and, over the years, built strong regulatory systems where Aboriginal people had a significant role to play in public government structures.

Because of the piecemeal way these systems developed, they became somewhat cumbersome and perhaps skewed toward environmental concerns over economic ones. However, as Aboriginal people grew more confident and involved in the economy and as the institutions of public government in the North were strengthened, we eventually reached the point when these regulatory systems could and should be reformed to make development simpler while still ensuring environmental protection. The process of reform undertaken by the Harper government has been controversial at times—largely because of a lack of appropriate consultation—but, in my view, is a good initiative for the future of the North. It will be important to ensure the pendulum doesn't now swing too far the other way.

Finding ways to both benefit from development and protect the environment always involved competing interests and points of view. Take the issue of national parks. Parks have long been proposed as a way of preserving the land for future generations and protecting watersheds from contamination. In the Northwest Territories, Parks Canada has actively pursued the creation of huge national parks on the Arctic Coast, in the Nahanni watershed and on the East Arm of Great Slave Lake. They've been supported in these initiatives by environmental groups like the Canadian Parks and Wilderness Society, which mobilizes southern support and money for their campaigns. Aboriginal groups, too, have often been in favour of creating parks, especially in areas where land claims haven't been settled. For example, the Deh Cho First Nations were active participants in the expansion of the Nahanni National Park. Parks Canada encouraged and promoted their involvement as a demonstration of their collaboration with Aboriginal people. Caution is needed on both sides, however, as once park boundaries are drawn on paper, nothing can change them. Like diamonds, they are forever.

Parks assure Aboriginal people that lands and the environment will be protected forever. No development will occur within the park boundaries. This is often in sync with traditional values of protecting the lands and leaving them in their natural state. On the other side of the coin, as Aboriginal people develop and set up their own governments, they need money to run their governments and the mineral and fossil resources to provide jobs for their people. Fifty or a hundred years from now, they will be frustrated when they realize that these resources are not available to them. Parks mostly benefit a few people who venture north in the summer, while we give up our economic future. First Nations are always promised economic benefits from national parks, but the reality is that few jobs or business opportunities result. In fact, all the parks in the North together have not provided as much economic benefit to communities as a single mine.

In my view, there have always been better ways to promote both environmental protection and economic development. In 2005 I outlined some of those ideas in a newsletter entitled "Nahanni Forever?" I circulated a copy to every household in the Northwest Territories, which made me quite unpopular in certain circles, but for which many individuals thanked me. In it, I said, "The best protection we have for our traditional lifestyle is to limit the size of the park and keep control of the land for ourselves…. Any future Deh Cho government will need economic development to generate revenues for their services and programs. Parks don't have a history of creating many jobs and business opportunities for local people. Nor will an expanded Nahanni park provide significant revenues to a Deh Cho government."

A few years later, after learning about the process that created the Spirit Bear reserve in British Columbia, I hired Yellowknife consultant Jamie Bastedo to write a paper called "Seeking Certainty" that looked at ways land management in the North could be reformed. I've often felt that if the Harper government had paid attention (and it was sent to many federal ministers and officials) to its advice, their efforts at regulatory reform would not have been so uncertain.

I have contracted a number of special studies over the years, using funds either from my research budget or acquired by applying to the Senate's Liberal Caucus Research Fund, which has provided me with several grants. One of my first reports, researched and written by Lutra Associates of Yellowknife, compiled a list of all Aboriginal-owned or -controlled businesses in the Northwest Territories. With the rapid growth of the Native business sector in the first decade of the twenty-first century, it soon was out of date, but it was the first directory of its kind and proved useful to government and business alike for several years. I also directed my policy analyst to prepare a number of discussion papers that I circulated to many stakeholders and posted online. Among the topics covered were guaranteed Aboriginal representation in parliament, the effectiveness of Aboriginal immersion programs on education and the selection of Northwest Territories premiers.

Much economic development in the North has occurred in waves of resource exploitation that have created a boom-and-bust economy and an unequal distribution of jobs, opportunities and wealth in the North between individuals and communities. In 2012, I turned my attention to economic opportunities that could help smooth out the peaks and valleys and spread the benefits of development more smoothly. The result was "Plugging into the Future: Boosting the Northern Economy through Small-Scale Science and Technology." Researched and written jointly by Bastedo and my policy advisor Hayden Trenholm, it sets out a vision for development that is both progressive and sustainable. It is too early to tell what outcome it will have but I hope it will be a significant one.

ONE ENVIRONMENTAL ISSUE that has become more and more obvious and urgent over the years is climate change. Like many Canadians, I was only vaguely aware of climate change and its ramifications. Once I became a senator and began visiting communities in the High Arctic, many of which I hadn't been to in decades, the reality of climate change quickly hit home. In all instances, the people living there have told me that they like it cold. They are bothered by the more frequently erratic weather and earlier open water. In 2008 I hired Jamie Bastedo to look at the effect of climate change in the North. The resulting paper, "On the Frontlines of Climate Change," provided a detailed and dramatic account of global warming and its current and future consequences in the Arctic. Like most studies of five or six years ago, we are finding the impacts on the land and water even more significant and worrisome than we predicted.

Over the last few years, in my travels to northern communities and conversations with northerners, the reality of climate change has been brought home. From slumping riverbanks to receding sea ice, the effects of global warming are real; they're happening now and they're going to get worse. Warmer winters and wilder weather have already affected our ability to travel on the land and sea and altered both traditional and modern economies. We all have to act both to slow down climate change and to adapt to the changes that have and will inevitably occur. I truly believe future generations will look back on us in horror that we have done so little as a country to prevent this terrible environmental and economic disaster from happening.

FOR THE FIRST seven years of my time in the Senate, the Liberals were in power. While I was not part of the government when parliament was sitting, I had weekly access to ministers and the prime minister at our Wednesday caucus meetings. I often raised matters affecting the North and Aboriginal people and was able to directly question ministers in a forum where they could be frank and open. I never hesitated to criticize our leadership officials when I thought they were wrong and I like to think I had some influence on their attitudes, particularly with respect to the North. I worked closely with our MP and minister, Ethel Blondin-Andrew, on a number of issues. As well, it was never difficult to get a meeting with a minister for me or for people from the North. I recall a delegation from Yellowknife who were in Ottawa and were touring parliament. Someone suggested that they would like to meet the prime minister, who was then Jean Chrétien. I called Chrétien's office and within the course of a couple of hours we were ushered into his office and had a short meeting and pictures taken with him.

I was appointed by Prime Minister Chrétien based primarily on my accomplishments as the first northern Aboriginal lawyer and my contributions as a northern politician, not because of my party politics. I was a member of the Liberal party from time to time and had attended a number of Liberal events over the years, but I was largely non-partisan. Still, I was proud to be appointed by Chrétien and admired his abilities as a prime minister and party leader. What really stood out were his finely honed political instincts, a characteristic that all successful politicians must possess. Over the years, I've served under five Liberal leaders and have seen the party suffer under the hands of those who didn't share Jean Chrétien's ability to measure the pulse of the public or to recognize when political opportunities arose.

Paul Martin had been a successful businessman and an even more successful finance minister. He provided a strong policy and fiscal presence in cabinet and caucus that balanced nicely with Chrétien's political instincts. It was clear the two men were rivals—sometimes bitter ones—but for many years they worked extremely well together. Martin wanted to be prime minister and actively campaigned for the job even before Chrétien was ready to leave. Eventually, he did succeed him, though the circumstances were hardly ideal, as Martin was labouring under a sponsorship scandal. Some argued that Martin should have called an election as soon as he took over the leadership. Instead he chose to wait (in part to allow electoral boundary changes to come into effect) and had to respond to the emerging scandal, which he did quite forcefully. However, the public did not see it that way and he was reduced to a minority government and eventually defeated by the Harper Conservatives in 2006.

In the subsequent leadership race, I initially supported Michael Ignatieff. He seemed a likely winner—good-looking, a dynamic speaker, fluently bilingual. However, at the leadership conference in Montreal, a number of delegates from the Northwest Territories strongly supported Stéphane Dion. I was caught up in the excitement of the crowd and eventually went with the other Northern delegates in supporting Dion.

The Conservatives immediately launched a highly negative campaign, using unflattering photographs and out-of-context quotes to denigrate Dion's abilities. He seemed unable or unwilling to defend himself and couldn't shift focus to his significant accomplishments as the author of the Clarity Act or as environment minister. His Green Shift policy—taxing carbon while reducing income taxes—was complicated, and the party was never able to really communicate it to the public. I raised the matter of the negative Conservative ads several times in caucus, as it was clear to me they were effective and needed to be countered. Although the powers-that-be said they had a strategy, nothing emerged, and Dion's leadership was weakened from the outset.

Nonetheless, the Liberals remained competitive right to the last days of the campaign, when reporter Mike Duffy broadcasted tapes of botched first-takes of an interview that made Dion look incompetent. The Conservatives increased the size of their minority government as the Liberal vote stayed home.

After the 2008 election, it became clear that the Conservatives could be stopped only if progressive parties came together to do so. I was in the room when Dion, Jack Layton and Gilles Duceppe signed an agreement that would create a coalition between the Liberals and the NDP, which would govern with the support of the Bloc Québécois on specific issues. Although I was never as against the Conservatives as some of my colleagues, I did hope that the coalition would succeed and provide a more progressive government. However, to avoid a non-confidence motion, Prime Minister Stephen Harper persuaded Governor General Michaëlle Jean to prorogue parliament while the Conservatives launched a massive ad campaign against the coalition. By the time parliament resumed, the coalition had collapsed and the Liberals had chosen a new leader.

Again, Michael Ignatieff seemed the logical choice. He was intelligent and articulate and had finished second in the previous race. He didn't have the baggage that former New Democrat Bob Rae carried (though Rae proved a highly capable interim leader). I also felt that he did the right things—touring the country and rallying the troops at caucus meetings and other events. Yet the Conservatives were once again able to demolish his character through negative ads that attacked his long history of working outside of the country. Like Dion,

Ignatieff was an academic who lacked real political instincts, a fatal flaw for anyone who aspires to the top political job.

Justin Trudeau has yet to prove himself and show that he is more than simply his father's son. Thus far, his ability to mobilize youth and unite the party has been impressive, as is his popularity in Quebec. He certainly showed a decisive streak when in January of 2014 he decided to remove senators from the Liberal Parliamentary Caucus. The next few years and the election in 2015 will show whether he achieved leadership on his father's coattails or his own merits. The durability of current scandals and missteps by the Conservatives will be a key factor in the result, as will the ability of either Trudeau or the NDP's Thomas Mulcair to become the focus of progressive votes in the country.

I BELIEVE THE current troubles in the Senate arise from the growing partisanship of the chamber and especially the excessive partisanship of Harper's appointments. Senators Mike Duffy, Pamela Wallin and Patrick Brazeau were all suspended in 2013, largely because of the expense claims scandal. Liberal Senator Mac Harb, also involved in the scandal, has retired. During the 2006 election that led to Martin's defeat, Patrick Brazeau, then-chief of the Congress of Aboriginal Peoples, sided with Conservative claims that the Kelowna Accord had been "written on the back of an envelope." In fact, the negotiations had been going on for some two years; I attended several of the early meetings, as did Brazeau. A few months later—despite questions about his integrity and personal relations—he was appointed to the Senate. Brazeau was always in conflict with other Aboriginal leaders in Canada and as the government tried to mend relations with them, I noticed Senator Brazeau became less visible. The Conservatives were certainly quick to expel him from caucus when his private troubles became public. However, in the cases of both Duffy and Brazeau, Prime Minister Harper overlooked the well-known character flaws of these men in a rush to reward hyper-partisan behaviour.

Not all of the current prime minister's appointments have been strictly partisan. Senators from all walks of life have been appointed over the last nine years and most have served admirably. One of the most interesting appointments from a personal point of view was that of Dennis Patterson, my former adversary, who was chosen to represent Nunavut in 2008. Dennis had deep Conservative roots and had retained ties to Nunavut. He has been a reliable spokesman for the Harper government agenda across the North.

I have often proposed to the prime minister and other ministers that I should travel with them in the Northwest Territories or attend events held there. I've assured them I would be non-partisan and never cause any problem. To date, I have had no success. Since Senator Patterson's appointment, he has often been included while I, the representative of the area, have been ignored. On one occasion, when Prime Minister Harper came to my hometown to announce changes to Nahanni Park, the prime minister acknowledged every dignitary in the crowd except me, even though I was standing right in front of him. It was humiliating. This, I thought, is not the way we treat people in the North.

Dennis and I buried the hatchet after his public admission that his treatment of me had been unfair. Our relationship in the Senate has been cordial, though it seems funny for us to be sitting on opposite sides of the chamber. It never occurred to me when we were in the legislature or even in cabinet together that we were so politically different. We serve together on two committees and have collaborated on issues directly affecting the North; Dennis does his best to keep me "in the loop" when he can. For many years, one of Dennis's closest advisors in Ottawa was George Braden, the very first elected government leader of the NWT. During one 2014 meeting of the Energy, Environment and Natural Resources committee, when the current premier, Bob McLeod, was testifying, it was a bit like old home week.

I have been proud to serve in the Senate. I believe it is an honourable place where good work is done and I'm pleased to have made some small contribution to it. My appointment, as I said, was not particularly partisan, though obviously I have served as a Liberal senator and generally though not always voted along party lines. The party system is what we have in Canada, so I know it is sometimes necessary to appoint loyalists, but a balance is needed. Generally, prime ministers have appointed slightly more meritorious senators than purely partisan ones, but recently that balance has seemed to tip the other way. Hopefully, the recent difficulties in the Senate will both reform and clarify its procedures and also change the attitude of both the current and future prime ministers on how appointments should be made. I welcome and support the changes proposed by Mr. Trudeau to reduce the connection of senators to political parties (which of course will require similar initiatives by other parties) and to have a merit-based public process for future appointments.

AFTER THE CONSERVATIVES took power in 2006, it took me a while to adjust to my new role in Opposition. Whereas before I could question ministers directly in caucus, now I was reduced to dealing with the government indirectly through the government leader in the Senate. Ministers, too, were less accessible, a situation that got worse once the Conservatives had a majority. I've been blunt and truthful to people who have come to me for help, telling them I don't have the contacts and influence I once had when the Liberals were in power and have directed them to see Conservative Senators in their quest to meet with ministers.

Virtually my only direct contact with ministers in the last few years has been during private dinners organized by various senate committees. While we sometimes can have frank conversations, it is not always the case, as everyone is careful around members of the opposite party. Everyone in Ottawa feels pressure to follow the party line. I've always resisted that—my training in consensus government runs deep—but it still has an effect on my work.

Not that it was all bad when the Conservatives took power, despite what the various Opposition parties have said. On some issues, such as justice and the approach to Aboriginal consultation, I strongly disagree with the Harper government. On others such as the abolition of the gun registry and support for economic development, I'm more supportive. While I like the prime minister's interest in the Arctic, I often feel he cares more about militarizing the North than supporting the people who live there by investing in community infrastructure.

A good example of the pros and cons of the current government is reflected in the Conservative government's actions on Aboriginal issues. A few years after the defeat of the Martin government, I had my policy advisor analyze the performance of the Conservative government with respect to the Kelowna Accord—the agreement negotiated over a two-year period and initialled by Prime Minister Martin and Aboriginal leaders a few weeks before his government fell. Some of the results were surprising. On things like infrastructure—housing, water and sewer systems, and so on—and land management improvements, the Harper government spent as much as or more than had been promised in the Kelowna Accord. On other things—education, health and other people services—they came nowhere close, though one hopes the recent focus of the government on Aboriginal education will change that. The biggest surprise came in the area of directly supporting economic development activities of First Nations. The Conservatives, despite their supposed pro-business attitude, provided even less than the small amount contained in the Kelowna Accord.

Despite my occasional disagreements with my colleagues, on balance I still believe the Liberals have a better vision for the country and for the North, though some of the proposals of the NDP are appealing. It will be interesting to see what the Canadian people think in the election in 2015.

Chapter 19: Closing the Circle

WHEN I WAS a small child living in Fort Simpson with my grand-mother Ehmbee and my mother, I was happy. That happiness was shattered by my experiences at residential school, and I believe that those experiences are at the root of my later alcohol abuse, relation-ship difficulties and depression. In addition, I sometimes wondered as I grew older about who I was. I sometimes identified myself, like my mother, as Métis, a person who bridged two cultures. Yet because of my grandmother's teachings, the way I was raised and my ability to speak Slavey fluently, I more strongly identified with my Dene roots.

Although I gradually dealt with the effects of depression and grew more healthy, I continued to feel that the sources of my problems—residential schools and not knowing where I came from—remained unresolved. I had worked hard on dealing with the symptoms ever since they first appeared in the 1980s, but it was only during my time in the Senate that I was finally able to tackle the underlying issues.

WHEN I WAS a small child, the lack of a father didn't trouble me much. My aunts and uncles told me time and again that my mother, Laura, had been involved with Sergeant Walker of the American army, who had helped build the airport in Fort Simpson during the early 1940s. When my mother became pregnant, my uncle Charlie Hansen con-fronted the married sergeant, who didn't deny his relationship with the young Laura. Charlie went to the RCMP and asked that something be done. A week later Walker was shipped out, never to be seen again.

From then on it was presumed that Walker was my father. I was even nicknamed Walkie, as my grandmother couldn't say "Walker" properly. I also vaguely remember my mother showing me a picture of a man dressed in an army uniform and hat. This led me to believe that my aunts and uncles were right. It didn't much matter to me, though I sometimes wondered why I didn't have a father like everyone else and the other children occasionally called me a bastard. By the time I was old enough to perhaps ask my mother about it, I was away at residential school and she was hospitalized in Edmonton.

It was only when I was approaching forty and struggling with alcohol, infidelity and depression that the matter of my father began to loom in my mind. The resilience that I'd developed to get through adolescence and early adulthood was failing as I faced the grown-up challenges of family and work. I had come to realize that my experiences in residential school—being torn from my family, neglected by the nuns and sexually assaulted by an older student—were a big part of my problems. Now I thought that growing up without a father was perhaps also a part of it. Also, the lack of a role model left me with no grounding in how to be a good husband and father.

It was the mid-1980s when I finally dug up the nerve to ask my mother about my father. In the cultures of my mother, who was a Métis but raised as a Dene by her adopted parents, these things were not talked about. It was an embarrassment to have given birth to a child without being married. But one day as I was driving back to Yellowknife with only my mother with me, I posed the question to her. I was afraid that she might be insulted and close up, but I felt that I had to take the chance. I asked her in Slavey, the only language she spoke, "Who's my father?"

Her face drained of colour. There was silence. Many miles went by before she said, "*Soan dih,*" which means "I don't know."

I said, "I'm not a dog. I want to know."

Again there was silence, but finally she said, "Dalziel."

It was a name I hadn't heard before, which confused me, so I let the matter lie.

A couple of years later I again broached the issue, and this time my mother wrote the name George Dalziel on a piece of paper. She told me he was from the Yukon and that it had happened in the course of a party. That was all she would tell me.

So when I was next in Edmonton, I visited Charlie and Edna Hansen. Uncle Charlie listened to my story and after a long time said, "I didn't know George Dalziel was that kind of a guy."

I smiled to myself: these kinds of things don't happen in the light of day. They happen late at night in the dark under a blanket, while everyone else is asleep.

Charlie went on to say that George Dalziel was a bush pilot who flew in and out of Simpson and always conducted himself respectably. He still thought Sergeant Walker was my father because Walker had had a stout build and I had a similar body structure and height. I thought maybe so, but my mother was the one who should know. I wondered if anyone else had ever bothered to ask my mom about that whole matter.

I began making casual enquiries about George Dalziel in Fort Simpson. Morris Lafferty, a teenager when I was born, said that Dalziel was a prominent man in the community, as he had a plane and flew people out to their traplines. Morris's older brother Eddie used to fly with Dalziel out to Sibbeston Lake to haul fish for the mission. Planes were being introduced into the North and apparently it was quite a novelty. The better-off trappers would hire Dalziel to take them out to their traplines. Whenever a plane flew over the community, people rushed out to the snye at the back of the island to watch the plane land on the ice. Many of the old pictures that my mother kept show her standing by an airplane in the snye. When I asked a few of the older women about Dalziel, some of them smiled and said he was quite a guy; I wasn't sure if they were thinking of his flying exploits or more personal experiences they had with him, and I didn't ask. Mary Krause said that once when she and her husband, Gus, were living in Nahanni Butte, George Dalziel landed in his plane on the ice in front of the community and everyone went out to see him and later the people held a dance in his honour. A friend of mine, Edwin Lindberg, told the story of the first time he ever saw a plane, one summer day when he was a young boy. A plane landed in front of their home along the Liard River and taxied onto shore, and out came a wild-looking man who called himself Dalziel and said he was short of gas. Gasoline was always in short supply, but Edwin's father agreed to lend Dalziel the gas if he replaced it later. Edwin didn't re-call whether Dalziel ever did replace the gas, so I agreed to pay him for the sins of my father and gave him gas money some fifty or so years later.

It was only after I became a senator that I finally decided to take the plunge and make serious inquiries into my paternity. Claire Bar-nabe, who had helped set up my senate office and done some research work for me, agreed to look into the matter on a confidential basis.

George Dalziel was prominent in the Yukon in the Watson Lake area. In Whitehorse, he is featured as a pioneer bush pilot in the Avi-ation Museum. In 1941 he worked as a civilian flying instructor for the Armed Forces in Portage La Prairie, Manitoba, and was loaned to the US Armed Forces to instruct search-and-rescue crews in the North. Dalziel was also involved in training rescue dogs, who could be dropped by parachute to the scenes of accidents. He provided recon-naissance services for the US Army while they built the Alaska High-way and the Canol pipeline. When the war was over he started an air charter company in the Watson Lake area and throughout his life was a bush pilot, flying a total of over twenty-three thousand hours. Later, his airplane charter company expanded to include a big game hunting operation in the Dease Lake area in northern BC. He also lived many years in Watson Lake, where he had a hotel and a museum with all the stuffed wild animals he had hunted around the world.

Under the guise of doing northern research, Claire got in touch with a number of members of the Dalziel family. George Dalziel had died in the early 1970s, and his wife before that; their four grown chil-dren lived in various parts of northern BC, Watson Lake and White-horse. After Claire had gathered enough information, I wrote a letter to Dalziel's oldest son Robin, who had been a lawyer in Whitehorse but was retired and living in northern BC. I told him my name and early life history, including that "my mother Laura says George Dal-ziel is my father."

A month or two later I received a phone call from Sherry Brad-ford, Robin's younger sister. Sherry was pleasant and forthright, but skeptical. Sherry didn't seem closed to the possibility of her father having a wayward son, but asked if I could send pictures of myself to her so her family could look at them to see if there were any resemblances. I gathered all the pictures I could, particularly those from my youth, and sent them on to her.

It was again weeks before I received a phone call stating that she liked my pictures, but she was still unconvinced. One reason for the initial reluctance to embrace me, I discovered later, may have been that the family had just finished a big court fight over the estate of their father. I assured Sherry I was doing this for my own emotional well-being. I had been blowing in the wind all my life not knowing who my father was, and I was looking to have closure on the matter.

I suggested that I pay for a DNA test. She agreed, and I had blood samples from myself and my mother tested by a lab in Vancouver; Sherry and her brother Byron did the same. It was months before we got an answer, but when we did it was positive. An analysis of the blood samples showed a 99.9 percent certainty that our DNA was from the same father. (The 0.1 percent uncertainty could only be eliminated if all the people in the world were also tested to rule out any other possibility.) I was elated. Finally I knew who my real father was, and I had brothers and sisters out in the big world. I need not feel groundless, fatherless anymore.

I immediately phoned Sherry, who had also just received the results. She said that she gladly accepted me into her family as her brother, and was especially glad that I was Aboriginal. We made plans to meet, and that Christmas Karen and I went to Watson Lake to stay with Byron, the youngest sibling, and spend time with our new family. It was a joyous occasion.

One interesting thing that happened while we were there was during a visit to some friends of the family. One of them said, "I thought George Dalziel walked in the door." Apparently of all the children, I look most like him.

Since then I've learned a great deal more about my father. He was an important figure in opening up the North as a bush pilot and was a highly successful trapper, pilot and businessman. He was no slouch academically, either; he had been studying in Vancouver to be a doctor when the call of the wild lured him away from university in 1925. He never looked back. He featured prominently in many articles in the *Edmonton Journal* and newspapers as far away as New York, and was discussed at length in several books about the North.

Dalziel trapped for eight years along the Liard River and up into the Nahanni mountains. Tales of his exploits filled newspapers across the south, and other stories are recounted in a book about the "Colourful North of L.A.C.O. Hunt," who had been the HBC manager in Fort Simpson for many years. Hunt describes how the first time he met Dalziel he simply walked out of the bush with a single pack dog and a load of furs. He had walked from BC, living off the land, using only a revolver for hunting. He sold a pack of prime marten pelts and used the money to fund his continued life in the bush. In 1929, travelling only with a pack dog and carrying nothing but a blanket, gun and axe in his small pack sack, he made his way by foot across the mountains from Telegraph Creek to Fort Norman in an amazing twenty-nine days. While there, in 1933, he was introduced to flying by Wop May and he went on to become a legend among bush pilots.

Dalziel's exploits as a flying trapper became so infamous that they reached the floor of the House of Commons in 1937, where concerns were expressed that white trappers—using planes to increase their range and efficiency—were threatening the livelihood of Native trappers. In fact, the areas exploited by Dalziel were not ones Aboriginal people trapped in.

These days I keep a large, blown-up photograph of George Dalziel in my senate office and on the walls of my house in Fort Simpson. He is standing in the bush with a caribou skin wrapped around his shoulders and his hair and beard rimed with frost. He is staring fiercely at the camera, and you have the sense that he wasn't afraid of anything or unwilling to take on any challenge. I never had the chance to meet him, but it makes me proud to think of him as my father.

IN 1995 THE ROYAL Commission on Aboriginal Peoples (RCAP), established by Brian Mulroney in the wake of the Oka crisis, issued its multi-volume report. Although the vast majority of its specific recommendations were not immediately implemented, over time it has had a significant influence on Canada's approach to Aboriginal rights. For example, the recognition of the "inherent right to self-government" as

an Aboriginal right under the constitution and the long process to improve dealing with specific claims arose directly from RCAP's report.

Another major issue highlighted by the commission was the legacy of Indian residential schools. From the late 1800s, governments
had promoted the policy of forcing Aboriginal families to send their
children to school, either day schools if they were near large population centres or residential schools if they lived in more rural areas. It is
significant that almost the only thing the Indian Act has to say about
education were draconian measures to deal with truancy. The purpose of residential schools was clearly stated as "to educate the Indian
out of the child." For more than a century (the last school closed as
recently as 1996), governments funded and churches operated dozens
of these schools from coast to coast to coast.

The work being done by RCAP was echoed throughout the North
as more and more people started talking about their terrible experiences in residential schools. In the mid-nineties a number of us began
to compare our life experiences and found that most of us were stuck
in a somber, sad and discontented state of existence. We found that it
related back to our years in the residential school. The people I spoke
with had all been in the Fort Providence school when we were very
young and felt that this had an adverse effect on our lives. These discussions were the beginning of our decision to deal with those sad
and melancholy feelings and hold meetings and workshops to get at
their source.

We approached Bishop Denis Croteau, then the leader of the
Catholic Church in the Mackenzie–Fort Smith area, and asked for
some money to hold a healing workshop. With a five-thousand-dollar
grant and a few other dollars garnered from other sources, we held our
first residential-school meeting in Fort Providence with the theme of
"I just want to be happy."

The effect of residential schools has been enormous. Although
some Aboriginal people credit the schools with giving them an education and providing an escape from difficult family or community situations, the vast majority, myself among them, experienced the schools
as places of misery. Thousands of children died and were buried in un-
marked graves, their families never knowing of their fate. Thousands

more experienced crippling emotional, physical and sexual abuse or had their cultures and self-esteem stripped away from them. Not only did students suffer directly, but they took their suffering back to their communities and families, creating multi-generational abuse. I know that my own experiences affected my children and I can only be thankful that in later years, as I became healthier, I've been able to in some measure make it up to them. I live each day conscious of trying to be a good husband and father.

Subsequent to RCAP's report, the federal government began to look at their role in residential schools from a different perspective. In 1997, in response to the commission's recommendations, the Chrétien government adopted an Aboriginal action plan, "Gathering Strength," which built "on the principles of mutual respect, mutual recognition, mutual responsibility and sharing" that were identified in the RCAP report.

One component of this new action plan was the creation in March of 1998 of the Aboriginal Healing Foundation (AHF), a national, Aboriginal-run organization with an eleven-year mandate and a $350 million endowment to address the effects of the residential school experience.

I immediately saw the benefits of what the AHF had to offer. I had attended many counselling programs and taken treatment for my depression and addictions; others less fortunate than me hadn't necessarily had the resources for those measures. Building on the healing session we had already held, I worked with other former students to create the Fort Providence Residential School Society. We received funds from the AHF and instituted healing programs and workshops for former students. Over the next decade, we were able to help hundreds of former students. We had an office with an executive director, and workshops were held every few months. Field workers in each of the Deh Cho communities visited former students, hearing their stories and arranging for them to attend healing workshops.

There were some who didn't want to participate, who wouldn't come to the gatherings or if they came, wouldn't speak. I remember one man who refused for several years to come to our meetings in Fort Providence but was eventually persuaded. He sat silent for two days listening to us all tell tales of our experiences, the many bad things that had happened but the good things too. Finally he piped up and said, "Oh it was tough, we ate fish three times a day for 365 days a year." We were all amused, but it was clear that he had issues and this was just his way of breaking his silence. After that, he was able to talk a little and participate in the sharing.

There was one woman who said she could not forgive the nuns for their cruel treatment. She seemed stuck in her healing, so we took her to Montreal to visit the Grey Nun sisters who were still living in the original house in which Mother D'Youville, their founder, started her work with the poor. Although all of the sisters who looked after children in the North were dead, it was a good experience to see where the sisters originated and took their training as young nuns before they came north to work in the residential schools. The trip helped the woman, as she seemed less burdened and more spirited. After a while, having had an opportunity to express her anger to people who shared her experiences and understood, she was able to laugh a little and even began to perform little acts of kindness for some of the other students, something she hadn't done in many years.

MEANWHILE, EFFORTS AT financial compensation were ongoing. By 1998 a series of class-action suits had been initiated by residential school survivors and their lawyers in every province and territory. The federal government's initial response was to issue a statement of reconciliation and establish the Aboriginal Healing Foundation. After a series of pilot projects, Canada set up an alternative dispute resolution process in 2003 to provide some compensation to those willing to forego legal action. The system was bureaucratic and frustrating—I went through it myself and helped several others with their claims—and offered minimal compensation based on narrow criteria. In my case, for example, where I was assaulted by a bigger boy, the process for claim recognition and compensation required that I had told persons in authority about the assaults at the time they occurred. I couldn't fulfill that requirement, because as I child I did not understand what had happened and in my child's mind, telling Sister anything would have led to reprisals by the bigger boy against me. It was a totally unrealistic requirement. Eventually the government realized this approach wasn't going to work, and it entered into negotiations with survivors' groups and national and regional Aboriginal organizations. By this time there were thousands of civil suits that had been started by former students against the churches and the federal government. The goal of the new process was to reach a settlement with those who had directly experienced the damages caused by residential schools—some eighty thousand people.

The negotiations went on for many years, and it was only in the dying days of the Martin government that an agreement in principle was reached. That day I rose in the Senate and said, in part, "Honourable senators, today the federal government announced compensation for Aboriginal people that have been in residential schools. That decision is a very good and touching one. When I heard the decision this morning, I shed a tear, because I was five years old when I went to residential school.... A number of years ago, when we started our healing process, many of us said, 'We do not want money; we just want our life. We want to experience happiness.' Fortunately, some of us have made progress; unfortunately, others have not.... [T]his is a monumental day—not so much because of the money, but because of the gesture and the recognition that it has been really tough on those who attended residential schools."

Before the final agreement was reached, the government had changed but the commitment to do the right thing had not. In 2006 Minister Jim Prentice announced the terms of the final agreement. The $2.1 billion settlement had a number of components including a common experience payment to every surviving student based on the number of years they had been in school as well as a fund to compensate students who had suffered physical and sexual abuse. For the latter there was an arbitration process, which was lengthy and at times frustrating, but it was more open and accommodating of victims than earlier efforts had been. Survivors could make an application for compensation and have their cases heard by independent adjudicators; provisions were made for legal counsel and for applicants to have comprehensive hearings in a non-confrontational setting.

For my own application process I hired Tony Merchant, a lawyer who had started many of the court actions that eventually led to a class action against the government and churches. On April 1, 2008, I filed an application for compensation for sexual assault as well as a number of other less serious assaults and incidents. The process was time-consuming, requiring the procurement and gathering of a lot of documentation and information touching on all aspects of my life, particularly about how the assaults had affected me. It took several years before all the information was gathered and a date set for me to appear before an adjudicator in August 2010. When the two-day hearing was completed, the adjudicator indicated he was satisfied that the assaults against me had in fact occurred and he wanted a psychiatric report assessing the harm the assaults caused me.

That December I was interviewed and tested for a full day at the office of a psychiatrist identified by the Crown. The psychiatrist's report was submitted in June 2011, and my lawyers began negotiating a settlement with the lawyers of the Department of Justice. In January 2012 agreement was reached, and in March I received the payment. All in all it had taken six years from the time I began seeking compensation through the alternative dispute resolution process until settlement was completed under the independent assessment process. Finally I felt I had been truly listened to and my suffering acknowledged. For many former students, that was the important thing.

STILL THERE WAS one thing missing: a formal apology. On May 17, 2007, Senator Charlie Watt introduced the following motion to the Senate: "That the Senate take note and concur with the resolution of the House of Commons apologizing to the survivors of Indian Residential Schools for the trauma they have suffered as a result of policies intended to assimilate our First Nations, Inuit and Métis children, causing them harm and the loss of their aboriginal culture, heritage and language while also leaving a sad and tragic legacy of sexual, emotional and physical abuse." Following the motion's introduction, I spoke at length about the issue. In fact, it was the longest speech I ever gave during all my years in the Red Chamber. I spoke about the financial elements of the settlement agreement, the steps being taken toward healing and the forthcoming Truth and Reconciliation Commission. Then I stated that the one thing missing was a simple apology from the government. I expressed how important that apology was and why:

> "In the end, I feel that the federal government, as the government of the people, ought also to apologize, and this is what we are working towards and we hope that it will eventually occur. There have been vague, general attempts at apology.... An apology is not simply a matter of saying 'I'm sorry,' but requires an acknowledgement that actions have caused harm, an acceptance of responsibility for that harm and the promise to do something about it. Through the settlement agreement, the government has already promised to do something about the harm that was caused. They are making payments, and that is very good, and we are generally very grateful for that. As I say, an apology is important because to make an apology is also to ask for forgiveness and to forgive is always the first step towards true personal healing. I know this to be true."

I spoke about other apologies issued by the government, and the calls from various organizations, media and individuals for a formal apology about the residential schools. I spoke about my own experiences. When I finally sat down, to resounding cries of "Hear, hear," the motion was immediately adopted.

Later that year, Prime Minister Harper did make a full apology to residential school survivors, one that was echoed by every other political leader. It was sincere and well-received and I know I speak for many others when I say I am grateful for it. The date and the time of the apology was well-known in advance and I made the decision to stay home in Fort Simpson and watch it on television with a group from our healing society. We were deeply moved and many, including me, wept silent tears as we listened.

Did it solve all the problems faced by Aboriginal peoples in this country? Not even close. The terrible conditions faced by too many citizens were created by centuries of oppression, colonialism and racism and will take years and even decades to fix. The periodic, but ever-growing protests by Aboriginal people across this land, most recently exemplified by the Idle No More movement, show that words are not enough. The struggle for healing never ends.

Epilogue: The Future of the North

IN NOVEMBER 2013 I turned seventy. I'm healthy and happy and enjoying all that life has to offer. My marriage and spiritual life sustain me, and my healthy and prosperous children and many grandchildren make me proud.

I can honestly look back on my life so far and say that despite the hardships, it has been a life worth living. In some respects I feel that my most important political work was done many years ago in the 1970s and 1980s when I fought to make the territorial government more responsible and accountable to northerners. My time in government was exciting and productive as well, establishing the Northwest Territories on the national stage for the first time and fighting for Aboriginal languages and rights. It was certainly those years that made me feel most alive.

Life after elected politics has been more tranquil, more focused on personal healing and finding contentment. Still I'm proud of the work I've done in the Senate, especially in terms of improving economic opportunities for Aboriginal people and northerners and fighting to support and improve the land claims process. The most personally satisfying work has been my contribution to the healing discussion around residential schools. I suspect it will be those speeches and activities I'll be most remembered for.

I've also found a great deal of comfort and hope from my relationship with God and the Catholic Church. Karen and I do the occasional marriage preparation course, and whenever I'm in town I play the guitar, help with the music and translate the gospel into Dene. As I always say, you should come out of church feeling better than when you went in; as another phase of my life—the Senate—comes to a close, I do. With each passing year, I become more interested in the next world and am spending more of my time and energy helping bring about positive changes in the Catholic Church in the North.

MY "EARTHLY" WORK is not done yet, not quite. In the fall of 2013 a devolution agreement was signed to grant control over land and resources to the territorial government. Transfers of federal authority began years ago, and I know from experience that one has to be diligent to make sure Canada keeps her word. I'll spend some of my last few years in the Senate keeping an eye on that development.

Climate change continues to trouble me, especially as I see how little has been done by governments around the world to stop it or to prepare for its serious effects. I've heard the argument that Canada is too small a player to have any real significance but I don't buy that. Leadership comes in all sizes. Back in the 1980s the Northwest Territories was a small player in the constitutional debates, but that didn't stop us from standing up for what was right and doing everything we could, even at the risk of biting the hand that fed us: the federal government. Climate change isn't going away and neither will my insistence that we do something about it.

HAVING SPENT MUCH of my life overcoming addiction, depression and the effects of residential school, I finally feel well. I feel I have something to tell people about living a good life, a healthy life. Recently, I took up the challenge of being a spokesperson for mental health in the North. I'm not sure yet what I can contribute—beyond the stories I've told in this book—but it seems like another interesting and useful way to spend the rest of my life.

Index

Photographs indicated by roman numerals in bold